Praise for *No Scrap Left Behind*

"When you stop wasting food, you save time, save your money, and help the planet. Teralyn Pilgrim's book will guide you to do that in simple and easy steps."

—**Selina Juul,** founder of the Stop Wasting Food movement

"Teralyn dives into the largest source of food waste in America: our home kitchens. And unlike many pressing issues of our time, she shows that individuals have the power to make an immediate difference that will lower climate emissions and help feed more people."

—**John Mandyck,** co-author of Food Foolish: *The Hidden Connection Between Food Waste, Hunger and Climate Change*

"Cooking at its best is an act of conscious love, for the people we feed but also the source of our ingredients, the earth, the sea. Like Teralyn, we're at our best as cooks when we're present, engaged and respectful of every morsel life gives us."

—**Michael Smith,** chef and author of *Real Food Real Good*

"In a fun, often funny, and always accessible style, Teralyn Pilgrim makes the serious and compelling case that what we do every day in our kitchens sends ripples around the world. Americans waste 40 percent of the food we grow and produce, much of it in landfills. Consumer waste hurts people, the environment, and the global economy. Her response to this crisis is smart and inspiring."

—**Eric B. Schultz,** former CEO of Sensitech and co-author of *Food Foolish: The Hidden Connection* [illegible] *Food* [illegible]

"Teralyn Pilgrim is the funny, no-nonsense, heart-of-gold friend you want alongside you in the kitchen. When it comes to reducing food waste at home, she calls out advice that's fussy or just doesn't work and keeps things real with hard-earned insights and ideas. As I read her stories of low-waste-living trial and error, I found myself alternately laughing out loud, nodding heartily, and feeling the emotional highs and lows of her journey. Sometimes hilarious and sometimes so poignant it hurts, this book will help you make practical shifts to both make the world a better place and save you money and time."

—**Rachael Jackson,** journalist and founder of EatOrToss.com

"*No Scrap Left Behind* is filled with everything you need to start reducing food waste in your home. With practical tips and very human stories of one family's messy, often frustrating, and sometimes delicious journey to save money and heal the planet, this book belongs next to your favorite cookbooks."

—**Katherine Miller,** author of the James Beard Award nominated *At the Table: The Chef's Guide to Advocacy*

"I raise a reusable stainless-steel canister to Teralyn Pilgrim for writing this important book, which is filled with revelatory facts (e.g. the world wastes 730 stadiums of food each year) and helpful tips on how to reduce your own food waste."

—**A.J. Jacobs,** bestselling author of *The Year of Living Biblically*

No Scrap
Left Behind

No Scrap Left Behind

my life without food waste

Teralyn Pilgrim

Health Communications, Inc.
Boca Raton, Florida

www.hcibooks.com

Library of Congress Cataloging-in-Publication Data
is available through the Library of Congress

ISBN 13: 978-0-7573-2516-8 (Paperback)
ISBN 10: 0757325165 (Paperback)
ISBN 13: 978-0-7573-2517-5 (ePub)
ISBN 10: 0757325173 (ePub)

Publisher: Health Communications, Inc.
301 Crawford Boulevard, Suite 200
Boca Raton, FL 33432-3762

Cover, interior design, and formatting by Larissa Hise Henoch

To every mother
who has lost a child
to hunger

Contents

Part 1:

Becoming a Food-Waste Warrior

Chapter 1:

Why I Stopped Wasting Food

My husband held up the remains of his meal. "This is just soggy bread. No one is going to eat it," he said.

The soggy bread was once a shrimp po-boy sandwich. The restaurant hadn't added nearly enough shrimp, which left us with the thick ends of sauce-smeared bread, sprinkled with relish and lettuce shards.

I lowered my hand, which was raised to ask the waitress for a takeout box. "What's wrong with it?" I asked.

"Look at it," Andrew said, turning a piece over in case I needed a better view.

It was our first time going to a restaurant since I had announced we would stop wasting food the week before. He had been on board when we were at home, but keeping unwanted food from restaurants was too much.

"You said you were going to support me," I answered. "No food waste, ever. Even at restaurants."

"Teralyn, this is *gross.*"

"How do you figure? You ate most of that bread five seconds ago. It wasn't gross then. Plus, if I gave you a bowl of shrimp right now, you'd put it on that bread and eat it happily."

His shoulders sank in defeat. "You seriously want to take this home?"

I folded my arms firmly. "It doesn't pass the Hungry Kid Test."

He frowned because that was the end of the argument. With his head lowered in shame, he asked our waitress for a takeout container so we could keep eight pieces of po-boy bread, sans shrimp.

"It'll be interesting to see what you do with that," he said.

To be fair to my husband, when I told him I wouldn't waste food anymore, it took him a while to understand what counted as "food" and what counted as "waste." He saw me pick onions off my hamburger once and wondered if that was all right, since onions are technically food.

A lot of my friends felt the same way. When I announced my new lifestyle on social media, they bombarded me with questions.

"What about orange peels?" they asked. "Potato peels? You can eat dandelion leaves, you know."

They sent me recipes for banana peel cake and orange pulp muffins. I was touched by their support, but something felt off. It didn't make sense to bake a banana peel cake every time I wanted a banana. (By the way, never make a vegan pulled-pork sandwich out of banana peels, no matter how much a blog article insists it's good. It tastes just as awful as it sounds.)

My husband and friends made an interesting point: If throwing away onion slices and orange pulp wasn't wrong, what *was* wrong?

I came up with the Hungry Kid Test.

Imagine you want to throw out some food. To one side of you is a garbage can, and to the other side, there's a hungry kid. If you would put your food in the trash with a hungry child watching, throwing it out is okay. For instance, if a kid asked me for some food and I had a banana peel in my hand, I wouldn't hand it to him. I would say, "Sure, just let me throw away this banana peel first." If you would give the food to the child, throwing it out counts as waste. I would never hand a hungry child slivers of raw onion.

Another example: Once when I was eating enchiladas, the skin on the peppers was too thick to chew. I picked them out until there was a pile of pepper peels on my plate. (Say that five times fast.) If a kid had asked for those skins, I would have said, "No, sweetheart. Let me get you something else." If a kid had asked to eat the last bite of my enchilada, I would have said, "Of course you can!"

You get the idea.

I wouldn't throw out po-boy sandwich ends with a hungry kid watching me. Ergo, I had to take it home . . . and figure out what to do with it.

The po-boy challenge almost stumped me. I would have eaten the bread the way it was if I absolutely had to, but maybe I could take the bread from being just edible to being desirable. It needed to be toasted so it was no longer soggy. While it sat in the toaster oven, I scrounged around my kitchen until I had the idea to caramelize cheddar cheese on the bread. Then I topped it with dollops of mayo-and-relish tuna fish.

It was really good. The po-boy sauce on the bread paired well with the cheese and tuna, plus I thought the shape of my mini-sandwiches was fun.

After my creation was complete, I arranged the pieces on a plate and presented them to Andrew. In my best waitress voice, I said, "Would you care for some open-faced tuna-melt sliders?"

We laughed until we cried.

Not too long ago, I didn't think twice about throwing away food. Granted, I would frown on people who tossed food that was perfectly good. There are starving children in Africa, after all. I would do the much more responsible thing and leave my leftovers in the fridge to rot.

Back then, I went on huge grocery trips. There wouldn't be enough room in the fridge for what I had bought, so I'd take everything out that was no longer edible. A stack of Tupperware containers would accumulate on my counter—sometimes two or three stacks. I'd plop all the rotten food in a garbage bag, which would be very heavy, and drag the bag outside as a trail of putrid fluid drizzled behind me.

Then I'd mop the floor.

Well, I'd at least mop up the putrid fluid.

I didn't *waste* food. We ate leftovers, after all. Plus, I judged wasteful people with righteous indignation. You can't be judgmental if you're guilty of the same thing, right?

Despite my denial about our waste (and most of us are in the same denial), I knew what I was doing wasn't okay.

I knew this because of the Ghost Baby.

Hopefully, this doesn't make me sound too crazy . . . though after reading the title of this book, perhaps that ship has sailed. I read once that most American families throw away enough food to feed an additional family member. This altered my attitude about food. Whenever I dumped out container after container of leftovers, I imagined the ghost of a fifth member of our family. He was a hungry African child like you see in the news, and he would be watching me. Frowning at me.

I threw away food so often that my kitchen felt haunted. Yet I ignored my Ghost Baby and continued to waste stacks of food year after year after year.

Then, on April 2017, a news article came into my life and changed everything.

I was scrolling through my phone, avoiding housework, when I saw it. The article was about famine victims in Yemen, South Sudan, Nigeria, and Somalia. It had all the typical stuff you'd expect: unfathomable numbers of people suffering in ways none of us could understand. As I read about the tens of millions facing illness and starvation, I figured I would do the same thing I always did: feel sad for a while and move on. We have no choice but to move on.

But this article was different. It was more descriptive than all those other articles, painting a picture that I couldn't get out of my head. It talked about people walking for days in search of food, many of them women with children in tow—children who were dying from exposure, malnutrition, and sickness. That image, more so than the big numbers, stuck with me. I could see those mothers' faces. I felt like they were looking right at me, saying, *Help me. I'm so tired.*

I was still free to move on at that point. Then I got to the last sentence of the article, and I haven't been the same since. It said that in Nigeria, some communities have lost all their toddlers.[1]

I wept.

I couldn't stop crying. Adalyn was a toddler at the time, and so were my four nieces. Most of our friends had toddlers. Several of our cousins did, too. I thought of all those lives—gone—and the holes that would be left by such a loss.

Usually, a good cry will make me feel better about anything. This was the opposite. Crying made me feel worse somehow, even though I cried a lot over the next few days. Once in the shower, I leaned my hands against the wall and let the water run over my head as I sobbed.

I had already seen horrific pictures of starving children. It's not like I didn't know that stuff was happening. The thing is, they never show you pictures of *dead* children. I vaguely believed charities swooped in right after the pictures were taken and that they were feeding those kids. It's funny what you can believe when you put zero thought into it.

Later, after reading this article, I would learn a horrific truth: Globally, we waste enough food to feed every hungry person three times over.

Just like that, those hungry children would never again be just a passing thought. Every time I wasted food, the image of those mothers' tired faces and those communities without their toddlers would come back and cause me the same pain. The only way to get them out of my head was to stop throwing away food completely.

I'd had enough of my guilt and enough of my ghosts. It was finally time to do the right thing. I stood in front of my refrigerator and made a vow never to throw away food again.

It was just the sort of thing I would do. I had always felt a restless urge to do *big things*. My favorite thing was to write novels, but when I was between projects, I'd get restless, and Andrew would often come home and get bombarded with new plans. "I had a great idea for a podcast/blog/website," I might say, or "I'm going to start a new club/group," or "There's a new hobby I want to pick up," or "Listen to my great business idea." My brain wouldn't *stop thinking*, even when I told it to shut up.

Some ideas I would reject after sleeping on them for a night, like learning to paint or building a website where agents find writers instead of the other way around. There were many ideas that Andrew had to talk me out of. Opening a bookstore, a knitting shop, or a barre studio (sometimes all three in one space) were common discussions between us. There were others I tried and didn't pursue, like becoming a professional organizer, and some I pursued and wasn't successful at. Finally, there were goals that I finished, and I was ready for something new.

I wanted to explore, invent, try crazy things, and tell people about my experiences. More than anything, I wanted to do something that had never been done before. I was a stay-at-home mom who needed a new adventure but wasn't sure where to find one. What better place than the kitchen?

"You're *never* going to throw out food again?" Andrew clarified after I announced what I wanted to do and why.

"Never," I said while bouncing my four-year-old on my knee. It occurred to me that I didn't know if my new goal was feasible . . . or even possible. *I probably should have tested this before making a lifetime commitment,* I thought.

"Maybe never," I added. "I mean, a lot of people do stuff like this for a year. It could be a yearlong challenge sort of thing. Or longer. Then I could decide if I want to keep it up. . . ." I shrugged and laughed. "I've never done this before."

Our two-year-old, who was climbing over Andrew's shoulders, kneed him in the face and he grunted. "It isn't possible to throw out *zero* food," he said as he struggled to pull her off.

"I just don't want to live the way we've been living. You know what? I want to see how low I can get with my food waste," I decided. "Like an experiment. Can I make it to zero? If so, what would it take?"

His response caught me by surprise. Andrew shrugged and said, "It's a great thing to try."

Just like that, I had his complete support.

Andrew extricated himself from our daughter, who whined in protest as he lowered her to the ground. "I'm going to make white cupcakes," he said on his way to the kitchen. She followed him with her hopeful arms outstretched.

"Could you add some almond extract to the batter?"

"Why?" he asked.

"Because almond is awesome. It's one of the world's most underappreciated flavors."

He chuckled. "How much should I add?"

"No idea. To taste, I guess."

From my spot on the couch, I could see him separating the egg whites from the yolks. "Oh no," he teased, "I'm going to throw out three egg yolks!"

I rolled my eyes. Three silly egg yolks. Who cares? Then I thought, *Yolks are still food, right? Still edible?* If I was going to do this—to *really* do this—then I should take it as far as I could.

"Actually," I said, "could you put them in a Tupperware container?"

His smile faded. "Seriously?" he asked. "What are you going to use them for?"

"I dunno, I'll figure it out later."

This was when he fully understood the lifestyle I had signed us up for.

TIP: If a recipe calls for egg whites only, you can add the yolks to scrambled eggs, omelets, frittata, or quiche. It should be about one yolk per whole egg.

Ten minutes later, Andrew approached me as I was folding laundry in the bedroom and the girls played with toys on the floor. He couldn't look me in the eye, and he had a sheepish, embarrassed grin. All he could say was "Um . . ."

Uh-oh. I was familiar with that look.

"What happened?" I asked.

"I meant to put in the almond extract," he explained, "but I accidentally grabbed the mint instead."

"Mint!" I cried. "In vanilla cupcakes?"

"Yeah."

"Couldn't you smell the difference?"

"I did once I added it to the batter, but by then, it was too late. You said 'to taste,' but I put *way* too much in."

"Andrew! I have to eat all those cupcakes!"

"Sorry."

I put my palm on my forehead. Clearly, my noble intentions were going to be more difficult than I had thought.

There had to be a way to salvage the cupcakes. The girls would still eat them, of course, though I didn't want my daughters to finish twenty-four cupcakes by themselves. Nor did I want to give them to the dog. That would be difficult to explain to the vet. Andrew would of course eat zero, and I would eat one and wish I had eaten zero. We certainly couldn't give them away. Freezing them would only delay the inevitable. I couldn't compost them because of Rule #2: Composting Counts as Waste, which we'll get into later.

The only thing I could come up with was to make chocolate-dipped cake balls in hopes that chocolate would mask the vanilla and dilute the mint. But this reminded me of a story my mom told me:

Early in my parents' marriage, my mom cooked liver because she'd heard it was healthy. The liver was too gross to eat. In an attempt to be resourceful, she chopped the liver up and added it to a pot of beans, which only made the beans inedible, too. She had to dump it all down the sink.

"Don't throw good at the bad to make bad better," she said. She told us this story often because it's a metaphor for life.

In all likelihood, I'd go to the effort of making cake balls only to end up with a less healthy dessert that was just as horrible.

The oven timer went off, and Andrew brought me a steaming cupcake.

"How is it?" I asked dubiously.

"It's . . . well . . . here, just try it."

I took a bite. It tasted like almond.

I jabbed a finger at him. "You tricked me!"

"Gotcha," he said with a grin, and he popped the rest of the cupcake in his mouth.

The Many Problems of Food Waste

You might be wondering if food waste matters. Sure, it's throwing away money, and it's a shame when so many people go hungry. But it's a renewable resource, and in the end, all food turns to dirt that's used to grow more food. How much does waste actually *matter*?

Food waste isn't just a shame. It's a disaster. I didn't know food waste was a problem when I started this venture. As I learned about food waste around the world, what I discovered was staggering. Preventing it should be a top priority. If you drive an electric car home from the local farmer's market and unload organic food from reusable grocery bags, but ultimately put that food in a compost bin, you are contributing to one of the top environmental problems of our time.

Before I send your mind reeling with my mad research skills, I want to emphasize that even if I had never read any of the stats I'm about to share with you—even if I never knew that my actions affected anyone—I still would have stopped throwing out food. I still would have written this book. When all is said and done, it doesn't matter if I'm the only one doing the wrong thing, and it doesn't matter if I'm the only one doing the right thing. Wrong is wrong; right is right.

Now, brace yourself. This is going to be a bumpy ride.

The Natural Resources Defense Council published a report on how much of America's food goes to waste. Care to harbor a guess?

Forty percent.

Almost half of all the food produced in the United States goes uneaten.[2] That's enough food to fill 730 stadiums every year.[3] The money spent on wasted food is more than the budget for national parks, public libraries, veterans' health care, all the federal prisons, the FBI, and the FDA—*combined*.[4] Around twenty pounds of food is wasted per person each month.[5] Even more shocking: 90 percent of that food is tossed prematurely,[6] meaning someone could have eaten it at the moment it was thrown away.

Those are all very big numbers—so big, they're hard to process. The numbers hit home for me after watching videos of food dumped in landfills: truckloads of packaged goods and mountains of fresh produce.

How is so much waste even possible?

It's tempting to point the finger at big corporations, but most food waste happens at the consumer level. You and me.[7] The American consumer spends 25 percent of their food budget on food they never eat.[8]

No one believes me when I say this. Once, I posted on Reddit a chart of where food waste happens, and it attributed 40 percent to consumers. Readers were outraged. Someone accused me of diverting attention away from corporations, who are the true culprits of this problem. Such a high level of consumer waste was so unbelievable that I got reported for posting misinformation and had to take it down.

After doing the research that I should have done before posting that image, I can assure you that 40 percent is accurate . . . depending on whom you ask. The Commission for Environmental Cooperation said 45 percent.[9] Both the USDA[10] and the Food and Agricultural Organization of the United Nations put consumer waste at only 22 percent, which accounts for 37 percent of carbon footprint wastage.[11] The National Resources Defense Council echoes 40 percent.[12] The

Environmental Protection Agency puts it as high as 40 percent to 50 percent.[13] That's a pretty big spread, but everything I've read is unanimous about one thing: In the United States, most waste is caused by consumers.

Even if consumers didn't carry so much of the blame, waste from consumers is more dangerous to the environment than waste from farms and grocery stores. The Food and Agricultural Organization of the United Nations says,

> The further along the chain the food loss occurs, the more carbon intensive is the wastage. For example, a single tomato spoiled at the harvesting stage will have a lower carbon footprint than tomato sauce wasted at the retail store, since the harvesting, transportation and processing accumulates additional greenhouse gases along the supply chain.[14]

Most people think they're an exception to all this. Few of us would readily admit to throwing out twenty pounds of food per person every month.

The next time you clean out your fridge and your cupboards, I challenge you to put the garbage bag on a scale before taking it out. Those numbers add up quickly.

If appealing to your better nature doesn't convince you, think of the *money.* American consumers waste an average of $1,300 worth of food per family each year.[15] When I read that, I thought, *Seriously? I can save that much every year, and all I have to do is eat the food I bought? Why doesn't everyone do this?*

I'm citing a lot of American stats just because I am an American, so that makes it easy for me. That doesn't mean my country is the only one at fault. Italy's food waste can feed all the starving population in Ethiopia. France's food waste can feed the entire population of the Congo.[16] I could go on.

Food waste is a worldwide problem, and it costs the global economy $936 billion a year.[17] Percentage wise, every country in the world wastes about the same amount, even developing countries. It seems weird, but it's true. Developing countries don't have the resources to store and deliver food safely—like refrigeration, for instance—so a lot of what is produced perishes before it can be sold. However, once the food gets to consumers, they don't waste it. Not like developed countries do.

We should probably do something about this food-waste problem sooner rather than later because scientists predict that there will be over 9 billion people on the planet in 2050. Some say that if we continue producing and wasting the way we do, we will run out of food. Scientists indicate that the world will need 70 percent more food to accommodate the population boom.[18] (I'm not entirely sure how a 34 percent increase in population will require a 70 percent increase in food, but who am I to argue with science?)

Okay, so we waste a lot of food. Big deal. It's a renewable resource. When most of us spoon rotten leftovers into the sink, we think, "That's a shame." We tend to have the same feeling about global food waste: what a shame.

But it's not just a shame. Food waste wreaks massive havoc on the environment, on global warming, and on the worldwide economy.

Don't believe me? Buckle up; I got more stats.

The Environment

My father-in-law was in church when the president of the congregation stopped the service. He stood at the pulpit and asked every able-bodied man to go to a church member's chicken farm—immediately.

All the men went home and changed out of their suits and into work clothes and headed to the chicken farm. The owners guided them into a chicken house, and when my father-in-law stepped inside, he thanked his lucky stars that he had the foresight to bring his boots.

Certain chicken corporations will convince farmers they can make a lot of money raising poultry for their company, even if they've never farmed before. The farmers have to buy the company's feed and sell the chickens to them at the prices the company chooses, and sometimes people start the farms with no idea what they're doing.

This family quickly discovered keeping chickens was much harder and less lucrative than they had thought. The day before that fateful Sunday, no one turned on the fans to keep the chicken houses cool like they were supposed to.

It cooked all the chickens.

The stench was unreal. Hundreds of dead birds lay limp on the ground. My father-in-law tapped one with his boot and the insides sloshed. He said it was like carrying Ziploc bags of hot Jello. (He couldn't eat chicken for years.)

A tractor dug a mass grave, the helpers tossed the chickens in, and the tractor buried them. My father-in-law went home and burned his clothes. He says he will always remember that smell.

What the farm owners didn't know is that when you bury so much bio waste, you have to install a vent. Otherwise, the gases released from the rotting waste will cause an explosion.

Which is exactly what happened. The tractor had to scoop all the corpses back into the hole.

It wasn't until I researched food waste that I understood the science behind the explosion. The rotting chickens were making methane. Methane gas is released when bio waste decays in anaerobic conditions, or in other words, without air. Like chicken graves. Bio waste that decomposes out in the open releases carbon dioxide instead.

Consider: Exhaled breath is carbon dioxide. Farts are methane.

The way biomatter degrades is important because methane is twenty times more potent than carbon dioxide.[19] The vast majority of our food doesn't decompose in the open, but in landfills where it is buried under layers of garbage. This prevents it from getting the air it needs to rot safely.

That means methane, and lots of it. One-fifth of landfills is food, which makes it their single biggest occupant.[20] There's more food in landfills than *plastic*.

If a pit of chickens makes enough gas to literally explode, imagine what is happening with the 2,600 landfills in the United States alone.[21] Landfills are the third largest source of methane in the United States, behind gas emissions and cow farts. (Seriously, cow farts. Look it up.)[22]

Compost is twenty times better than landfills because the waste gets rotated, adding air that helps it decompose faster. Unlike landfills, compost bins release carbon dioxide. But remember: Carbon dioxide is still a greenhouse gas. It can make explosions, too. Wet haystacks have been known to spontaneously combust because bacteria feeds on the moist hay. The bacteria generates CO^2, which creates heat, and *boom*![23]

There's no good way for food to decompose, not even in a compost bin. This is one of the many reasons we shouldn't produce more than we need.

Many landfills have gas collection systems that convert methane into usable fuel. This is called anaerobic digestion . . . which reminds me: It doesn't just cost us money to *make* wasted food. With the expense of both trash collection and running the landfills, it costs Americans $1.5 billion a year to *dispose* of wasted food.[24]

Anaerobic digestion might sound like a clean and responsible thing to do—expensive, but responsible. Still, I don't like it. If you're going to make that much methane gas anyway, I suppose you might as well use it, but pumping edible food into factory equipment doesn't sit well with me. I do support using anaerobic digestion on animal waste. A single cow produces about eighty-two pounds of manure a day,[25] and I don't think we need that much compost.

I can see it now: the new Prius . . . runs on cow poop.

Buying food locally is much better for the environment than getting it shipped from another country. Transporting food uses resources, including fossil fuels. On average, food at grocery chains travels 1,500 miles to get from farm to table,[26] which means we contribute to climate change pretty much every time we go shopping.

If greenhouse gas doesn't keep you up at night, food waste causes plenty of other environmental problems. It's a major squandering of resources. Food-waste activist Rob Greenfield said, "When we waste food, we don't just waste the food; we waste all of the land, the water, the fossil fuel, and the labor that was used to grow that food. Because we waste so much of it, it's one of the leading causes of rainforest deforestation, depletion of fish in the ocean, and biodiversity loss."[27]

Let's talk about deforestation. Three-quarters of endangered animals face threats from agriculture and overexploitation of plants and livestock, while only 19 percent are affected by climate change. That's 5,407 species threatened by agriculture alone.[28]

A whopping 40.8 percent of American land is used for farming, but 30 percent of the land used for farming is squandered on food that doesn't get eaten.[29] That means 12 percent of American soil is being used to make wasted food.

Think about all the trees that were cut down and all the animal habitats that were destroyed so that we could use pesticides, fertilizers, water, and fuel to grow wasted food that releases methane as it rots in a landfill. It sounds pretty silly when you phrase it that way.

I haven't even mentioned water. Food production swallows 80 percent of fresh water consumed in the United States,[30] and 25 percent of all the water consumed in the United States is used on crops we don't even eat.[31]

Plastic is a hot-topic environmental problem, but no one connects the plastic problem to food waste. Try to picture all the food that is thrown out at restaurants, grocery stores, and homes, and imagine how much packaging is wasted with it.

Food waste contributes to just about every environmental concern. If you want to help endangered animals, prevent global warming, reduce plastic, and more, all you have to do is eat your food.

The Hungry

"Oh, those poor hungry people," we all say. "If only there was *something* we could do to help them. Alas, there is no solution to world hunger . . . right?"

After all, people talk about the need to solve world hunger all the time. It's hard to believe anyone would be scratching their head over this issue when the answer is right in front of us.

But, remember, food that is wasted globally could feed every hungry person in the world three times over.[32, 33] Sit with that for a moment. There are 828 million people suffering from chronic hunger around the globe,[34] and we make enough food for all of them.

If the United States cut food waste by just a third, we could feed every single American,[35] which is no small feat, since 34 million of us are food insecure.[36] I had to look up "food insecure," so if you're like me and you've never heard that term, "food insecure" means that a household lacks access to enough food for an active, healthy lifestyle for all household members.[37] One in eight of us are in such a precarious situation. Out of the people who aren't food insecure, many of us can afford enough food to live but can't afford healthy diets.

I knew there were a lot of hungry people in America, but one in eight? It was difficult to wrap my head around this. Once I heard how bad hunger was in America, I looked at people suspiciously, wondering which of the eight customers I met at the grocery store was going hungry and how many of my friends were keeping secrets about their finances. Then I realized (duh), I didn't go to neighborhoods where impoverished people live. I had a middle-class life with my middle-class family and all my middle-class friends, completely isolated from food-insecure families. It's easy to think everyone lives the way we do, isn't it?

Everyone has heard a mother say to her child, "Eat your food. There are starving children in Africa." The kids think, *Whatever. It's not like I can mail it in a package and send it to them*, and that's true. We can't give our food back to hungry people around the world. But we're part of a global food market, and the way we eat affects people all over the world.

According to Selina Juul, the founder of the organization Stop Wasting Food, "Wasting so much food is affecting the global demand for food and the global food prices. What we do here actually affects people on the other side of the planet."[38]

Some of my readers might say, "Time out. World hunger is a lot more complicated than you're making it out to be. We can't just stop throwing away food here and every country will magically have enough to eat."

True. Much of the world's hunger has nothing to do with food quantity. Venezuela is dealing with sky-high food prices because of the drop in the price of gas and the government's mismanagement of funds. Yemen is suffering from famine because of civil war. There's nothing we can do in those situations except offer aid where we can.

The thing is, we can't always afford to offer aid. Our country has so much need and is in so much debt. In 2022, the United Nations asked for a record $41 billion to give assistance to the 274 million people worldwide in dire need of humanitarian assistance. (To give you some context, there are 331 million people in the United States.) Getting those funds was unlikely since funding has fallen short of the need every year since 2007.

Sadly, they raised only $13.5 billion. Countries like Yemen, Syria, and the Democratic Republic of Congo received less than half of what they requested. The United Nations warned that growing global humanitarian needs are vastly outpacing donations.[39]

I haven't told you yet how much all our wasted food is worth. Just in America, we throw away $165 billion worth of food every year.[40]

Forty-one billion is needed. One-hundred and sixty-five billion is wasted.

Imagine what we could do with that money.

Obviously, if our country saved $165 billion a year, it wouldn't go toward hungry children in Africa. I know full well we would spend that money on other things—although I did read an article by Global Citizen that the United Kingdom spends more money on food waste than foreign aid, so I'm not the only person who's made this connection.[42]

My point is, how can we sleep at night when we can't afford to help others, and at the same time, we waste so much? It's like someone casually setting wads of cash on fire, and when a friend asks for financial help, the person says, "Sorry, I can't. I'm broke."

I have no problem with people spending their money on themselves. They earned it, so they have every right to enjoy it. When people waste their hard-earned money while others go hungry, that's infuriating.

How Food Waste Happens

Even though consumers carry a great deal of blame, food makes a long journey to get to us. There are many casualties along the way.

Food waste starts on the farm level. Most of the waste is inevitable. Fruit and vegetables rot, get bruised, or get nibbled on by animals and bugs. That's natural but there's nothing natural about the fact that up to 30 percent of edible produce doesn't leave the farm[43] and entire fields often go unharvested.

That might not seem like a big deal because all that extra food becomes compost. It all goes back to the soil, right?

Not exactly. Remember, farming uses resources. Think about the pesticides and fertilizers, the water, the land, and the gas from machines, all for produce that didn't need to be grown. It's not about the nutrients of the food going back into the soil. Food production itself is a wasted resource, not to mention that decomposing biomatter produces greenhouse gas, as I mentioned earlier.

Why do farmers waste so much food that is perfectly good to eat? This happens because of:

1. **Market fluctuations.** An item might become too cheap to be worth harvesting.
2. **A lack of labor.** Fieldwork is hard and pays little, so farmers struggle to find employees willing to do it.
3. **Overproduction.** Smart farmers plant more food than they can sell in case they lose fields to weather and damage. If no disasters occur, they end up with a surplus.

Donating all that unsold food seems like an obvious answer but it isn't as easy as it sounds. It's prohibitively expensive to harvest, prepare, and store food that won't bring a profit. There are tax incentives for donating food that help cover this cost, but the laws around these incentives are ever-changing. Farmers can't be expected to eat the cost of food donations in hopes that the incentives will still be there when they file their taxes.

Volunteer organizations harvest surplus produce and donate it—this is called gleaning—which is great. But they rescue very little in the grand scheme of things, and everything else stays in the field.

I understand the challenges of unharvested fields. What drives me insane is when farmers can't sell their edible food not because it was damaged or it wasn't profitable, but because it wasn't "perfect." The USDA specifies the shape, color, and size of sellable produce. Carrots have to be perfectly straight. Bananas can't be too curved or too flat. Peaches have to be perfectly round. Some of that makes a little bit of sense; misshapen fruit is harder to ship and shelve because it doesn't stack as well. Still, I don't understand why the government feels the need to regulate the appearance of edible food.

Supermarkets are even pickier. Trucks of food that meet federal regulations can still be delivered to the store and then rejected.

Whole truckloads of edible produce are thrown into landfills every day. It makes me sick. It makes the farmers sick, too.

This brings us to our next culprit: grocery stores.

Supermarkets are picky because they do not believe customers will be enticed by "ugly" food. I wonder how much the shape of produce really matters to consumers. They assume perfect fruits and vegetables will turn a better profit, but if all their produce was abnormal, I don't see why we would buy any less of it. I make a point of buying misshapen produce whenever I find it. Some grocery stores sell misshapen produce at a discount. If that was available to me, I would never buy flawless fruit and vegetables ever again!

Supermarkets cause farmers to waste massive amounts of food, but they also waste food after it enters the store. On average, supermarkets throw out 10 percent of their supply. The USDA estimates that this waste costs supermarkets $5 billion every year.[44]

Not only will grocery stores only stock perfect produce, but they will stock much more fruit and vegetables than will sell. They think customers are enticed by displays piled high with abundance, but their gratuitous stacks and pyramids squish the produce on the bottom, and the fruit and vegetables get overripe because it takes too long to sell such large quantities. To compensate, supermarkets buy food that is underripe so it will last longer. This is frustrating for customers who can only find produce that is either underripe, overripe, or squished.

I hate taking produce home only to discover that it tastes awful. It makes me want to buy candy instead. I might have wanted a peach more than a Snicker's bar, but at least I know the Snicker's bar will be good.

Supermarkets throw away a lot of ready-made food too, like the fried chicken or potato salad at their delis. They make way too much for the same reason: They think people want to see bowls and trays brimming with food. One supermarket manager said he throws out 50 percent of his rotisserie chickens because he wants the shelves to be full all the way to closing time.[45]

It's insane, but I understand the reasoning. Think of it this way: A grocery store might only get a handful of people who want rotisserie chickens at 7:00 PM. If those customers keep coming for their chicken late in the evening and the grocery store is always out, they will take their business to a store that always has it. Fifty percent of a store's rotisserie chicken might seem a small price to pay to retain customers in a competitive market. I'd have trouble explaining that to the chickens at the farm, though.

While we're on the topic of grocery stores, some products you buy generate more waste than others. Take celery hearts, for example. I used to buy celery hearts in hopes that getting celery in smaller amounts would prevent it from going bad in my home. Then I watched the documentary *Just Eat It,* and a farmer demonstrated how much celery has to be cut off in order to sell just the heart. His field was covered in perfectly good celery stalks. Now that I know how much waste goes into harvesting celery hearts, I don't buy them that way anymore.

Greek yogurt is another food-waste culprit. It's called "Greek" when it's been strained and re-strained, making it thicker and more protein rich, but it takes four times as much milk to make the same amount of yogurt.

Supermarkets throw away packaged food too, not because it's bad or unsafe, but because it isn't at the absolute peak of freshness. They want customers to eat the food at its best. Since no one will buy packaged food that is labeled to expire in the next few months, supermarkets throw it out *before* the dates get close enough to deter customers. That often means dumpsters full of perfectly edible food, most of it packaged in plastic.

In *Just Eat It*, two people committed to only eating discarded food for six months. They bought misshapen produce from farmer's markets and accepted food from friends, but mostly, they ate out of grocery store dumpsters. Family members worried the two of them would go hungry. On the contrary, they were bombarded with more food than they could handle. The dumpsters were full of such a massive surplus of food that they could take home only a tiny portion of it, and even after giving food away to friends and family, they still had so much extra that the man gained ten pounds.

Rob Greenfield took things a step further. While on a cross-country bicycle trip, he discovered that he could go to any city at any time and in one day find enough food in dumpsters to feed hundreds of people. He would take dumpster food to parks, get the media to take pictures, and give away every single morsel.

After reading this, my first thought was that more people should raid dumpsters for their food. Ta-da: The hunger problem in America is over! That isn't a sustainable solution for many reasons, but mostly because grocery stores deter people from their dumpsters. They might lock the dumpster, and sometimes they even pour bleach on the contents. Makeup companies notoriously destroy products before throwing them away.

In February 2021, Oregon experienced a record snowstorm that caused widespread blackouts. A Fred Meyer grocery store lost power and couldn't refrigerate their food until they got the generator working, so they threw all their refrigerated food away, even though the power hadn't been out long enough for the food to go bad, and it was the middle of winter anyway. They even threw away apple juice. We were in the middle of a pandemic when many people couldn't work and were struggling to pay their bills!

People caught wind of the massive amounts of food available for the taking, and they swarmed on it. One person reached into a dumpster, lifted a tiramisu cake over his head, and shouted, "Let them eat cake!"

Store employees told the people to leave. When they refused, the employees *called the cops*. The cops came, the dumpster diving ended, and huge dumpsters full of edible food were wasted.

If it wasn't so sad, this story would be amusing because Fred Meyer began a "Zero Hunger, Zero Waste" campaign four years earlier. Their impact plan "reflects our efforts to increase access to safe, affordable food and other essential products for customers across our geographies. This includes improving food security, nutrition, and health."[46] Their goal was to eliminate their waste by 2025. I guess the manager in Oregon didn't get the memo.

If farmers and grocery stores didn't waste so much, maybe groceries would be cheaper, making food more accessible to low-income families.

Next up on our list: restaurants.

City Harvest is a food rescue program that started when a soup kitchen volunteer ordered potato skins at a restaurant. She asked what happened to the potatoes' insides and was told that the restaurant threw them out. Shocked, she asked if she could have them for the soup kitchen, and the restaurant donated 30 gallons of potato guts in a single day.[47]

I don't know what shocked me most: that they couldn't find a use for 30 gallons of the most versatile of vegetables, or that someone would pay money to eat a potato peel.

TIP: Don't throw away potato peels! They're nutritious and yummy. You can deep-fry them in oil or bacon grease, crisp in an air fryer, or cook them in the oven. Just toss with oil and salt, lay flat on a baking sheet, and bake in a 400-degree Fahrenheit oven for 15 minutes. Keep an eye on them because they burn easily.

Huge portion sizes are a problem. When I go out to eat, I expect to get two meals out of it—one that I eat at the restaurant, and one that I'll eat the next day—but people don't always take their food home. Those who do often let it go bad. Restaurant diners leave 17 percent of their meals uneaten. Only 45 percent of that gets taken home, and 38 percent of people who take home restaurant leftovers say they often let them go bad.[48]

Another problem is that customers expect everything on the menu to be in the restaurant at all times. Running out is unacceptable, and if it happens enough, we take our business somewhere else. This means restaurants have to stock up on more food than they plan on selling to keep customers happy (like the deli manager with the rotisserie chickens). I stopped eating at a KFC because every time I went there after roller derby practice at 8:00 PM, they were out of everything.

Companies will point their fingers at consumers and say they have to run their businesses a certain way to make a profit in a competitive market with picky, unforgiving customers. I believe American consumers aren't jerks. We're just spoiled.

In many countries outside of America, restaurants behave differently. When I was in Italy, every menu I saw said "hot chocolate," but there wasn't a single café in the country that would give me any because it was May. I was baffled. Hot chocolate was on the menu, and I wanted it. Whether the weather was warm wasn't any of their business.

Then there was the bakery in France that didn't keep regular hours. I couldn't get a chocolate croissant on my last day in Paris because, as a local told me, "They're open when they're open." I thought, *What kind of an anarchy are they running in Paris*? The locals don't mind. They buy what's available, not what they expect to be available.

Once I tried to get afternoon tea at a café in England, but they wouldn't sell it to me because I ordered it at eleven o'clock in the morning. They looked at me like I was crazy for expecting afternoon tea in the morning, and I looked at them like they had wronged me because I come from a country where I can order waffles at 3:00 AM. That's what we're used to, so that's what we expect.

It's a chicken-or-the-egg argument. If we grow up getting what we want all the time, we're going to pitch a fit when things don't go our way and then take our business elsewhere. That's human nature. But if every restaurant expected consumers to be more flexible, like they do in other countries, we would adjust, and life would move on.

If farms, supermarkets, restaurants, and consumers are stuck in a vicious cycle of meeting expectations that shouldn't be expected, at least the unwanted food can be donated, right? Except that only 10 percent of surplus, edible food is recovered.[49]

Laziness is probably the biggest factor, but donating food is more complicated than you might think. Finding places that can accept the food takes time, delivering the food costs money, and some donations aren't practical. You can't just show up at a food bank with a truckload of red onions and say, "The supermarket says these aren't round enough." It all takes resources that farms, supermarkets, and restaurants just don't have. Even if it were feasible, the food might perish before it gets to the people who will eat it.

Food rescue programs will pick up food at grocery stores and deliver it to the hungry themselves, but there aren't enough food rescue programs, and not enough stores are aware of them. Jonathan Bloom, the author of *American Wasteland*, suggested that we should have a database of food donors and recipients so that it's easier to transfer surplus food to the hungry. That's brilliant. Someone (who isn't me) should do that.

Even with food rescue programs hard at work, some store managers claim they're afraid of getting sued if they make a donation and someone gets sick. Actually, the law protects people who donate food in good faith. It's called the Good Samaritan law. Not a single lawsuit has ever been filed against a grocery store, restaurant, or food caterer for donated food, ever, and if a lawsuit ever were filed against donated food, it would get thrown out because the givers are protected.[50]

Finally, the last link in the food-waste chain: consumers.

I've been criticized for only addressing consumer waste problems because (as people have told me) consumers can only make a dent in the food-waste problem.

While those people say that I think too small, I would reply that they're the ones thinking too small. I'm not trying to change just consumers while other people are passing laws on corporations, farming practices, and so on. I'm trying to change an entire cultural mindset. At the end of the day, when we've left work, all of us go home to our kitchens. We are *all* consumers. We *all* need to think about food differently.

Imagine if every parent bought this book, read it, and changed their mindset about food because of it. Then they taught their children to value food. Later, one of those kids becomes a grocery store manager, and because of what she was taught growing up, she realizes that the grocery store is inefficient and wasteful. She brings about change in the store. Another one of those kids becomes the CEO of a restaurant chain and realizes the business does not abide by the values he was taught.

We don't need to fix one group of people and then another. We need to change the collective soul of the Western world.

How My Quest Became a Book

My quest to end food waste in my own home started with the article. My quest to end food waste in *every* home started with a Facebook photo.

Shortly after Thanksgiving, a friend posted a picture of turkey bones in a big pot of water with spices floating on the surface. She wrote, "Can't wait to have my way with this turkey carcass!" She boiled it for four hours, strained out the bones, added vegetables, noodles, and herbs, and voila! Delicious turkey carcass soup.

The name "turkey carcass soup" sounded overly morbid to me. I dislike the idea of eating carcasses, even though I do it every day. I nevertheless loved the idea of making inedible scraps edible. It's like free food. I say it's "like" free food because I did, in fact, pay for the bones when I bought the turkey.

I made broth out of our own turkey carcass from Thanksgiving, and I was hooked. Homemade broth is liquid *gold.* I can't make recipes with the store-bought stuff anymore. Broth in a can is mediocre, and don't even speak to me about bouillon cubes.

To make the broth into soup, I added onions, carrots, celery, bay leaf, garlic, parsley, and egg noodles. *Mmm.* Now we have a new Thanksgiving tradition.

This inspired a catchphrase: Whenever I came up with a clever way to rescue food, I would say, "Another scrap saved!"

Excited by my success with broth, I tried my hand at making stock, only with the carcass of a rotisserie chicken this time. Stock is broth boiled with vegetables—typically carrots, onions, celery—and herbs. After four hours, you drain the liquid and throw the bones and vegetables away. This makes for a more flavorful broth.

The ethics of stock are shady. You have to waste vegetables to make it. I'm also not sure why you'd boil vegetables to mush if you're going to cook vegetables in the broth anyway. Does that not give it enough flavor? But I had a bunch of unhappy vegetables that I didn't know how to save: the leafy parts of a wilted celery stalk, half a bag of shriveled baby carrots, and half an onion that was so old, I had to cut out the brown parts.

TIP: To make bone broth, submerge a carcass in water and simmer in a pot or a pressure cooker for four hours. If you use a pot, check on it periodically to make sure the water doesn't boil down and add more water as necessary. Strain the bones. Add salt to taste.

To freeze, store one-cup portions in containers or Ziploc bags or chill it in ice cube trays.

Four hours later, I sieved the liquid and served myself a big bowl of hot stock with slices of baguette. The mushy carrots I gave to my girls. They loved cooked carrots, and these tasted like chicken, so that's another scrap saved, too.

I raved to my husband between sips of the stock. "Making broth and stock is oddly fun," I told him.

"Of course, it's fun. You just made dinner out of garbage."

Dinner out of garbage . . . this got me thinking: *What other creative ways could I save food that I typically throw away? Would other people want to hear those ideas?*

"Hey, Andrew," I said, "what if I made a cookbook out of recipes like this stock?"

"That would be cool. Or you could do a blog. People can make a full income with a blog."

"Absolutely not," I said. I used to love blogging, back before articles became so weighted with ads, videos, and "please subscribe" popups. Blogs used to be stories that you could follow as they unfolded. You got to know the writer. Now they're just pages that appear in Google searches and are impossible to read.

I wasn't perky enough for a food blog, anyway. Almost every food article ever written goes like this:

"It was seriously the BEST recipe ever! My children gobbled it up. It's their new favorite! My husband is so picky, and even he couldn't stop eating it. I could binge on it all day, and my waistline does NOT need more goodies!!!"

I'm not sure I could drum up that much enthusiasm about anything.

Making a cookbook to help people use up their food was exciting for a while . . . until I realized a teensy-tiny logistical problem: *Every* recipe uses up food. It's not the recipes that will bring about change. It's our lifestyles.

Think of it this way: Once, I took all the extra vegetables in my fridge, simmered them in chicken broth, and blended them up to make a green sauce for penne pasta. (In case you're curious, it was 2 carrots, half an onion, 2 garlic cloves, 2 tomatoes, 2 handfuls of spinach, 1 green bell pepper, salt, and pepper in 1 cup of broth.) Super clever, right?

Except in order for someone to replicate that recipe, they'd have to buy all those vegetables. What would they do with the rest of the bag of spinach? The other half of the onion? Worse, they might not like the recipe and then not eat it. The whole meal could end up in a compost bin.

Another reason not to do a cookbook is cultural differences.

Love Food, Hate Waste is a British campaign to end food waste in the United Kingdom. Their website has scrap-saving recipes that are definitely worth looking at. Problem is, all the recipes are British. Every recipe I hadn't heard of before, didn't know how to make, or had no interest in trying: Mince pie brownies. Haddock lasagna. Colcannon. One-pan haggerty. Then there's my personal favorite:

haggis burrito. I will never have enough leftover haggis to necessitate putting it in a burrito.

Generational differences are a concern, too.

The I Hate to Cook Book by Peg Brackman is hilarious. In the "Skid Road Stroganoff" recipe, she wrote, "Brown the garlic, onion, and crumbled beef in the oil. Add the flour, salt, paprika, and mushrooms, stir, and let cook five minutes while you light a cigarette and stare sullenly at the sink."

The problem is that it was written in 1960. They're all grandma recipes designed for a time when ready-to-eat food was new and exciting, like SPAM and Jell-O. Pretty much all Brackman's recipes called for cream-of-something in a can. Nowadays, we're focusing on natural, local, farm-to-table, health-crazed food. Millennials and Gen Zers won't go nuts over lamb shanks cooked in ketchup.

If I wrote a cookbook, it would be useless to Americans who don't like the same food as me, useless to everyone outside America, and obsolete to the next generation.

What I really wanted was to learn how to get my food waste to zero. The problem with most books and articles is that hardly any of the writers have actually tried being waste-free. You can find a plethora of clever tips online, but it's much more difficult to find someone who knows from experience what works and what doesn't.

It's like the Nutella jars. To get all the Nutella off the sides, food influencers tell you to pour in hot milk, close the lid, and shake the jar until the Nutella melts. It becomes zero-waste hot chocolate. Sounds great, right? Except that I couldn't figure out how to add milk that was hot enough to melt the chocolate without also melting the plastic jar. They also didn't specify how vigorously to shake the jar, which I realized after the lid exploded off and sprayed scalding milk all over me.

I wondered if anyone had ever tried this trick or if everyone just liked talking about it, so I checked it out on YouTube. Turns out, this only works if you have a lot of Nutella left on the sides. Once you've melted everything you can without melting the plastic, you have as much stuck to the sides as you would have if you just scraped it out with a spoon. Thanks for nothing, Internet.

TIP: The easiest way to get food off the sides of a jar is to use a rubber spatula.

No Scrap Left Behind isn't a blog or a list of recipes. It's a lifestyle book I've honed down to nine steps after much trial and error. It has dozens of food hacks, many stories about my efforts and failures, more statistics than are strictly necessary (as I'm sure you noticed), and a few impassioned rants, all in an effort to help you live waste-free.

Chapter 2:

You Have Concerns. Let's Address Them

As a member of the millennial generation, I feel compelled to share my life on the Internet. It's like the proverbial falling tree in a forest that doesn't make a sound because no one hears it. If something happens to me and no one reads about it online, did it really happen? I can wish Andrew a happy birthday in person and say how much I love him to his face, but imagine how he'd feel if I didn't say it on Facebook where everyone could see it.

So, of course, I had to announce online that I had vowed not to waste food anymore. After the flood of questions, it became clear that I needed a system. I made a list of rules to give everyone an idea of how my process works, which I hope will answer all your questions, too.

The Rules of Food Waste

Rule #1: Food can be tossed if it passes The Hungry Kid Test.
Rule #2: Composting edible food counts as waste.
Rule #3: Animals can eat leftovers.
Rule #4: Almost always taste before tossing (unless the food is obviously unsafe).
Rule #5: No self-righteousness and no guilt.
Rule #6: Guests can throw away their own food.

Rule #1: The Hungry Kid Test

Like I said earlier, the Hungry Kid Test dictates that I cannot throw away food that I would feed to a hungry kid. I can throw away apple cores, the sauce from a pot roast, or the crispy ends of an overcooked fried fish, but I cannot throw out leftovers or table scraps.

Food counts as waste if it is still edible. Food does not pass the Hungry Kid Test if there's just one bite left. Let's say a kid didn't want the last bite of my enchilada because it's one bite. The kid would have wanted it when the bite was still connected to the enchilada. Food also counts as waste if it's no longer edible because of something I did to it, like if I burned it or the recipe didn't turn out.

Condiments are tricky because they're not really food. Salad dressing and Tabasco sauce won't fill any bellies, but I wouldn't toss out a bottle of ketchup or a jar of mayonnaise if someone wanted it. Soda passes the test because it's evil, and no one should drink it anyway. Especially not a malnourished kid.

Finally, there's the issue of junk food. I went back and forth for months on what to do with extra junk food. It would be stupid to force-feed my family stale cookies, freezer-burned ice cream, and vanilla mint cupcakes. They shouldn't be eating that stuff in the first place. Throwing away junk food felt less like a failure and more like a wise decision. But . . . it's still food, throwing it out is still wasteful, and I would still give it to a kid.

As a compromise, I have tips and tricks for making junk food last longer. That might sound counterintuitive. The purpose is to save you from eating more than you want when there's too much. Ideally, this will translate into eating less junk food because you can eat it a little at a time. It will also save you money. Junk food can be expensive, and the less you waste, the less you spend on it.

Tips to Keep Treats Fresh

- **Use your freezer.** Most baked goods can be frozen and still taste just as good once they're thawed. You can buy cupcakes, cookies, a pie, or a cheesecake, eat a serving or two, and freeze the rest to be eaten gradually over time.
- **Buy small quantities.** If you've got a craving for something sweet, perhaps get a single doughnut instead of an entire pack of Oreos. If your ice cream often gets freezer burn, buy a pint instead of a half gallon. You can also buy single servings of chips instead of a whole bag.
- **Bake small.** You don't have to make a dozen cookies or an entire cake. You can just bake part of the dough or batter and freeze the rest for later.
- **Toast stale food.** This works great for crackers, chips, and cereal. Spread the food over a baking sheet and bake on a low temperature for a few minutes. Keep a close eye on it so it doesn't burn.

- **To prevent freezer burn on ice cream:** Freezer burn happens when frozen food is exposed to too much air. Lay plastic wrap over the top of the ice cream to protect it.
- **To keep cookies fresh:** Add a slice of bread to your container of cookies to keep them soft.
- **When cookies are stale:** To make stale cookies taste like they just came out of the oven, toast them in the toaster. To take them out, tilt the toaster on its side and take the cookies out with a spatula. You can also reheat them in the oven.
- **Give food away.** This is my favorite way to use up excess food. It's easy, it's effective, and other people appreciate it. In the case of junk food, make sure you know the receiver's diet before sending it over. The person might be diabetic, gluten-free, recovering from an eating disorder, doing keto, or have other food-related restrictions. Your dieting friend isn't going to say thank you as you hand over a plate of cookies.

A staple in my home is freezer cookies. I bake a big batch of cookies and freeze most of them. Whenever I crave a warm, homemade cookie, I pop one in the toaster. It's a lot easier to resist a bag of frozen cookies than a plate piled high with cookies fresh from the oven, and they taste the same.

According to Pinterest, if you burn cookies, you can use a cheese grater to scrape off the burned parts. I haven't tried this method because I'm not a monster who burns cookies.

Rule #2: Composting Edible Food Counts as Waste

People keep telling me, "I don't waste food. I compost!"

A compost bin is better than a landfill. Whenever I see people throw biowaste in a garbage can, I cringe and think, *Another nutrient bites the dust.*

Not to mention that food in landfills creates methane and food in compost does not, like I mentioned before. Despite the benefits of composting, America only composts 5 percent of the food that's wasted.[1]

But . . .

I've angered a lot of people with what I'm about to say. I might get chased out of town for this, but you deserve to know, so please hear me out.

Composting isn't that great for the environment.

I understand the appeal of composting. Creating dirt is satisfying. It even feels god-like to literally make earth. Composting gives you an emotional high, too, because healthy dirt releases chemicals that make you happy. In the documentary *Wasted! A Story of Food Waste*, a farmer could tell when his workers had been in a healthy field by their mood when they returned from work, whether they were chipper or grumpy. That's one of the reasons gardening is so therapeutic.

It's a fun hobby, but no matter how you look at it, composting still means putting food in a bin and letting it rot. All the resources that went into making the food in your compost bin have already hurt the environment, and composting only recovers 1 percent of the energy it took to create the food.[2] Plus the food cost you time and money, and you could have given it to someone in need. Finally, while food doesn't release methane in a compost bin, it still releases carbon dioxide, which is still a greenhouse gas. There isn't much of a plus side here.

Just for the fun of it, let's discuss thermodynamics.

The second rule of thermodynamics states that natural processes tend to go only one way: toward less usable energy and more disorder. All exerted energy degrades into a weaker form of energy. For instance: A solid block of wood can be set on fire and converted into smoke, ash, and heat, and once the heat dissipates, it's gone. You cannot reuse campfire heat. What that means is you cannot "recover" energy by composting. It's gone and can't be brought back.

Wait before you burn this book! Rule #2 is for *edible* food. In heated conversations with compost fanatics (there have been several), I've had to repeat this multiple times before they would calm down. It does not apply to peels, cores, and shells. By all means, if you're not going to use it, compost it. I'm just saying that when you compost an apple core, there shouldn't be an apple attached to it.

How to Compost

I started my own compost bin around the time I stopped wasting food. Once I understood the dangers of landfills, composting just made sense.

There are whole books about composting, but after reading a few articles, it doesn't seem that complicated to me.

To make a compost bin, you need a container that's breathable. Otherwise, it composts without air, which will make it decompose more slowly. A head of lettuce at the bottom of a landfill takes twenty years to fully decay.[3] You can buy a bin specifically for compost, but I just used a plastic storage bin with drilled holes all along the sides and top.

You have to include plants like leaves and grass cuttings. It should be one-third food, two-thirds plants. Also, sprinkle in some dirt because the bacteria in the dirt works as a starter, or you can buy compost starter. Add water occasionally, stir it up with a shovel every now and then to add air, and voilà. You have created earth.

Here's the best part: If you do it right, compost doesn't stink. I was skeptical of this, but to my surprise, compost actually smells kind of good. Like potting soil. I can take a big sniff of my compost and get that feel-good high.

Foul odor in your compost means there's too much water, too little air, or not enough brown and green plants to balance out the food.

Meat and dairy can't go in compost, not only because they stink, but because they attract maggots and animals. I even heard about a guy who saw *bears* getting into his compost. Unless you plan on running a fly brothel or hosting a buffet for raccoons and rats—or possibly getting mauled by a bear—keep meat and dairy out of your bin.

Luckily, there's plenty of stuff besides food that you can add to your bin.

You can compost:

- Eggshells
- Cut-up cardboard egg cartons
- Coffee grinds and tea bags
- Sawdust
- Yard debris (leaves, grass clippings)
- Vacuum cleaner dust
- Shredded wet newspaper and paper bags
- Wood ash (not coal ash)
- Hair

- Paper, including paper towels, napkins, and paper plates
- Burned popcorn
- Old herbs and spices
- Used paper muffin cups
- Cotton clothing, cotton towels, and jeans cut into strips
- Dust bunnies and other debris in a dustpan
- Hay and straw

TIP: If you can't take your compost out to a bin immediately, keep it in a bowl in the freezer so it doesn't stink up your kitchen. If your freezer is too full to fit a big bowl, see Step 5: Don't Buy Too Much Food. You can also buy a countertop pail that's designed to prevent foul odor.

Adding worms helps the compost decompose, but I didn't try it. The worms need a specific environment that includes bedding and lots of water. I also couldn't figure out how to turn the compost without killing them. Anyway, I had a dog, a betta fish, two kids, and a husband. I did not need to be responsible for any more living things.

It's a good thing I was too lazy to try worms because my compost bin became infested with fire ants. Anyone who doesn't live in the South cannot comprehend the heinous nature of fire ants. They are tiny Satans who tunnel because they have to dig up to the surface from the depths of hell. When you step on an ant hill, fire ants don't just bite you. A mass of them will sneak up your leg like silent ninjas. Then they count to three and all start biting at once. Each ant will keep biting for as long as you let it, leaving tiny pustules on your skin that hurt for days.

Investigating this infestation, I moved the bin over and discovered tunnels burrowed deep in the ground, and one tiny tunnel running off to the side. I followed it under a tarp where I discovered the original hill, six feet away from the bin. If they had stayed under the tarp instead of eating my compost, I never would have found them and would have no reason to exterminate them. Their greed was their undoing.

If we didn't get rid of the ants in my compost, their hills would spread all over the yard and they'd declared war on my household. It was time to suit up for battle.

This was a bit of an issue. To get rid of ants, we would pour gasoline on the hill and set it on fire. The gasoline kills them. The fire is just for fun. I didn't want to pour gasoline on the quarter-of-the-way-full bin of compost that I had worked on, even if it was mostly leaves. Instead, I tried a natural approach: gallons of boiling water.

The water only killed most of the ants, and scared the crap out of a few worms, who wriggled out of the dirt in a panic. The surviving ants carried corpses to the surface and piled them onto a mass grave. I must have killed the queen, though, because we saw less and less of them until, finally, they were gone completely.

I needed to keep the ants from getting into my compost again. But how?

Here is an example of kismet: Citrus and vinegar are natural bug deterrents, and I just happened to have two pounds of orange pulp soaked in vinegar. I had bought a bag of oranges from Sam's Club, even though I'm the only one in my house who eats them. They were aggressively bitter. I juiced them, added sugar, and even put the juice in smoothies, but nothing I did could mask that flavor. We eventually finished the juice, even though I had to plug my nose and chug most of it down.

This left me with a massive amount of orange pulp.

This is controversial, but I believe pulp doesn't pass the Hungry Kid Test. The entire orange was edible before I juiced it, so anything left over after juicing it still needed to be eaten.

Juicing is not my favorite thing because there is virtually nothing you can do with pulp. There are recipes for pulp muffins, but an entire batch typically calls for only one cup. That means you can either make very little juice or an insane amount of muffins, neither of which is as good as just eating produce and not juicing it.

I've done a lot of creative things with my scraps, but in this situation, I was completely stumped. In desperation, I posted all over Facebook food forums asking for advice.

Someone suggested I use it for homemade cleaner, which isn't food but is at least not wasteful. You can make household cleaner by soaking orange peels in vinegar for three weeks. "Maybe pulp would work the same way," she wrote.

It did not work at all. The orange pulp soaked up the vinegar, and there was no liquid left to spray.

As I struggled to squeeze little drops of vinegar out of the pulp, I realized that I had unwittingly made the perfect insect repellent to stir into my compost. I never had a problem with bugs again.

Another scrap saved!

In summary, composting is great . . . but not as great as people think. Maybe we should just eat our food.

If You Can't Have a Compost Bin

Perhaps you live in an apartment and have no room for a bin. Or maybe you do have room for a bin, but you have unsupportive roommates who would rather not have it in the apartment. There are still options. Composting companies will take your food waste, including meat and dairy, to a processing plant. This is safer than doing it at home (compost facilities are protected from bears), and it has all the benefits of renewing resources and keeping food out of landfills.

Upper Valley Compost Company provides their customers with food-only bins that they pick up on a weekly basis. In a *Marketplace* podcast interview, the owner said many of her customers have canceled their garbage service. Composting reduced their waste so much that they preferred to save money by taking their remaining trash to the dump themselves.

Some states require that their citizens use food-only bins. In January 2022, California passed a law that all people and businesses need to separate their compostable waste from the rest of their trash so it can be taken to a composting facility.[4]

If you don't have compost companies in your area, check out the ShareWaste app. It shows you who is accepting waste for their compost bins, as well as people who are willing to contribute to other people's bins. You also might have a friend or family member who would take in your compost.

If none of this is a possibility for you, there is one last resort that might surprise you: your garbage disposal.

Food in your garbage disposal goes into the sewer instead of a landfill. Sewage is treated and filtered, and 55 percent of it is used as fertilizer for farmland while the rest goes in the ocean.[5]

Garbage disposals could solve many food-waste problems if it weren't for one issue: Our sewers cannot handle the sheer amount of waste consumers produce. There are also a lot of things you can't put in your garbage disposal without breaking it, like potato peels and large amounts of rice (as I learned the hard way). Still, if you're looking at a trash can as your only option to dispose of waste, a garbage disposal is a good tool to have.

Rule #3: Animals Can Eat Leftovers

Food can be recycled into other products besides compost, such as animal feed, worm castings, bioenergy, bioplastics, and clothing.[6] I cannot fathom making clothes out of food, but that's what it says on the USDA website.

If you ask me, human food is meant to be eaten by humans. It's too valuable to go to animals. It still wastes your time and money when you give animals food you bought and prepared for yourself. Still, animals have to eat, and feeding animals is definitely better than putting food in a landfill or a compost bin.

Giving my scraps to a pet might seem like a cop-out for my zero-waste goal, and I suppose it would have been if I owned a Labrador or an elephant or something. Instead, I had a Border collie who was so picky that she used her paw to push unwanted food from her bowl like a friggin' toddler.

I avoided using my dog as a catch-all for table scraps as much as I could. If anyone in my family dished up more food than they wanted, I would (a) put it back in the pan if it was for the most part unchanged, like if it was a roll with no bites taken out of it, (b) wrap up the individual servings for later, or (c) pass our table scraps to another family member. When all else failed, the dog got a treat.

I say "treat" because giving dogs scraps should be rare. (This doesn't include raw meat, which is technically the original dog food.) Human food is not good for dogs because:

- A dog's dietary needs are different from ours. If their diet relies too much on human food, they won't get the right nutrients.

- While humans thrive on variety, dogs thrive on consistency. Even switching from one dog food to another can upset their stomachs, and veterinarians recommend that you introduce new dog food gradually.
- Your dog can get pancreatitis if its diet is too rich in fat. This causes abdominal pain, diarrhea, and lethargy, among other symptoms. A dog with pancreatitis might need to be treated with medication. Veterinarians notice an increase in pancreatitis during the holidays.
- Some human foods are dangerous for dogs, like caffeine, chocolate, cooked bones (the bone shards can scratch their throat), grapes and raisins, macadamia nuts, onions, and corn on the cob (they can break off a piece of the cob and choke on it).
- They can't eat spoiled food. Their digestive systems are stronger than ours, but spoiled food can still make them sick.

There's a bit of debate about how much onion a dog can handle, if any. A friend once showed me a bag of plant-based Hawaiian teriyaki mushroom jerky and asked what on earth she could do with it. I said jerky makes good treats for dogs. Another friend nearby scoffed and said, "If you could get a dog to eat that stuff," but the friend making the request looked shocked.

"This has garlic and onion!" she said.

I looked at the long list of ingredients, and waaaaaaay down at #15 was onion powder, and at #16 was garlic powder.

"Are you *trying* to kill my dog?" She laughed.

For the record, I wasn't advocating that she feed her dog the whole bag in one go.

This was my first time hearing that dogs couldn't have garlic and onion, so I did some reading. Turns out that one medium onion would be enough to kill my Border collie.[7] I don't know how they figured this out. Onions aren't exactly a dog's favorite dish.

My first instinct is to brush this off my mind, especially in the case of the mushroom jerky, because giving my dog a small portion of spaghetti with a little onion on it is not likely to hurt her. Then again, while we might know how much onion it takes to make a dog visibly sick, we don't know how much makes a dog feel yucky.

Some people aren't comfortable giving dogs table scraps at all. That's fine! You can reduce waste in your own way without compromising your standards.

To summarize, I wouldn't hand my dog a pan full of leftovers or a stack of onion rings, but she's great for the little scraps on my plate that are too small to wrap up, or for the lasagna that my toddler spilled orange juice all over. If I *were* stuck with a pan of food that is safe and edible but tastes bad, and my dog will still eat it, I would give her small portions of it over the course of a week or more.

If you have pigs or chickens that eat anything and everything, your problem is solved. Farm animals are basically food processors; they convert food waste into meat, eggs, and milk, and they generate compost.

Feeding animals edible waste in America used to be common, but starting in the 1950s, concentrated animal feeding operations (CAFO) became the norm. Big farms have perfected their ability to keep more animals in smaller spaces, feeding them exclusively on grains for efficiency, which isn't as good for them. CAFOs cause many environmental and economic issues, one of which is that we no longer use waste to feed our livestock.

Thankfully, animal scientists and entrepreneurs are looking for solutions to this problem. They call it upcycling, which I think is cute; it makes giving garbage to pigs sound trendy. Maybe someday, upcycling food to animals will bring about meaningful change.

Although I'd be curious to know if our livestock could even eat all our waste. Forty percent of everything we produce is a *lot* of food.

Rule #4: Almost Always Taste Before Tossing

I used to toss food that I assumed must be bad because it was so old. Now, I check everything first. It turns out that I had been getting rid of a lot of food that was still good.

For my daughter's birthday party, I tried to make chocolate-dipped butterflies out of pretzels. You take one pretzel stick and four mini pretzels, use dollops of melted chocolate to glue them together to make wings, and then dip the whole thing in more chocolate. Cute, right?

There was only one color of melting chocolate at the store: green. The party was drawing near, so I bought the green chocolate, even though that's a strange color to use for a butterfly, not realizing until I got home that it was cookies-and-cream mint chocolate. The mint butterflies tasted disgusting, and the black cookie specks made them look diseased.

Defeated, I threw my hands in the air and threw the pretzels in the cupboard.

TIP: Using clips on your bags will do wonders for keeping your food fresh.

I decided to stop wasting food five months later. While rummaging through the cupboards, I discovered the open bag of pretzels. No Ziploc bag, no airtight container, and no clips. I didn't yet know about toasting stale dry goods in the oven, so out of habit, I almost threw them away without a second thought.

Then I remembered my rule: Unless the food is noticeably unsafe, always taste before you toss.

To my surprise, the pretzels were just as fresh as when I bought them. This made me concerned about the preservatives in our food, but the point is, you can't know food is stale until you try it.

Another example: I had some homemade yogurt and home-squeezed orange juice in the fridge, both of which had seen better days. The water in the juice had separated from the pulp and the yogurt had turned to foamy liquid. It was inconceivable that either of them would still be good, but believe it or not, the flavors were fine. No fermentation, no mold. I put them both in a blender with some frozen mango. Delicious yogurt smoothie.

TIP: If your yogurt is on the verge of getting old, you can make frozen yogurt pops or freeze cubes and defrost it to mix into smoothies later.

Sometimes food is bad enough that tasting it is unsafe. If your food has changed drastically in color, texture, or consistency (i.e., deli ham that is gray and slimy, or rice that has turned to liquid), don't taste it. Do not eat mold. With meat, it's better to err on the side of caution—but not a ridiculous amount of caution.

This often surprises people, but you can eat food that's freezer burned. Food cannot become unsafe in the freezer because bacteria can't grow at low temperatures. Food might change in flavor and texture to the point where you wouldn't want it, but often freezer-burned food tastes fine once you thaw it and cook it.

This reminds me of the Fresh Fish Fiasco.

I'm a city girl from Portland, Oregon, and I had never caught a fish. When I told my husband's family this, every one of their rural Southern mouths hit the floor. I hadn't gone hunting, either. I still use the phrase "he caught a deer" instead of "he killed a deer," much to my husband's dismay, and my uncle-in-law knows more about Pacific game than I do.

They decided to take me fishing.

I admire vegetarians, but I'm not against eating meat. If it's good enough for half the animal kingdom, it's good enough for me. Still, every now and then when I gnaw on a chicken bone I remember how much I dislike corpses. I don't get the appeal of killing an animal myself.

Still, I'm always up for an adventure, and catching a fish seemed as good an adventure as any. I had lusted after fresh fish for years, after friends raved to me of the pleasure of fish straight out of the river. They say it has no fishy flavor at all. I'm not sure why anyone would get excited about a fish that doesn't taste like fish, but I longed to try it all the same.

At the pond, I had my husband put the worm on my hook and looked away from said worm as I cast into the lake, reeled the line back in, cast, reeled, cast, reeled. The day was pleasantly warm, and the fishing was relaxing, even after we lost hope that any of us would get a fish.

Then, right as I was pulling up my line, I saw a big fish right below me. He was just chilling out close to the surface.

Light bulb.

I dipped my line right in front of his face, and as he opened his mouth, I jerked the pole so the hook went inside and yanked him up out of the water.

"I caught a fish!" I squealed.

Everyone was so excited about my first catch . . . until I bragged about the clever way I caught it. Their faces fell. Apparently I had violated an unspoken fishing code of ethics. I thought hunters and fishermen would have more of an all's-fair-in-love-and-war policy, but in their mind, the fish either bit the hook or I caught it "wrong."

Later that night when I was getting a snack from the fridge, I asked my husband how he was going to cook the fish I caught.

"You didn't actually catch it," he reminded me.

My fish wasn't in the refrigerator. I searched every shelf, but it was gone. Finally, my heart filling with dread, I checked the freezer. There it was. Covered in tiny icicles.

"What have you done?" I cried.

My husband's fight-or-flight response kicked in, and he tensed his shoulders. "What?" he asked.

"My fresh fish is in the freezer!"

"Well, yeah. I put it there to keep it fresh."

"If you freeze a fish, it isn't *fresh* anymore. It's *frozen*. I could have bought that at the store."

He thought about this for a moment. "Oh," he said.

I jabbed an accusatory finger at him. "You froze my fresh fish!"

"Yeah, yeah," he grumbled, which is his way of telling me he's really sorry.

I felt a responsibility to eat it, seeing as the animal's blood was on my hands, but my enthusiasm had bottomed out. We kept the fish in a corner in the freezer and never got around to cooking it.

Month after month, year after year, I couldn't bring myself to throw out that fish. He had been minding his own business in his pond, happy to be alive and to think happy fish thoughts, when someone caught him—dishonorably, I might add—and for what? So that my freezer could become his final resting place? I was 99.99 percent sure this fish was inedible, but I still kept it. I even brought the fish with me when we moved apartments.

Years later, when I vowed to stop wasting food, I finally faced my fish. The "always taste before tossing" rule still applied. I got the grill ready.

It took three Internet articles to convince my husband that food cannot become unsafe in the freezer. All the same, Andrew heated fish sticks for the girls to eat instead. Just in case.

We grilled the fish with butter and lemon pepper that I got at my bridal shower twelve years prior, which had more or less lost its flavor by then, but I was stubbornly trying to use up my spices. My friends were right; the fillets actually didn't smell or taste "fishy" at all. But they did have a weird texture. Firm and rubbery. I'm not sure exactly how to describe it. Sort of like a mushroom.

"This fish is really chewy," I told Andrew.

He frowned. "That's because it's been in the freezer for five years."

"It's not bad."

"It isn't good." He was a good sport and finished his piece, though the piece he took was the smallest.

Halfway through my second fillet, the texture finally got to me. "The more I eat, the worse it tastes," I said.

"Yup."

I pushed the rest of my fish away. "This is terrible."

"I'm telling ya," he said. He didn't say anything else because, in the South, that's a complete thought.

We gave the leftover fish fillets to the dog in small portions over the next few days. She loved it.

Another scrap saved . . . I guess.

Rule #5: No Self-Righteousness and No Guilt

We all have *that* friend—the one who makes a drastic lifestyle change and can't think about anything else. Vegans. Dieters. Religious converts. Pyramid scheme victims. We're happy that they're happy, but when will they ever stop talking about it? I'm not going to pretend that my friends haven't heard me talk about food waste a billion times. In all fairness, I have a short memory, and they've probably heard me talk about most topics a billion times.

But I decided early on that I'm not going to give anyone That Look. You know the look I'm talking about; it's the one you get when a vegan sees you eating meat or a fitness enthusiast can't get you to go jogging.

It would have been hypocritical to act self-righteous. I used to throw out a lot of food, too. Yet my friends and family still felt self-conscious around me and would overeat to keep from being judged. That didn't serve much purpose beyond making them uncomfortable. The point is to inspire others to be zero waste when I'm *not* around. I always said, "You can throw that out if you want. It's none of my business."

Going waste-free wasn't just an experiment, but a personal journey. Emphasis on *personal.*

I will say this, though: If we give others the slightest inkling that throwing away food is bad and even shameful, we will go a long way toward preventing waste. You can lure people with the promise of saving money, bombard them with sob stories, and threaten them with global destruction, but nothing works better than raising your eyebrows when someone tosses out half their meal. Social acceptance is the greatest motivator.

One more thing: It was also against the rules to feel bad about myself when I made mistakes.

I allowed myself to feel frustrated when food was forgotten or ruined, but I did not allow myself to feel guilty. There was no point in it.

Sometimes my female friends confessed to me how much food they wasted, their eyes averted and their heads hung low. Women feel ashamed over so many things. I thought, *What if I'm giving women one more thing to feel guilty about? Is that irresponsible?* I went back and forth on this for a while, trying to figure out how to inspire readers without making anyone feel like trash. The only thing I can do is implore you to think positively about your future and not negatively about your past. Resist self-righteousness and guilt. It will make you and the people around you much happier.

Rule #6: Guests Can Throw Away Their Own Food

We were getting the house ready for guests to come over for dinner when my husband suddenly spun toward me. Aghast, he said, "What are we going to do if they want to throw away food?"

In his mind, he saw me spooning tiny bits of our friends' food into separate Tupperware containers for them to take home or lecturing them about not taking too much and supervising every bite until their plates were clean. I assured him only a crazy person would do that, and he looked at me skeptically from the corner of his eye, probably because the verdict was still out on whether I qualified as a crazy person.

I think of food as being in a person's jurisdiction. When a friend dishes up food that I made, it is no longer mine and therefore is no longer my responsibility. It's theirs. If they want to throw what I made in the trash, that's on them, not on me.

Remember, this was a spiritual journey to free myself from the sin of waste. (Is sin too harsh a word? I'll use it anyway.) This was about making myself feel better, not policing the rest of the world.

Hosting parties and events is more challenging. You might think I'm about to say not to serve more than your guests will eat, but let's face it: We're all going to prepare way more food than we need. You can't predict how many people will come or how much they will eat, and no host wants to run out of food.

The secret: When you plan what you're going to serve, plan what you're going to do with the leftover food. Are you going to donate it? Take it home? Give it to the guests?

TIP: When you host parties, you can have containers, bags, or plates with tinfoil ready to hand out leftovers to your guests, or you can ask them to bring their own containers.

When I throw birthday parties for my girls, I only serve food my family will be willing and able to finish. I almost bought individual bags of chips for a party, then realized I didn't want my family to eat all the unhealthy chips that would be left over. I bought Pop Corners instead. I avoid too many sweets at parties for the same reason. If my family is going to eat half a cake after the party, we don't also need to eat doughnuts and candy and cookies. I talk about this more in Chapter 6.

The next question is what would I do with my food when I was a guest at other people's homes?

This was one of my greatest challenges. If I took a kiwi from my in-laws' fruit basket and it was terrible, I couldn't exactly put it in the freezer to make a smoothie later. If a friend had me over for dinner and I dished up too much food for myself or my kids, I wasn't going to ask for a Tupperware container and take it home.

TIP: Puree soon-to-expire fruit for smoothies or fruit pops or chop the fruit up and put it in the freezer to use for smoothies. You can keep a gallon-sized bag in your freezer and pop scraps of fruit in whenever you don't think they'll get eaten and blend it up later.

Portion control was the only option. I tried not to take anything I wasn't willing to finish, and I didn't serve my girls more than I could finish if they refused it.

Once my husband and I were talking to a friend at a pizza party when my daughters abandoned their half-eaten pieces of pizza to run after friends. Without saying a word to each other about it, my husband picked up one piece to eat and I picked up the other.

What can I say? We're a well-oiled machine.

There have been times that I've wrapped scraps like pizza crust in a napkin and snuck it into my purse when no one was watching. You can't say I'm not dedicated!

Myths and Misconceptions

When my husband and I were at a restaurant with friends, I mentioned to everyone at the table that I don't waste food anymore. One of the women curled her lip and scrunched her nose.

"So, what, are you like, the goulash queen?" she said.

Goulash is when you dump all your leftovers on top of each other and make it into a casserole. I was intrigued by the idea of a leftovers casserole, but that's beside the point. She thought I was gross . . . for eating food.

That wasn't the first time I felt misunderstood. When I ranted about inaccurate expiration dates, people often said it was a shame the government made food companies use them. Expiration dates aren't required by federal law, and only *some* states require that *some* foods have them, like formula and medicine.

So it seems necessary to discuss some myths and misconceptions about being waste-free. We should talk about food safety, too, to clear up misunderstandings in that department.

Here are the myths I hear most often:

Myth 1: "Being waste-free is too hard."

My goal to stop wasting food *completely* was overwhelming. But making a huge improvement wasn't difficult. After following the Nine-Step program in this book, I'd say 75 percent of what I used to waste was easily preventable.

The next 20 percent of my food waste was more difficult to save. The last 5 percent was downright *hard*.

But if you're worried about effort, think of how much work you put into eating. There's planning meals, making grocery lists, going shopping, preparing the meals, and cleaning up afterward, not to mention the time you spend at work to earn the money to buy groceries in the first place. Much of that effort is spent on food you don't eat. Reducing your waste can't possibly be more work than all that.

If you're concerned about how hard it is, I urge you just to try it out. You might be surprised at how much a little effort will affect your life.

Myth 2: "It's gross."

The key to reducing food waste isn't to eat gross food. The key is to not let your food get gross in the first place. Don't buy so much that it goes bad before you have the chance to eat it; don't let your food sit out on the counter all night instead of putting it in the fridge; and make sure you follow Step 9: Be Smart When You Cook.

The fact of the matter is that you bought food—which you paid for with your hard-earned money—because you wanted to eat it. It looked good at the time. If the food gets gross at any point after leaving the grocery store, it's because you did something to make that food gross. Do not do that thing.

Every family has different standards of sanitation. Some families won't eat food that has touched the floor while others follow the three-second rule. My family is fine finishing food off each other's plates, but I won't eat food off the cousins' plates when they come over. Sharing is an immediate-family-only activity for us.

Then there are some people I know, like my husband, who learned the hard way in college that if you leave a sausage pizza out overnight, it will make you sick, but if the meat was cured—like pepperoni or salami—you'll be okay. I emphatically do not recommend testing this.

I'm not a germaphobe, but I do have my limits. I've heard of people taking home restaurant leftovers from their plates *and* their friend's plates. Kudos to them for preventing food waste, but that's not for me.

At Reed College before COVID, the cafeteria had a long tradition of students without meal plans "scrounging" for meals. They'd sit at a table and wait for other students to hand them their half-eaten food.

No. Just . . . just no. Good for them, I guess, but that is *all* kinds of "no" for me.

My standards might not be the same as yours, but rest assured, I am not going to convince you to lower them. You decide as an individual/couple/family what makes you comfortable.

I'm also not going to convince you to raise your standards. (Unless you and your family keep getting sick, in which case, please make changes.) A woman on a food forum once asked if putting her toddler's uneaten food back in the pan was gross. Everyone unanimously agreed that no one should eat food her toddler touched because of spreading sickness and whatnot. I explained that any saliva from the toddler would degrade the rest of the food and make it go bad faster. A halfway-eaten bowl of applesauce, for instance, could ruin the whole jar.

The post itself puzzled me. Why does she need other people's permission to be gross? In the privacy of your own home, you can do what you want.

Keep in mind that the stricter your sanitation standards are, the stricter you'll have to be with your food to prevent waste. I have no problem shaving mold off a block of cheddar cheese. If you have a problem with that, you have to put more thought into your cheese. Maybe you can't buy as big a block as I can, or perhaps you should buy shredded cheese instead and put some of it in the freezer. If the members of your family won't eat off each other's plates, they'll need to practice better portion control. You get the idea.

TIP: Most dairy products can be easily frozen, like butter, cottage cheese, cream cheese, and milk. Cheese frozen as a solid brick will get crumbly, so it's best to shred it first. Cream will not whip as well after being defrosted. Sour cream, yogurt, and buttermilk will likely become grainy.

Myth 3: "I don't waste very much food."

Remember, the average American wastes 25 percent of the food they buy, $1,300 in food a year, and enough to feed an additional family member. Yet most people I talk to say they don't waste much food. The numbers don't add up. I recommend trying Step 4: Be Aware of What You Toss. Make a list of the food you throw out, or weigh it, just to see. You might be shocked by your results.

Myth 4: "It'll make me fat."

This was a top concern for most people I spoke to, including my husband. He didn't know how to support me without eating everything on his plate, even after he was full. That wasn't the right way to go about it at all.

If you eat food you don't want and your body doesn't need, you're still wasting it. You're just diverting the food from the landfill to your waistline.

Think of it this way: I stopped wasting food as a tribute to mothers who have lost their children to hunger. Imagine how those mothers would feel if I told them my tribute was to engorge myself at every meal. I wouldn't get many thank-yous.

If you're a loyal member of the Clean Plate Club, like I am, there are things you can do to keep your plate clean without overeating.

You don't have to gain weight to be waste-free, and you can even diet if you want. It all depends on how you go about it.

Depending on the food, I might put anything unfinished back in the pot if it was for the most part unchanged or untouched, like florets of roasted broccoli or a meatball. Don't forget that you don't want to reintroduce partially eaten food because saliva breaks things down. If you dip a used spoon in a bowl of yogurt or pudding, it'll get watery.

If the food is changed, like curry poured over rice, and there's a serving of it left, I might put it in a container separate from the other leftovers. If there's only a little bit left, we would give it to another family member, and if another family member didn't want it, I would give it to the dog.

Still, on occasion, the food remaining on my plate was in a limbo of can't save it, can't put it back, can't give it to the dog, and no one wants to eat it.

One of the key steps in maintaining a healthy weight is taking modest portions. This is also a key step in reducing food waste. The two goals can actually work hand in hand. If you do find yourself in a situation where you have to overeat to not waste food, I'll tell you this from experience: It only takes stuffing yourself a couple of times before you master portion control. Feeling stuffed and angry is an effective lesson.

If you still find yourself stuck with too much food on your plate, don't beat yourself up over it. Really. I'm not all that worried about table scraps.

I was staying with another family when for breakfast, they served leftover crepes from a party the day before. I wanted more than one crepe, but less than two. Instead of having the foresight to make myself one-and-a-half crepes, like a more intelligent person would have, I made myself two and soon realized my mistake. Andrew and the girls didn't want it. I wasn't at home, so I couldn't put it in the fridge for later or feed it to my dog. My goal was to waste *nothing*, so I had no choice but to finish it.

As I slowly shoveled in the last bite, the husband of the family started to clean up. He picked up a large platter full of freshly cut fruit . . . *and threw the whole thing in the trash.* Table scraps contribute so little to the global food-waste problem and saving them won't save the world. It's chump change for the hungry and the environment.

Just so you know, I didn't gain any weight after I stopped wasting food. I actually lost weight at one point. You can read about that in Chapter 6.

The Truth About Expired Food

Let's discuss expiration dates: their accuracy and their usefulness. Here's a summary:

Expiration dates are stupid. Ignore them.

Most of us treat expiration dates like gospel doctrine. If the stamp on the yogurt container says June 12, then the gods of expiration have spoken, and it shall be so. Ninety percent of Americans occasionally throw food away based on the label alone, and 25 percent *always* throw food away because of the label.[9]

If that describes you, get ready for your world to turn upside down. None of the dates on food is regulated, and except for a few things like baby formula and prescription drugs, they aren't even required by law. In the vast majority of cases, the dates indicate freshness, not safety. It's a way for companies to protect their brand. Companies understandably want you to eat their food when it's at its best so that you don't get a negative impression of their product.[10]

These businesses have no incentive to be accurate with their expiration dates. If you throw out food prematurely, you have to buy more, which means bigger profits. Even if they wanted to be accurate, it's not like they let their food sit in boxes for years, then opened a single box each month until they discovered one that didn't taste as good as the others. They're guessing.

And trust me, they're way off. Dried goods usually have an expiration date of only a few years. I inherited my parents' food storage, and my family has been eating through cans that were sealed twenty years ago. There was probably some loss of nutrients in that time, and the dried beans and the oatmeal have to be soaked longer, but they're otherwise fine, and the pasta and the rice taste exactly the same.

TIP: Water is one of the components that bacteria need to survive and multiply. Keeping your food dry will help it last longer.

Please don't close this book and tell everyone on Goodreads and Amazon to burn their copies if they want to live. I'm not just a nut job spreading food-borne illnesses; other people smarter than me hate expiration dates, too. The Smithsonian website published an article titled "'Sell By' and 'Best By' Dates on Food Are Basically Made Up—but Hard to Get Rid Of."[11]

Additionally, Emily Broad Leib, the director at the Harvard Food Law and Policy Clinic, and Dana Gunders, a former employee at the Natural Resources Defense Council and the author of *Waste-Free Kitchen Handbook*, both said the exact same thing: dates printed on food are chaotic and unregulated, and they have very little to do with safety.

Jonathan Bloom wrote this on his blog, Wasted Food: "Food doesn't . . . die at midnight on the date stamped on its package. Instead, it slowly passes from optimal to inedible. And that date stamped on the package—no matter what words precede it—tends to fall much closer to edible."[12]

Expiration dates didn't even exist until the 1970s. Consider this: in the 1970s, we wasted *half* as much food as we do now.[13] Might there be a connection? Companies are so dedicated to expiration dates that they even put dates on food that will never go bad, like honey, salt, and sugar. Archaeologists have discovered honey in ancient Egyptian tombs that is still safe to eat.

In 2018, I found a picture online of sea salt with a label that said, "Formed by the primal sea more than 250 million years ago." Its expiration date was 2019. The caption on the image read, "Just my luck. 250-million-year-old salt and it expires next year."

A reader commented: "I guess they dug it up just in time."

A comedian joked about the expiration dates on ipecac syrup. That's the medicine that makes you throw up if you drink poison.

"What's expired ipecac syrup going to do?" he asked. "Make you sick?"

Yet so many people believe expiration dates to be true. A friend of mine once found her roommate cleaning out the fridge. The roommate handed her a container of yogurt and said, "Do you want this? It expires at midnight."

She said, "That's not how it works, but thanks for the snack."

I know a family who frequently leaves their dinner out all night long. They once made a huge pot of soup for a party, left it out, and brought it to work to share with their coworkers the next day. No one got sick because it was a spicy soup . . . we'll get into spices later.

(Please, please, please do not start leaving your food out all night and tell people I said it was okay. Just because it worked for that particular soup doesn't mean it works with everything!)

The same family that leaves their food out refuses to eat *anything* past its expiration date. Even if it's one day past, they throw it out. I'm fascinated by the psychology of this. That family has no fear of getting sick from their food. They follow the expiration dates because . . . I honestly have no idea.

Whatever you do, for the love of all that's good, don't download one of those charts on Pinterest that says how long food stays fresh. I read one that said milk is still safe three days after its expiration date. Boy, that made me mad. Pinterest charts don't know how long your food was in the store before you bought it, how long it sat in the car on the way home or on your counter before you put it away, and they don't know the temperature of your refrigerator. The chart also said pasta lasts two years past its expiration date, which isn't true. They're just swapping one irrelevant date for another, and in their effort to prevent food waste, they're actually encouraging it.

The worst part is that "expired food" is considered ineligible for donations for hungry people. Activists are trying to change that law, and hopefully, that law will change soon.

In fact, I've heard multiple accounts of people going to food pantries because they couldn't afford to buy food, and when they got home, they threw out everything that was expired. They then posted reviews on Google about how the food bank didn't respect their health or their dignity enough to give them safe food. We trust food companies so much that some of us would rather go hungry than go against their dates!

My brother, on the other hand, disregards expiration dates like a good consumer should . . . though even I'll admit that he's reckless. One Christmas, he bought six containers of eggnog that he hoped would last him all year. Then he forgot about them. A year and a half later, I teased him about how the expiration date only mentioned the month it would expire. They didn't bother to say the year because surely, no one would be foolish enough to keep cartons of eggnog for that long.

Imagine my shock when he told me that a year and a half later, he was still drinking them.

"They're all sealed. Look at the containers," he said. "None of them are bloated. That's how you can tell when it's gone bad."

"And it tastes fine?" I asked.

"Yup."

"You didn't get sick?"

"Nope."

To each their own, I guess.

On another food forum, someone posted a picture of cold bone broth with a layer of white fat on top. The fat had congealed in a wrinkly way that made the poster wonder if it wasn't fat at all, but mold, even though he had put it in the refrigerator only the day before.

Most people agreed that it would only be mold if the broth smelled bad. One commenter suggested that he heat the broth because fat would melt and mold would not.

A single person suggested he just get rid of the broth and not worry about it.

"When in doubt," he wrote, "throw it out."

What the Expiration Dates Really Mean

- **Sell by:** This is when the store wants to sell the item. Stores aren't going to sell their food up until the day it will kill people, so the sell-by date is useful to the store, but irrelevant to you and me. Some stores use a code that is indecipherable to customers so no one gets confused and throws the food away too early.
- **Best by:** This is when the food is at its peak in quality and freshness. After this date, the quality of the food will gradually decline. The day after the best-by date on a carton of yogurt is not the day that yogurt becomes dangerous; it's the day that the yogurt becomes a teensy-tiny bit not as good as the day before. Some food still tastes the same for months and even years after the best-by date.
- **Use by:** This is a guess of when the food is no longer safe to eat. I've also seen the stamp "Use or Freeze by," which I think is helpful, especially with meat. The use-by date is still an estimate and not based on science.
- **Expiration date:** "Expired" by definition means "comes to an end." Food doesn't come to an abrupt end on a certain day. This date doesn't mean anything.

It would make sense to throw the broth out if he doubted its safety. But why would he doubt? The broth was twenty-four hours old. It didn't smell bad.

The old adage "When in doubt, throw it out" might have been good advice back in the 1960s when we didn't distrust food so much, but that's no longer the case.

I read a post by someone experiencing a food-related panic attack. She had cooked a tart, and to make the crust of a tart, you need something to weigh it down while it's baking so the crust doesn't rise into a pastry dome. Bakers often use beans, which they call blind baking. This person used chickpeas and then used the chickpeas to make hummus. Resourceful, right?

TIP: When you make a tart or a pie shell, you have to weigh it down as it's cooking with heavier food like rice, beans, or quinoa. You can still soak and cook the "weights" after baking them in the oven, though they might need to soak longer.

That same day, she watched a cooking show. The chef on the show said to throw away beans that have been blind baked because it makes them "inedible." The woman scoured the Internet to find out if the hummus was safe to eat, and when she couldn't find the answer, she went on the forum and begged people to help her. She said (and I quote) that she was "freaking out."

I resisted, but I wanted to respond with a snarky comment. *Are you still alive? Did you have to go to the hospital? Did you feel nauseous, or did you throw up? No? Then your hummus was fine.*

A friend told me she cut mold off a tomato and then cooked the rest of it, and she wanted to know "if that was okay." I'm starting to wonder if people's definition of "okay" is different from mine. Bad food makes you sick. If it doesn't make you sick, it isn't bad.

TIP: Solid foods with mold on the outside, like bread, hard cheese, and fruit, are still good to eat after all the mold is cut off. Soft foods, including soft cheese and liquids, are not safe once they're moldy.

Too many of us have a deep, irrational fear of spoiled food. I wonder why. Obviously, no one should eat anything that is decayed or contaminated, and I highly recommend that you do not drink eighteen-month-old eggnog. But with all the regulations from the FDA and developments like pasteurization, food is safer now than it's ever been. Yet we're more afraid of it than ever.

Our paranoia over food safety might be connected to how little we know about everything we're putting in our bodies. With all the medications, pesticides, preservatives, and other mysterious substances we consume, not to mention our awareness of illnesses like diabetes and cancer, we worry about safety even after we've eaten and nothing happens. Some people say red food coloring causes ADHD, which makes you wonder what other substances are making us sick that we don't know about.

But our paranoia over spoiled food shouldn't connect to our fear of cancer and mental illness because the consequences of spoiled food are immediate. You eat bad food, you throw up and get diarrhea, and you learn a hard-earned lesson about food safety.

I don't think our phobia is from pesticides and preservatives, though. If I were to guess, I'd say the advice from the FDA and others, combined with expiration dates, is the reason we don't trust our food.

Let's go back in time to the 1970s, when expiration dates first became a thing. You open a container of yogurt. It looks fine. It tastes fine. It smells fine. You would have eaten it, but now there's a stamp on the container saying it's no longer safe. You assume the expiration date is required by law and supported by science, not just a random number that the manufacturer pulled out of thin air.

If people you trust say you can't eat yogurt that you thought you could eat, you must not know what's good for you. You start to mistrust your senses. Eventually, you become so dependent on the rules that you put no thought into what you're throwing away and why.

Personally, I think instead they should print packaging dates and leave it to us to decide how long is too long.

You can't rely on companies to tell you when a food should be eaten. The only one who can tell if your food is unsafe is you. Keep reading to find out how.

Bacteria Makes Food Unsafe

It was Andrew's birthday, and I handed him a box with a tie inside.

"Thanks," he said sincerely. It had the blueprint for the Millennium Falcon on it.

"That's not your present," I said slyly. "That's a blindfold for you to wear on the way to your present."

We loaded the girls into the car, and he wrapped the tie around his head. "I'll know where you're going," he bragged, "even with the blindfold on."

"Challenge accepted!" I declared.

For twenty minutes, I drove all over town in circles and zigzags, trying to get him lost. Every turn I made, he'd say, "We're on Hardy Street. We just passed the university. We're at the zoo."

He was impossible to trick, so finally I pulled the car up to a small mom-and-pop grocery store.

"Ta-da!" I said.

"Why did we stop at a liquor store?" he asked, taking off his tie and looking at the building to our left instead of the grocery store to our right. He didn't even know we had a mom-and-pop grocery store in that area. I could have taken him straight there and he wouldn't have known where we were.

"Are you ready for your surprise?" I asked.

"Sure," he said, though he wasn't convinced anything in a grocery store could be exciting.

"This place has *aged steaks.*"

He raised his eyebrows. "Really," he said.

"Yup! You've always wanted to try one. I planned this months ago."

An aged steak is refrigerated in specific conditions for an extended period of time. Thirty days is typical, though some steak is aged for as long as 120 days. Meat loses moisture as it ages and the enzymes in the meat break down proteins and fibers that make beef tough. The end result: the two of us swooning over magnificent steaks that were so tender, our jaws weren't even tired after eating them.

The moral of the story: "old food" is not the same as "bad food."

Another example: Once when I was a kid, my parents bought four ginormous cabbages to make sauerkraut. I think their purchase had less to do with their love of sauerkraut and more to do with the irresistibility of such a big cabbage. My parents took pictures of each of us holding one, our little bodies straining under the weight.

My parents shredded the cabbages, put them in ten-gallon ice cream containers with brine, and let them rot. I'm not joking. We used weights on top of plates to press the sauerkraut down, and each morning we'd lift the weights and scrape the mold off the surface.

Once the cabbage was fermented, we put it in jars and stored them in the basement.

The sauerkraut was *delicious.*

Sauerkraut is not the only fermented vegetable people regularly eat. I have a jar of kimchee that's been in my refrigerator for years, and it tastes just as terrible now as when I first opened it.

Understanding food safety will do a lot to change how we treat our food. People unaware of safety rules will freak out over milk one day past its expiration date, yet they'll eat cheese and yogurt, both of which are just milk that was intentionally left out until bacteria thickened it. Hundreds of Internet articles say you can't leave sour cream out for two hours, but cream has to be at room temperature for twenty-four hours to even become sour cream in the first place.

Since my more skeptical readers might not take my word on this, here's some expert advice from Dana Gunder, the pioneer of food-waste research:

> Many people don't really understand how or why food makes them sick. . . . Most food-borne illnesses come from food being contaminated, not from its natural process of decomposition. . . . Foodborne illnesses generally fall into two categories: 1. Infections from living microorganisms or toxins produced by these organisms, or 2. Poisoning caused by harmful toxins such as those of poisonous mushrooms or chemicals that have contaminated the food.[14]

Food with salmonella, listeria, and *E. coli* is contaminated before reaching your kitchen. That means most of the illnesses you're afraid of are completely outside your control, and you wouldn't know it was unsafe until after you got sick. I had to toss a whole head of lettuce because of an *E. coli* outbreak at a farm in my area. That made me grumpy.

TIP: For leafy vegetables like lettuce, celery, broccoli, and green onions, rinse them thoroughly in water and wrap them in aluminum foil when they're still dripping. This will keep vegetables crisp and make them last longer.

You can't protect yourself by throwing all your food out early. That does nothing except waste your money. Instead, you should worry about bacteria. Safety has less to do with age and more to do with how food was prepared and stored. I used to think the fact that Cheez Whiz doesn't need to be refrigerated means it isn't real food, but the reason is that bacteria can't get inside the pressurized can.

The temperature of your food is important. Perishable items need to stay below 40 degrees or above 140 degrees Fahrenheit to prevent bacteria from growing. Think about buffets that leave their food sitting out on hot tables for hours on end. They're able to do this because the hot plates keep the food at a safe temperature.

When food isn't cool or hot enough, the FDA says you should throw it out after it's been left out for two hours. I swear, so much food is wasted because the USDA and FDA like to slap rules on things that don't need to be regulated, like the shape of produce.

How long food can sit out depends on a lot of things, like the temperature of the room, the temperature of the food when it was served, what kind of food we're even talking about, how much of it there is (a big pot of stew will take longer to reach room temperature than a small pot), and what spices are in it.

Did you know spices act as a preservative? I have a theory that this is why countries in hot climates rely on spicy cuisine. It probably isn't the right time to mention this since we're talking about food, but spices were used to embalm dead bodies as a way to preserve them.

I guarantee that whoever came up with the two-hour rule didn't systematically serve room-temperature food at different intervals and keep track of when the test subjects got sick. They just felt like they should make a guideline, even when there can never be a true guideline, and some suit-wearing schmuck in a conference room raised his hand and said, "Let's just tell people two hours."

If we're going to go overboard with the rules, why two hours? Why not one hour, or thirty minutes? There's no value in picking a number that doesn't mean anything. Meanwhile, many people in developing countries don't have refrigerators or freezers, so the two-hour rule isn't even an option.

Another rule I can't stand is that you have to eat defrosted food within twenty-four hours. The Food Standards Agency, and many other official-sounding groups, say this without giving a reason.[15] It's untrue, plain and simple. Bacteria can't grow in a freezer. Why would defrosted food decay any faster than food that was never frozen?

That same group says on its website, "You can freeze pre-packaged food until midnight on the 'use by' date."

Yeah, okay . . . or I can freeze food whenever I darn well please. Your use-by dates aren't the boss of me.

When is it safe to leave food out, and when is it not safe? My advice: It doesn't matter because we have refrigerators. When all is said and done, the two-hour rule is good advice. As soon as your food reaches room temperature, the clock starts ticking and there's no way of knowing when the alarm will go off. All I'm trying to say is don't throw out a big pot of soup when the timer hits 2:01.

Keep in mind that even if your food doesn't go bad after two hours, it will go bad faster if it ever reaches room temperature for very long, even if you put it in the fridge afterwards. Our goal is for food to stay good for as long as possible to keep it from going bad.

TIP: How cold is your fridge? It should be no higher than 40 degrees Fahrenheit, or 5 degrees Celsius, according to the Food Standards Agency.[16] A warmer fridge will cause food to spoil faster. The dial in fridges isn't always accurate, so it's best to use a fridge thermometer.

Not putting hot food in your fridge is also good advice. Hot foods raise the temperature of everything in your refrigerator. This might not make your food unsafe, but again, raising the temperature in your fridge will make everything go bad sooner.

There are hard-and-fast rules you *should* follow. Meat usually has to cook to a certain temperature before it's okay to eat. Fish is safe to eat raw—assuming the fish wasn't sick or wasn't already poisonous and the fish is fresh and prepared properly. I don't feel confident preparing it myself, but hallelujah for sushi.

Believe it or not, one of the riskiest foods in your house is rice. *Bacillus cereus* is a bacteria that can cause food poisoning, and it can live on rice. Cooked rice is safe to eat, but the spores survive the cooking process and can develop if left at room temperature. If you've eaten old rice dozens of times without any ill effects, it doesn't mean old rice is safe; it just means that particular batch didn't have any bacillus cereus spores. The food poisoning is relatively mild and usually lasts twenty-four hours, but I'd still rather not roll the dice when I can just put my rice in the refrigerator.

After you've handled raw meat, don't go around touching everything in your kitchen. Wash your hands, the counters, and any dishes you use. Put the meat in a bag before placing it in the fridge, and if the meat has leaked juices in the fridge, clean it with soap and don't eat food the juices have touched.

Once I was dumb (it's been known to happen) and kept beef on a refrigerator shelf instead of in the meat drawer. It leaked all over a 3-pound Sam's Club bag of shredded cheddar cheese. I found out about the leak not because I saw the juice, but because I made grilled cheese sandwiches and the whole kitchen smelled like death. It was a pretty good indicator that the cheese wasn't safe to eat.

This leads me to my next point.

How Do I Know My Food Is Safe?

I can tell what many of you are thinking. *If I can't trust the FDA and I can't trust expiration dates, whom can I trust? Is there no one who can protect me? Is my whole life a lie?*

Relax. I believe this is an issue we don't need to worry about. The human body is designed to detect when food is unsafe. It smells bad, tastes bad, or has a gross texture or color. Raw chicken turns green and gets slimy. Produce gets mushy and moldy.

Listen to your body's cues. Examine the food and see if any of your senses raise a red flag.

Our bodies are so adept at being revolted by bad food that I don't think people can eat mold even if they want to. My husband and I disagree on whether a person could eat a fuzzy green slice of bread for a million dollars. I believe you cannot stifle those survival instincts for any amount of money, but Andrew says there isn't much he wouldn't eat for a million dollars.

TIP: While it may not look appetizing, food is still safe when it's brown, bruised, discolored, scarred, stale, and wilted because bacteria doesn't cause those issues.

Our instincts are efficient, but they can get confused. Have you ever thrown up after eating something and then you couldn't eat that food again, even if that wasn't the reason you got sick? My sister got violently ill after eating strawberry shortcake, and she couldn't eat it again for years. This is because your body has made an incorrect association and believes the food itself is unsafe. You might know after barfing strawberry shortcake that it had nothing to do with the shortcake, but you can't talk your brain out of being nauseated around that food. Your instinct is too strong to battle.

Except when a million dollars are on the line, in which case, apparently, all bets are off.

It's also easy to tell when food is too old, even if it's still safe. Old, packaged goods smell terrible. I wanted to make strawberry milk, but the syrup tasted old. Come to find out, the syrup expired three years ago. I knew not to drink that milk without having to look at the date.

This doesn't necessarily mean you can't still use old, packaged food. Stale food might taste fine once cooked. I accidentally used old cocoa to make homemade brownies, and the batter tasted like mummy bones. I baked it anyway, just in case (see Rule #4: Almost always taste before tossing). The icky flavor cooked out, and the brownies were delicious.

Of course, some people can't depend on their common sense because they don't have any. A friend of mine had a mother-in-law who would leave her groceries in a hot car for hours, feed her children balled-up bits of raw ground beef while making dinner, and this isn't unsafe, but she would make spaghetti sauce out of tomato juice and gelatin. Gross. When my friend went to her house for Thanksgiving for the first (and last) time, everyone got food poisoning.

Another friend of mine grew up in a single-parent household, run by a mom who was too busy to cook dinner every night. She would make a huge pot of soup, which she left on the stove instead of storing it in the fridge. For the rest of the week, the kids would ladle out a bowl whenever they were hungry. The rule was that when bubbles formed on the surface, it was time to throw it out.

It's too bad I can't tell you that story in person. I love seeing the look of horror on people's faces when I tell it.

For most of us, the concept is simple: don't be neurotic, but don't be a dummy.

Part 2:

Let's Get Started

Chapter 3:

A Somewhat Bumpy Beginning

We're done with the rules and statistics. It's time to change your life. I dove headfirst into my new resolution with certainty that I could stop wasting all food forever, and I learned two things very quickly.

1. Everyone can cut their food waste down by 50 percent, easily. I'm talking *overnight* easily. It takes only slight changes and a little effort to make that big of a difference.
2. Cutting food waste down to zero, on the other hand, was not so easy.

Stuff got thrown away the first month, and I let it go, figuring I'd get better, but month after month, food would slip beyond my grasp. Food got dropped, smashed, burned, doused with orange juice, or forgotten in a corner of the shelf. Once my youngest wanted to watch *Toy Story*, and as I reached into the entertainment center, I grabbed an apple that one of my girls had hidden and left to rot. It was like baby poop surrounded by a thin membrane of skin. There wasn't much I could have done to prevent that. If you'll forgive the pun, one might say that I bit off more than I could chew.

The biggest reason I couldn't suddenly go waste-free was that I didn't know how. There were books and blog articles that helped, but they weren't enough. I had to learn a lot by myself. For instance, I couldn't figure out what to do about milkshakes. You can't freeze them because they get hard as a rock. My mom would always put half-eaten milkshakes in the freezer. Let's just say they never got all-the-way eaten.

My original tactic was for me and the girls to split a milkshake, but they had to get their own once they were past the age of civil sharing. I found myself coaxing them into eating more than they wanted and coaxing myself into eating everything they refused to finish. Then I realized how absurd I was being. At 1,000 calories each, shoveling in spoonfuls of milkshake was ridiculous. This is when I first had my doubts about junk food passing the Hungry Kid Test.

I read dozens of articles like "Ten Ideas to Reduce Your Food Waste," and many books like *Waste-Free Living*, but no one taught me what to do with a melted milkshake.

TIP: To save smoothies and milkshakes, pour them into ice cube trays and freeze. Once frozen, dip the bottom of the tray in hot water until the cubes get loose. Store the cubes in a sealed bag or container. When you're ready, blend the cubes in a blender with just a splash of milk.

I called myself "waste-free," but it would be more accurate to call myself "waste resistant." Especially in the early days. Still, just putting forth the effort changed my life. You would think the benefits of going waste-free would emerge gradually as I got better at it. Instead, I noticed differences within the first month.

Less Waste . . . Obviously

In the first week, Andrew said the garbage can was lighter. That is *super* embarrassing. I had no idea we were wasting so much food that the can would be noticeably less heavy as he rolled it to the curb.

My new lifestyle didn't just affect the way we ate. Food rescue in my home inspired me to waste less of other things. One good decision leads to another. I started the compost bin that I mentioned before, and I started recycling.

Feel free to gasp or roll your eyes. Yes, despite my love of the environment and my abhorrence of waste, I wasn't recycling at the time. It hurts to admit. Although if it makes me look any better, your recycling isn't always "recycled" in the way you might think. I can't give you a statistic because everyone says different things, but a disconcerting amount of our recycling ends up in landfills. It used to be shipped to China where much of it went into the sea. I didn't know this at the time, though, so it's not a good excuse.

I *used* to recycle, back when I was growing up in Portland. Then I moved to an apartment in Utah where recycling wasn't an option. Every sheet of paper and every cardboard box that I put in the garbage made me cringe. After years of apartment living, I got used to it, and when we moved into a house where recycling became an option again, I didn't get around to asking the city for a recycling bin. It was on my to-do list but never made it onto my "done" list.

When I stopped wasting food, I finally got my bin.

The city charged me three dollars a month for recycling. That wasn't very much, but it still struck me as ironic. Wouldn't it make more sense for *them* to pay *me* to recycle? It felt like being punished for doing the right thing, which was especially irksome considering that they would probably sell my recycling to a third-world country for a profit.

Before, if we ever forgot to take out the trash, we'd be in a bad way for the rest of the week. That changed once we started recycling, composting, and eating our food. Andrew often didn't bother taking the trash to the curb. There wasn't enough in the can to be worth it. On more than one occasion, trash day came and there was only one solitary kitchen bag in the can from the entire week.

More Money

Once I stopped wasting food, everyone asked if our grocery bill went down. We saved almost exactly what the statistics said we would: about $1,300 a year.

I kept pretty close track of our bills, especially our grocery bills, so I noticed when the bill changed. There was a jump in our spending when Rose started eating solid foods, and there was a sharp incline as she went from being a toddler to a kid.

I've heard several experts say a leading cause of food waste is the low cost of food. I don't know where they're shopping. When have you ever looked at your grocery bill and felt relieved that the cost of food was low?

When I stopped wasting food in 2017, saving money on groceries was a top concern for my family. Our income wasn't the issue; the problem was medical bills. We had signed up for the cheapest insurance because no one in our family had any health concerns. Why pay a big premium for a low deductible that we would never use?

Little did I know how much the medical system will skewer even healthy people with outrageous expenses. Over the course of only a few years, we spent tens of thousands of dollars on typical procedures like childbirth, gallbladder surgery, root canal, ear tubes, and two emergency room visits where the doctor told us to go home and wait for the problems to resolve themselves. Then one of our kids started having seizures, and we discovered she had periventricular leukomalacia (PVL), which is damage to the white matter of her brain. We don't know how it happened. That year, an eighth of our income went toward medical expenses, and we were still thousands of dollars in medical debt. We hit our $6,000 deductible that year . . . in December!

Needless to say, we were eager to save money wherever we could.

I stressed over ways to cut down on food costs but hadn't found anything that made a noticeable difference. I read online articles and forum posts. Not a single one of them offered tips on avoiding food waste, so saving food to save money never occurred to me.

Instead, most of the articles were written by rich people who tell you not to buy things that I couldn't pay for in the first place. Make your own coffee instead of going to a café every morning. Make your own pizza instead of ordering delivery once a week. Instead of buying prepared food, cook from scratch. Buy a deep freezer so you can stock up on bulk items and sales. Use Groupon when you eat out.

I get really keyed up when every single article says to buy store brands instead of name brands. Oh, really? If I want to save money, I need to buy cheaper stuff? Gee, why didn't I think of that?

Other tips either weren't helpful or I didn't know how to implement them. "Shop on sale"—just because it's "on sale" doesn't mean it's cheaper than buying off brands or in bulk. "Use coupons"—the only coupons I could find were for expensive items or food I didn't want to eat, and clipping coupons took up so much time. "Shop

Costco or Sam's Club"—buying in bulk means you have to buy enough groceries to cover not only the current month but also subsequent months. Besides, the cost of bulk food didn't seem to be *that* much cheaper than Walmart, and you have to pay a membership fee to earn the privilege of buying it. "Shop discount grocery stores"—we didn't have any in my town.

This last tip killed me. Any time I saw an article on Pinterest with the headline "We only spend sixty dollars a week on groceries," the author always shopped at Aldi. If I wanted to drastically cut down on our grocery bill, it seemed I had two options: 1. Shop at Aldi, or 2. Give up, because you can't have that low of a bill without shopping at Aldi.

Some advice was downright ridiculous. Forage for edible plants in the wild. Volunteer at a food pantry and see if they'll let you take home the leftovers. Ask the grocery store manager for discounts.

Finally, I joined a frugal budgeting forum on Facebook and wrote, "Help! I spend $750 a month on groceries for four people. Is that normal?" I got close to fifty comments back, and they all agreed that I shouldn't have to spend more than $100 per person each month. (Food was much cheaper back in 2017.)

I wrote down all their advice and made a plan. The plan didn't include avoiding food waste—no one even recommended it. When my husband came home that day, I announced to him that we weren't going to spend more than $450 a month on groceries from then on. He was significantly less enthusiastic about this than when I would later stop wasting food. I guess that "Buy whatever you want and eat all of it" is easier to swallow than "Stop eating what you want if it's expensive."

These budgeting tricks helped:

One: Eat healthier. With more fruits and vegetables and less meat and junk food, not to mention water instead of juice and soft drinks, our bill went down. This confused me. I kept hearing that food-insecure people can't afford healthy food and that unhealthy food is cheaper, but then everyone told me the opposite. If my junk food and my healthy food were both too expensive for them, what were they eating? It made me realize how little I understood about how the poor live.

TIP: Avoid precut produce. When fruit and vegetables are cut up, they go bad faster.

Two: I kept track of how much things cost so that I knew what a good deal was, instead of trusting stores. I used to snatch up every "Buy 1, Get 1 Free" deal without realizing the items were often twice as expensive to balance out the deal, so learning typical prices kept me from buying overpriced things.

Keeping all those prices straight in my head was a challenge. I put a chart on the fridge of foods we usually bought and how much it cost at every store (Sam's Club, Walmart, Winn-Dixie, and farmers' markets). I learned never to buy chicken breast that was more than $2 a pound, never buy ground beef that was more than $3.50 a pound, and if I saw shrimp that was $5 a pound, it was time to load up the freezer. When I had it more or less memorized, I took the chart down.

Three: I cut corners wherever I could to see if the savings would add up. Here's the list of everything I tried, in case you're curious:

- Potty-trained my youngest kid early to save on diapers.
- Made household cleaner out of orange peels and vinegar.
- Made my own laundry detergent.

- Used rags instead of paper towels.
- Stopped using paper plates.
- Bought dried beans instead of canned beans. Also, started eating beans.
- Limited how much milk we drank. (The girls were drinking a *lot* of it.)
- Made my own bread, rolls, and herbed toast.
- Baked treats instead of buying them.
- Used containers more often instead of Ziploc bags.
- Bought food that came in large containers instead of individual servings, like yogurt, for instance.
- Included cheap sides with our meals.
- Stopped buying already-prepared snacks for my daughter's lunches, like Go-Gurts, Lunchables, bagged crackers, and so on.
- Made my own playdough, since my children went through that stuff like you wouldn't believe.
- Stopped eating dry cereal for breakfast and ate hot cereal instead.
- Ate fruit and vegetables that were in season, instead of just getting whatever I wanted.
- Downloaded grocery apps, like the Walmart Savings Catcher app where you scan in your receipts and get refunded the difference if another store is selling it for cheaper.

TIP: Keep a table of when fruits and vegetables are in season in your kitchen. In-season produce is cheaper and often local, and produce bought locally is fresher, will last longer, and causes less pollution.

I also bought whole chickens and cut them up myself to freeze the portions. It took forever and I hated it. But the whole chickens were only $1/pound, and I could use the bones for broth.

The day after I cut up my first chicken, Andrew had the impulse to make buffalo chicken dip and didn't think to check if we already had the ingredients. He bought breasts that were $3.50 per pound.

I could have happily killed him.

These ideas helped, but as you can imagine, doing it all took time and effort.

After I stopped wasting food, our grocery bill went down $100 in the first month. A hundred dollars a month is how much I expected *other* people to save but believed my home would be the exception. I also thought the improvement would be gradual, instead of noticing a difference overnight. Instead, it was by far the easiest and most effective money-saving tip I tried. Much better than clipping coupons, scanning receipts, or foraging for food in the wild.

More Time

Saving food didn't only save me money. It saved me time! For a mother of two young girls, time was almost as valuable as cash. We had always eaten leftovers, but I noticed a huge difference when we ate *all* our leftovers. I didn't need to cook as often. We would also repurpose leftovers into new dishes, which felt like a new meal but took less time than starting a meal from the beginning.

TIP: You can save a ton of time in the kitchen by repurposing food you've already made into a new dish.

For example, I had leftover roasted potatoes but didn't have a main course to serve them with. I heated them in a sealed container with some water so they'd get soft, topped them with melted cheddar cheese, and served them with fried eggs that were so over easy, the potatoes were soaked in the runny yolks. It was delicious and incredibly easy.

TIP: Eggs can transform many leftovers into breakfast. You can add food to scrambled eggs, for instance, put eggs in a breakfast burrito, or top leftovers with a fried egg.

My mother-in-law had her own version of repurposing. She often would serve two or three sides with her meals, and one of the sides would typically be from the night before. It was a constant rotation of new + leftover dishes.

I also got in the habit of freezing food before it went bad. Our freezer was soon full of meals that only needed to be defrosted, which also cut back on how often I needed to cook.

It might seem like an exaggeration to say I cooked *half* as often, but that isn't too far from the truth. I enjoy cooking, but making dinner with a toddler and a hungry four-year-old in the house . . . not so much. Between 4:30 PM and 6:30 PM is the worst time of the day. Everyone's hungry and tired, the girls want my attention, I want my husband's attention because he just got home, and he just wants to rest on the couch. Andrew would often be asleep while I was at the stove with a screaming kid hanging on my ankles, tears streaming down her face because I couldn't hold her and fry pork chops at the same time. I told them, "Not now, I'm busy," so many times, I considered recording myself saying it and playing it on repeat while I cooked.

After going waste-free, I spent more evenings playing with my kids.

I cooked dinner so infrequently that I even started to miss it.

Less meal prep wasn't the only reason I had more time. Cooking less often also meant washing fewer dishes, and I'll do just about anything to avoid washing dishes. I also had to do less grocery shopping and less meal planning, neither of which are my favorite activities.

More Space

The space in my kitchen completely changed once I followed Step 2: Clean and Organize Everything, Step 3: Eat What You Have, and Step 5: Don't Buy too Much Food. No longer drowning in food, my kitchen had room to spare. There was no food in the laundry room like before. I even dedicated a kitchen shelf to art supplies for my kids.

New Recipes

When I was faced with a food that I didn't know how to use, I now needed to apply a bit of creativity. Sometimes my creativity got pushed to the limit, and that's when I discovered new recipes.

Like the time I had half a potato. I was making gnocchi from scratch—a favorite dish in my household—and I wanted to measure the ingredients exactly for once so that I could write the recipe down. I'm pretty sure my grandchildren would be irritated if I wrote, "Cook some mashed potatoes and add flour until it's enough."

Because of how the measurements worked out, I found myself stuck with half of an uncooked potato.

I did not want to cook half a potato. That was all the potatoes I had, so I couldn't add it to a new potato dish. Luckily, I was roasting a chicken in the oven at the time, so I cubed the potato and tossed it in the juices.

The potato was incredible! The four of us had to share the small portion I made, and we wished there was more. Now every time I roast chicken, I add potatoes and carrots to the juice.

Another time I was shuffling through my pantry—this was before I came up with Step 2: Clean and Organize Everything—and discovered two bulk-sized boxes of individual-serving strawberry instant oatmeal. They had expired three years ago. This was baffling because I made oatmeal from scratch, so I didn't know when or why we had bought instant oatmeal, and also because I didn't like strawberry oatmeal. It was also frustrating because, after too many messes and unfinished bowls, I had just decided not to serve the girls oatmeal for breakfast anymore. The strawberry oatmeal still smelled and tasted good, so I had to find a way to eat forty-five bags of it.

To my relief, I discovered a muffin recipe on Pinterest made out of oatmeal and milk. Just mix 2 cups of oatmeal, 1 cup of milk, ½ teaspoon baking powder, any flavoring you want (which I didn't have to do because they were already strawberry flavored), pour into cupcake tins, and bake twenty minutes in a 375-degree oven.

It was exactly what my family needed. They weren't messy like oatmeal served in a bowl. I could make them the evening before and heat them in the microwave one at a time. If one of the girls didn't finish a muffin, I just put it back in the fridge for the next day. I even froze some of them.

Another example: I love berry pies, but whenever I made pie, my family members only ate one slice. Six slices of pie was too much for me, and let's face it, pie is always best straight out of the oven.

One day I was puzzling over two pieces of blueberry pie that no one in my household wanted to eat. Then I remembered that once at a milkshake parlor, I saw a guy take a whole slice of pie and blend it up with ice cream. Now we make them at home. I call them pie-scream. I wondered what else I could mix the pie into. I liked oatmeal for breakfast. Why not stir in chopped-up chunks of blueberry pie?

It was delicious. I especially loved getting a big chunk of piecrust in my oatmeal. Piecrust is awesome in almost every dish.

Finally, I started making half pies. Instead of putting the crust in a pie tin and filling up the tin, I put the crust on a cookie sheet, topped it with half as much fruit as before, and wrapped the dough around the top. Problem solved.

Improved Marriage

Andrew has always been a supportive husband, so I knew he would support me, but I had no idea the lengths he would go to for the sake of making me happy.

There was a bit of a learning curve, of course. He would toss things out without thinking, and I'd correct him—gently, I promise. Like once I ate half an avocado on toast and left the other half on the windowsill. The surface turned brown, so he tossed it. The avocado was perfectly fine because, first, food only turns brown because it was exposed to air, which doesn't affect the taste or safety, and second, the brown part is only a thin film on the top. If he was grossed out by the brown part, he could have just scraped it off.

"Sorry," he said.

"It's fine," I said. "Just ask me next time."

TIP: When food turns brown, it is caused by oxidation, not decay, so it's safe to eat. To prevent browning, you can keep food sealed and away from the air, or you can splash some foods with lemon juice, like apples, avocados, and pears.

We developed an unspoken rule that I would be the only one who could decide what got thrown out and what didn't. Once after he fed the girls breakfast, I saw that he had actually saved two bites of uneaten oatmeal. Just two bites! I would have either eaten it myself or given it to the dog, but I never would have wrapped it in plastic wrap and put it in the fridge. Isn't that sweet?

I made fried chicken once, and it was a disaster. The breading fell apart and formed a slimy black film at the bottom of the pan. (Chicken is supposed to be coated in flour before dipped in batter.) We still ate the chicken after scraping off the breading, though all the burned stuff went to waste.

I realized too late after dipping raw chicken into the batter that I had just ruined a bowl of edible food. Used vegetable oil passes the Hungry Kid test (though I usually strain it out and reuse it anyway). Flour and milk do not.

I was pretty irritated with the situation and with myself. There's not much you can do with milk, flour, and raw chicken juice. Yet as I was leaving the room, I saw Andrew in front of the stove, making boiled dumplings for the dog.

TIP: After frying food, keep the used vegetable oil in an empty container to use later. You might want to strain out the gunk with cheesecloth, a paper towel, or even just a colander.

You'd think this meant he was getting into the no-waste lifestyle, and he made the dumplings because he wanted to. Nope. He just cared about me, and I would always remember that.

No Guilt

They say no one ever does anything for selfless reasons. What did I get out of all this, besides money and time? No more guilt!

We are social creatures, and our social structures exist because of our need for community. A tiger or a pangolin can mosey along without a thought for other animals. Humans, on the other hand, have to experience empathy for our society to function. When a human learns that another human is suffering, we feel pain. A human who feels no pain from another person's suffering isn't functioning properly, and that person is diagnosed as a sociopath. Not only do we feel pain when others suffer, but we feel joy when others feel joy. That joy is magnified when we are the ones who gave that person joy. It's a biological incentive. Being selfless isn't selfless at all. When we solve a problem and help others, we experience joy through empathy.

Remember the Ghost Baby that haunted my kitchen? The second I decided not to waste food ever again, I stopped imagining my ghost, and an enormous weight lifted from me. My soul felt lighter, freer, and happier. Even when I failed—and at first, I failed a lot—at least I was trying my hardest.

That was the greatest benefit to this whole thing. If zero guilt was my only reward for going waste-free, it was worth it.

I Made a Difference

Everyone was excited about what I was doing. Friends approached me left and right to talk about it: at the park, in church, at birthday parties, at playgroup. Once I ran into a group of friends at a farmers' market, and they surrounded me, speaking over each other about food waste. They had recipes to share, questions to ask, and compliments to shower on me.

When they heard I was working on a book, they were much more supportive of it than my other projects. One friend said it was the best idea I'd ever had; after posting some excerpts from the book, another said I had "found my voice"; and another said I should drop everything I was working on and focus all my attention on this. It actually hurt my feelings because all three of them had read my fiction, but still, their encouragement bolstered me.

TIP: Before throwing your apple cores, orange peels, or lemon peels in the compost, you can simmer them over the stove to make the house smell good. You can also use orange and lemon zest in recipes, boil apple peels and cores in water for syrup and jelly, or use apple cores and peels to make apple cider vinegar.

An amazing thing happened; they started to share their stories with me. One of them used leftover corn and potatoes from a crawfish boil to make bisque, which sounds amazing; another used Thanksgiving leftovers to make stuffing muffins; my mom mixed a mashed-up old banana in her pancake batter. Many of them experimented with homemade broth. More and more, I was seeing posts with the hashtag #anotherscrapsaved.

My sister told me, "Before you started this, I threw food away without even thinking about it."

Whenever my friends had leftover scraps they didn't know how to use, they also asked for help: the severed tops of baking apples (apple syrup, apple chips, apple jelly, apple cider vinegar, or boil with cloves for air freshener), a hundred crepes (freeze them, crepe cake, savory crepes, crepe casserole, enchiladas), the pulp from juiced produce (stop making juice and eat your vegetables). It was like solving fun little puzzles.

I was making a difference. That was a great feeling.

Step 1: Think About Food Differently

A quick disclaimer before I discuss these steps in depth; too often in self-help books and blogs, the writers keep interrupting themselves to say, "I'm not perfect at this," or "I don't do this all the time." It drives me nuts. I already assumed the writer wasn't perfect. Reminding me he has flaws is as pointless as saying I am going to put a period at the end of this sentence.

Then there's my least favorite but oft-repeated line: "You can't eliminate food waste completely." They try to motivate people while repeatedly reminding them they're going to fail.

It would be cumbersome to preface all my advice with confessions, so I'm just going to make a blanket statement: I've failed at all the advice I'm going to give you, and I undoubtedly will again. Please don't search through my trash or peek through my kitchen window until you see me throw something away, then jump out of the shadows and cry, "Aha!"

I follow these rules and do all the steps to the best of my ability all the time, and even though I'm not "perfect" at it, I know they work.

Another pet peeve of mine, since we're on the topic of pet peeves: Please, stop saying your food "won't get eaten," or say, "that food didn't get eaten." That's called a passive sentence. You've removed the subject (you) and left only the object (the food) and the verb (to eat), leaving the person performing the verb absent. It's a useful tactic in avoiding blame. Who didn't do the eating? The sentence didn't say. Instead, tell the truth: "I did not eat my food."

Now that we've got that unpleasantness out of the way, here's Step #1: Think About Food Differently.

First things first: you must question everything you think you know about food.

The turkey carcass soup became a beloved tradition in my home. It's a symbol of gratitude for me. Thanksgiving is for enjoying our abundance, so it seems incredibly ungrateful to throw away the abundance you've just given thanks for. (Thirty-five percent of edible turkey meat in the United States is wasted by consumers.[1]) I enjoy the symbolism of eking every last morsel from the turkey.

Thanksgiving Leftover Ideas:

- Mashed potatoes freeze well, and so does the gravy. There are lots of recipes that call for mashed potatoes. My go-tos are gnocchi, potato patties, smearing it over casseroles, or mixing it with cheddar and French-fried onions to use as a shell for casseroles.
- Turkey potpie. Cooked turkey doesn't freeze well, but chunks of turkey in a pie freezes perfectly. This is also a good opportunity to use some of the broth you made for sauce and any vegetables you might have left over.
- Turkey sandwiches are a tradition almost as important as the turkey itself, but there's more than one way to eat it: with mayonnaise, Dijon mustard, cranberry sauce, avocados, bacon, provolone, or Swiss cheese, for example. You can experiment with different kinds of bread, and you can grill the sandwich.
- Potato peels are delicious roasted. Just drizzle with oil, sprinkle with salt, lay flat on a cookie sheet, and bake at 400 degrees Fahrenheit for ten to fifteen minutes. You can also deep-fry them in oil or bacon grease.
- Turkey salad is a great way to transform leftover turkey. Using grapes, dried cranberries, and pecans in turkey salad is delicious.
- You can shred the turkey to use for all kinds of recipes, like sprinkling over chips with barbecue sauce and cheddar and baking in the oven, adding to a barbecue pizza, or using on burritos with salsa and Mexican spices.
- Turkey can go in soups, too, and turkey chili.

I made the soup for another couple once. It did not go well. They were revolted that I had boiled garbage for dinner.

Guess what? *All* meat broth is made from bones. Cup of noodle soup, Campbell's chicken soup, bouillon cubes. The flavor doesn't come from the meat.

Most people don't realize this, but Jell-O is also made out of animal bones. Seriously, Jell-O. You can tell your bone broth is done if it gets gelatinous in the fridge. Gummy bears are made from boiled bones, too, so vegans won't eat them. How they get the meat flavor out of the gelatin is beyond me.

That same couple made rolls to go with the soup that they ultimately refused to eat. The rolls rose too high and melded together to form one big loaf of bread. Seeing the bread no longer in roll form, the wife said, "Oh, that's too bad," and scraped all the dough into the trash.

Unexpected things happen in the kitchen all the time. Being waste-free means seeing the potential in every food, no matter what wonky things it decides to do.

TIP: Eat broccoli stalks! After you peel off the woody exterior, the inside flesh is delicious. You can dip it in ranch, shred it for slaw, boil it with salt, roast it, stir-fry it, steam it, or just prepare it right alongside the florets.

My dad reacted negatively when I cooked broccoli stalks. I had roasted five heads of broccoli for dinner and boiled the stalks in salt water. Since the stalk is my family's favorite part, I had made sure to buy heads with the longest stalks I could find. I wish they sold just the stalks at grocery stores.

At the dinner table, I set out a plate of steaming hot broccoli stalks that were sliced down the middle.

"Yay!" said my daughter Rose as she snatched one up and began chewing out the insides.

My dad leaned away from the plate with distrust. "What is that?"

"It's the stalk," I explained.

He shook his head. "To me, that's garbage," he said.

I'll admit to having a few wrong ideas about food, too. When I found a gallon of forgotten milk in our fridge, I knew that pasteurized milk was safe to drink even if it has gone sour. Buttermilk, sour cream, and yogurt are made by letting milk sit out until it changes flavor and consistency.

TIP: Sour milk is safe! Dana Gunders wrote, "As milk ages, it becomes more acidic, which creates an environment that is unfriendly to microbes that might cause illness."[2]

I decided to make ricotta, so I added lemon juice and salt, heated it in the microwave until foamy, strained out the curds, and voilà! The sourness of the milk didn't affect the flavor because the cheese was supposed to be tangy from the lemon juice.

Yet as I ate ricotta sauce poured over pasta, it made me queasy, not because it tasted bad, but because I knew the milk had gone sour. I had a hard time enjoying it even though it was safe. The next day when no one in my family got sick, I felt much more at ease and the pasta tasted better to me than it had the day before.

(In the end, we threw out most of the pasta because we didn't like it enough to finish it. This just goes to show that clever recipes aren't the solution to food waste.)

Before we can change the world, we have to change the way we think. Food isn't an aesthetic, a status symbol, or an intricate display of etiquette. It's a resource—a life-saving one. Listen to me carefully, and post this on your fridge if you have to: *There's no such thing as edible garbage.* Stems, leaves, peels, stalks, bones. Everything that's edible is *food.*

Most of our food-waste issue boils down to attitudes that need to be adjusted. I said this was a lifestyle book, but lifestyle changes might not matter as much as adjusting our perspectives.

Step 2: Clean and Organize Everything.

Empty all your cupboards, empty your fridge, and empty your freezer. Throw out everything moldy, freezer burned, stale, or too old to eat, and set aside for donation the good food you don't like. There's no point in holding onto the mistakes of the past. It's just clutter to distract you from what you *can* eat.

Don't just look through your cupboards. You'd be surprised at how much stuff you don't notice because you're used to it being there. Trust me: every nook and cranny of your kitchen has to be *empty.*

Now, scrub and wipe down every dirty surface. Once it's all clean, organize the food that's left and put it all back. The cleaning part of this step might seem symbolic. After all, you can eat food from a dirty fridge just as well as you can from a clean one.

And yet, the symbolism is important. Getting out a bucket of hot soapy water and a scrub brush tells your mind and your family that this new goal of yours is for real. Your kitchen has changed because your life has changed. Not to mention that when your kitchen is dirty or in disarray, you want to avoid it, which means ignoring your food.

Plus, it just seems a shame not to clean those shelves when they're already empty.

It might be a good idea to do this once a year, though hopefully after you've finished this book, you won't have to do it ever again.

"Clean and organize" is a pretty obvious first step to running a waste-free kitchen, so it's embarrassing to admit that I put it off for months. I get easily overwhelmed by chores. Writing books and cooking food is fun, but wiping up a puddle of juice in the fridge that got sticky and became a graveyard for fruit flies (not based on a real-life example, of course) is sometimes too much to handle.

Instead, I would cheat by combing through my cupboards for expired stuff without emptying them out. This was not good enough.

Let's just say my past lifestyle was counterintuitive. I had a Sam's Club membership, for one thing. That was my first mistake. I also shopped buy-one-get-one deals, like I mentioned before. In the cupboards, I'd shove things around as best as I could to get it all in. Everything that didn't fit would get tossed in the laundry room. Bottles, jars, boxes. I tried to eat through it all, but we were still buying food faster than we were eating it.

I felt overwhelmed by the sheer magnitude of the food we owned. Finally, I made peace with the fact that to have any control over my kitchen, I needed to take drastic measures. I needed to get organized.

I brought in everything that was stored in the laundry room under chairs, on tables, and on top of the washer and dryer. I emptied the fridge and the cupboards. Then I laid all the food we owned on the counters . . . and on my daughters' Minnie Mouse table . . . and on the kitchen table.

I cried out, "What is all this stuff? Why do we have so much of it?"

There was enough food to survive the zombie apocalypse! No wonder I felt overwhelmed. My food situation was a hot mess.

The oldest item had expired *nine years ago*. It was a box of Abuelita hot chocolate tablets. They tasted like nothing. The spice drawer was overflowing with containers, some of which I bought back when I was an undergrad in college and by now had lost their flavor. The condiments were the worst. I counted them all: ketchup, peanut butter, soy sauce. We had 114 condiments!

Part of the problem was that we had multiples of the same things. There were three full containers of corn syrup. I can't recall a single instance of my life when I used corn syrup. Mathematically, I must have used it at least three times. I also had four half-empty bottles of Worcestershire sauce, for heaven's sake. What kind of person owns four half-empty bottles of Worcestershire sauce?

My kitchen had been too unorganized to find anything. When we couldn't find a condiment we needed, we thought we were out and bought more. It was a vicious sauce cycle. Some of the containers I found were *completely empty*. That part makes the least sense to me. I spent a full minute puzzling over an empty bottle of sesame seed oil.

TIP: There are a lot of products to help keep your kitchen organized. You can use sliding shelves, racks, baskets, lazy Susans, over-the-door organizers, drawer dividers, and lid racks, for instance.

Before you judge me too harshly, I'd like to point out that the worst food wasters have spotless kitchens. It's much easier to keep a kitchen organized when you throw away stuff without a second thought. I had always felt guilty about throwing out food but didn't know how to avoid it, so I just kept everything.

Not anymore! It was time to make a permanent change.

I filled a bucket with hot soapy water and got to work. Once I organized the food and put it away, my kitchen felt like a work of art. My spices were even in alphabetical order. For the first time, I knew where everything was, and eating through what we had seemed like no trouble at all. I can't tell you what an enormous relief it was.

That night when my husband came home from work, he was about to plop down on the couch when I stopped him.

I said, "Wait, wait, wait, go look in the cupboards."

He gave me his *Do I really have to?* look, because he had very much been looking forward to the couch. I insisted.

He went into the kitchen. I heard the cupboard doors open and knew he was standing before my glorious achievement of cleanliness, order, and beauty.

"Did you do something different here?" he asked.

"Oh, shut up," I said.

TIP: When organizing your pantry, put the stuff you know you'll use (such as flour, sugar, rice) in the back, and put the stuff you're likely to forget about in the front.

Unwanted Food: Pantry Swap Parties

Organizing my kitchen was great, but it left me with one rather large dilemma. I had set aside the food my family would never eat, like an unopened jar of green curry. (The fact that we owned this jar was peculiar because we also had an opened jar of green curry in our fridge that we were never going to eat because we don't like green curry.) There was no point in putting all that unwanted food back.

Some of it was left in our house by the previous owners, like crab boil spices and four boxes of tapioca. Some of it was gifted to me, like WIC baby food from a friend who had way more than she needed.

All that unwanted food felt like weights around my neck. I couldn't force my family to consume all our thoughtless purchases like canned sweet potatoes, canned collard greens, and spicy V8 juice, but I couldn't throw it away because it was still good. What to do, what to do . . .

That's how I came up with pantry swap parties.

I made an event on Facebook and invited every friend I had in town. "Bring all your unwanted food," I said, "and swap it out for food you like!"

TIP: If you have a lot of food in your kitchen that you don't want to eat, throw a pantry swap party.

Five of my friends came over, set their kids down in front of my toy bins, and hung out in my living room as I unloaded their bags and boxes onto my kitchen table. Once everyone had arrived, I brought them into the kitchen and said, "Take what you want."

They stood awkwardly around the fully laden table for a while. No one wanted to grab something another person wanted. Maybe I should have made it into a game, like Dirty Santa, or maybe a version of Planet Hollywood where you hit a timer every time you take an item and go around until a player takes too long to decide and the timer runs out.

I finally grabbed a carton of couscous just to get the ball rolling. People started to pick things up here and there. Then it started to gain momentum. Soon each of my friends had bags of free food. My favorite find was twenty cans of tuna fish.

Not only was the pantry swap party useful, but it was fun, too. We chatted while sharing a six-pack of what ended up being the worst soda pop in the entire universe: chocolate and sea salt caramel. That flavor is ingrained in my memory, stored in the section of my brain labeled, "Sensations I Hope to Never Feel Again."

Hosting a pantry swap party could be good in January when everyone is looking for fresh starts, or maybe during spring cleaning. Does anyone actually do spring cleaning?

The best time to do a panty swap party, though, is right before someone moves. Part of the reason the party went so well was that one of the attendees was moving out of state, so she had a lot of extra stuff she couldn't take with her.

This seems like a good time to mention a cool charity called Move for Hunger. The founder, Adam Lowy, worked for a moving business and saw so much food get thrown out by people moving to a new house that he started asking if he could donate it.

Now, he's signed up 600 moving companies that transport their clients' food to food banks. In the year 2021, the program fed 4 million people. Lowy hopes that the program will become irrelevant soon because whenever people move, they will donate to food pantries without his help.[3]

TIP: If you want to clear out your pantry without throwing anything away, plan to include at least one item in your pantry for every meal you make. You can do the same thing with your freezer.

This brings me to my next issue:

The best part about being the host was that I got to keep everything that was left. The worst part about being the host was that I had to keep everything that was left—and there was quite a bit I didn't want.

The next step was to donate the remaining horde to a food pantry. The food pantry in my area handed out full paper bags to anyone who asked for one. A person's presence was proof enough that they needed it. The bags were given not just to the unemployed or homeless, but to people who got hit with medical bills they couldn't afford, people who had taken in either a family member's child or an elderly parent, and others with expenses they couldn't cover. It's an incredible service, especially when hunger catches people by surprise and they need food right away.

I had never donated food before, and I felt awkward. It was the most random mix of food you can imagine, like canned beets, ranch croutons, and a bottle of sparkling mango-apple cider my husband had bought. (He's a smart man, but everyone has their bad moments.)

Food Drives

Food drives are a great way to feed the hungry while helping people clear out their pantries, which prevents food waste. Here are some ideas:

- **Library Fine Forgiveness.** My library hosted an event where they forgave two dollars of fines for each item donated. It was a massive success.
- **Bags in the Mail.** My mailman left a paper bag in our box with instructions—and advertisements for the sponsors—to fill the bag with food and leave it beside the mailbox for the mailman to pick up.
- **Pay in Food.** You can host a fundraiser where people give food instead of money. They can "buy" tickets to an event, treats at a bake sale, books at a used book sale, raffle tickets, etc.
- **Grocery Store Food Drive.** With the manager's permission, you can set up a table asking for people to donate food as they walk out of the grocery store. They will see the table as they walk in and then buy food to give you.
- **Food Drive Competition.** Have two groups of people compete against each other: offices or classrooms, for instance. Post the results daily as motivation.
- **A Marathon.** Sponsors pledge food instead of money.
- **Offer a Service.** Volunteers can wash cars, wrap Christmas presents, clean yards, and so on, in exchange for donated food.
- **Little Free Pantry.** Instead of building a Free Library where people swap books, you can build a Little Free Pantry where people donate and take food.

I thought, *No way are they going to want this bizarre assortment of weird sodas and curries.* Then I thought, *What if a person loves curry, but never eats any because it's too expensive? Maybe someone would be thrilled to see it at a food pantry.*

Just to make sure, I called the food pantry and asked if they had any restrictions on what I could donate.

"We'll take anything!" the woman on the phone said, using that chipper-sweet voice that's typical of charity workers.

"It's just stuff from my pantry," I clarified.

"Sounds great!"

"Okay, if you want it, I'll bring it by. . . ."

"Thank you so much!"

I loaded the food in the car and buckled up my kids. In the pantry drive-thru, I knocked while my car was still running, and volunteers opened the door. Inside were shelves filled with row after row of your typical bulk foods: canned corn, canned green beans, canned tuna fish. It looked like Costco. Compared to their industry-sized boxes of red beans and dry milk, my box of curry and beets seemed not only strange, but lame.

When I sheepishly handed over the box, I clarified, once again, that I was just bringing a random assortment of stuff. The woman peeked in, brightened up, and said, "Wow! We never get items like this!"

The experience reminded me of a chapter from *Sh!t My Dad Says.* The narrator's mom worked in a food pantry, and to help her children sympathize with others less fortunate, she fed her children welfare food for a month. The writer described the bland, cheap, horrible meals he had to endure.

It got me thinking; if the only food welfare people get is cheap and boring, it might be nice for them to mix things up every now and then with a bottle of spicy sauce or a jar of oregano. So I think I did a good thing.

When I went home, I realized every single container of food in my house was both edible and desirable. No more clutter. No more eyesores. No more feeling overwhelmed by all the food I couldn't possibly keep track of.

I once heard a yoga instructor say, "Now, take a delicious, cleansing breath of fresh air," and that's exactly what it felt like: cleansing and delicious.

I can do this, I thought.

Step 3: Eat What You Have

After going waste-free for about four months, a friend asked if it was getting easier or harder not to waste food. I said easier in some ways and harder in others. The truth is, I was struggling.

The first and second months were easy because I was excited about my new idea. The third and fourth months were somewhat miserable. Not wasting food is not as simple as "Just eat everything." You might have too much food to eat it in time. You might not know what to do with every item in your kitchen. I had yet to learn the skills I needed to make it work (including Step 2: Clean and Organize Everything, which I still hadn't done). There were days when I longed to throw something away because it was such a strain to store and use so much food.

The benefits of zero waste made it worth pushing through, but still. I was tired.

My advice: Stop grocery shopping as much as you can for as long as you can. Your kitchen is your new grocery store: Shop your kitchen.

TIP: If a vegetable is wilted and then cooked, it doesn't taste any different than if the vegetable hadn't been wilted.

You've already cleared out all the food in your kitchen that you can't or won't eat. Now, look through what you have left and come up with ways to cook the most stuff in as few recipes as possible. Don't just do it once. Continue to treat your kitchen like a grocery store every time you plan meals. Scan through your fridge, freezer, and pantry on a regular basis. It might even help to empty them on occasion to make sure you catch stuff that got pushed to the back. If emptying your fridge is a huge chore because you can't even see to the back of it, it might be time to do Step 5: Don't Buy Too Much Food.

There's actually a trendy term for shopping your kitchen. It's "shelf cooking." That means basing your meals on ingredients you already have, instead of coming up with a meal you want to make and buying everything you need to make it.

Facebook groups on shelf cooking have thousands of members. There are bloggers who brag about doing this, and some of them even host monthlong shelf cooking events.

It feels a little silly to make a big deal out of eating food you bought to, you know, *eat.* But shelf cooking is kind of fun. The reason it's trendy is that most of us have never done it before. It takes ingenuity, and I love the aha moments when I turn butter chicken into pizza and meatballs into hand pies.

Dig deep. Be as creative as you can. Toss random ingredients together to make soup, pasta, or pie. If you do need to buy more food, get as few ingredients as possible to make a dish that uses ingredients already in your kitchen.

There are websites and phone apps that let you enter ingredients you have on hand and suggest what to make using those ingredients. Examples include Allrecipes.com, Plant Jammer, Super Cook, Ready Set Dinner, Love Food Hate Waste, and Save the Food. That should be enough to get you started!

I hate to brag (ahem, I actually love to brag), but I was awesome at shelf cooking even before my waste-free journey. My husband might have said we needed to run to the store because there was nothing to eat in the house, and an hour later I'd made a roast with carrots and canned potatoes using an au jus sauce that expired two years ago, ranch dressing, and pepperoncini peppers. *Excellente!*

I don't know what was better: the taste of the roast or feeling so clever.

The first time I tried this hard-core, I planned seventeen meals and three desserts . . . and only needed to buy eight ingredients. The crazy thing is, I had thought that I needed to go grocery shopping. Then I raided my pantry and discovered we already had everything we needed to eat for weeks. Clearly, I wasn't as good about shelf cooking as I thought.

I'd like you to try a little exercise. With a pen and paper, write down every single thing in your refrigerator that you can think of without looking. (You don't have to do condiments; that would take all day.)

TIP: Food will stay fresh longer if you don't overcrowd your fridge. This allows the cold air to circulate around the food.

On a different sheet of paper, write everything you can think of that's in your freezer. Now, do the same thing for all your cupboards. If you have food stored anywhere else (garage, a second freezer, a pantry), write down everything in there you can think of as well. These exercises might take a long time—sorry—but bear with me. When you're done, take your lists to the various places you store food and see how far off you were from reality.

Did you write down most of what you have? Half of what you have? Did you struggle to think of anything at all? I recommend eating the stuff you forgot about first. People struggle to remember what's in their kitchen, even if there's a container of their favorite meal made only two days ago. My husband frequently sees delicious food in the fridge and exclaims, "I forgot we had that!" It's so much easier to eat what you have when you know what you have. I improved on this step so much that, at any given moment, I could list off every item in my fridge without looking.

Sometimes, food gets stuck in a limbo of don't want it, can't improve it, can't donate it. Once I bought a box of pancake mix, only to discover that I had grabbed blueberry by accident. Gross. Determined not to waste it, I made a batch of pancakes anyway and the whole house smelled like blue vomit. Since I had already opened it, I couldn't bring it to a food pantry.

What do you do with perfectly good food you won't eat and can't donate?

Give it away!

Nobody gets excited about this advice. It isn't as much fun as finding hacks to use up twenty pounds of carrots or three pounds of honey (based on real examples people have told me).

That's a shame because giving away food is the easiest solution. Everyone has people in their lives who would appreciate free food. Senior citizens who maybe have trouble cooking for themselves. Low-income families. Sick people. Disabled people. Parents with a new baby. Mothers who barely have the energy to cook, especially if they're single parents. College students who don't know how to cook yet. Friends and family who don't necessarily need more food but would appreciate the gesture of a free hot meal.

Once I went to a birthday party and the hosts were expecting seventy people. It was a one-year-old's party, which is the party where parents invite every single person they know. About thirty people showed up, which meant twelve extra boxes of pizza.

The hosts begged everyone to take the boxes home. Looking back, I should have offered to bring it to a soup kitchen. Instead, I agreed to take three boxes home with the intention of putting them in my freezer. Except I had yet to master the eat-what-you-have step, so we didn't have any room in our freezer.

I was at a loss of what to do with the pizza until I decided to give it to to the Church of Jesus Christ of Latter-day Saints missionaries. The LDS missionaries are hardworking twenty-year-olds with a small food budget, and they appreciate everything I give them.

The missionaries agreed to come by and pick up the pizza, and I included the blueberry pancake mix. We also had some soup I had frozen that my family would likely never finish. . . . It was good, but not fantastic. Then I threw in some Texas toast to go with the soup.

They did me a favor by taking three headaches off my hands—soup, pancakes, and pizza—but they were grateful. Giving away food is a win-win for everyone.

As for my three- to four-month slump, just like any new skill, I got better and it got easier. Step 2: Clean and Organize Everything and Step 3: Eat What You Have were the hardest. Once they were done, everything went so much smoother.

Waste-free living shouldn't be a burden. Learning how, on the other hand, is a challenge. To all of you who are struggling: Hang in there. I have a lot more tips that will help.

Enjoy Your Leftovers

I adore leftovers. My favorite food will be sitting in the fridge, waiting for me, and I don't have to do any work to get it. For a mom who does all the cooking in the house, leftovers are a gift that I make for my future self.

Not everyone feels the same way. A friend told me she loved my food updates on Facebook, and that she tried not to waste food, but it was really hard. I asked her what she struggled with the most.

"Leftovers," she said. "My kids and husband don't eat them, and I can't finish them by myself."

Her daughter, who was standing behind her, wrinkled her nose and shook her head.

I hear this a lot. Only the mom will eat a meal the next day, while the rest of the family snubs their noses at it. I'll betcha anything I know the reason moms eat leftovers when the rest of the family won't: The mom is the one cooking the meals. Why would the kids eat an old meal when Mom will just make a new one?

If we were to assign dinners to our kids, and they had to choose between spending an hour cooking a meal or heating up food that's already made, they'd learn to appreciate those leftovers!

TIP: Put up an "Eat Me First" sign in your fridge and store your most perishable food behind it.

Despite Rule #5—No Self-Righteousness and No Guilt—I do have trouble not being judgmental when people refuse to eat leftovers for no reason, except for the fact that they are leftovers. I can't even wrap my head around that way of thinking.

I mean, you go to the store, and you put your ingredients in your fridge, and at that point, they are considered desirable. Then you assemble the ingredients in a pleasing way—into a stew, a stir-fry, a casserole—and the meal is desirable. The next day, the same meal with the same ingredients is considered to be *un*desirable, even though it hasn't decomposed or changed in any way. It has nothing to do with age. If you waited a day to make the same meal, the ingredients would still be fine. The ingredients in your assembled dish are undesirable the next day because. . . .

Honestly, I don't know.

Remember how I said we need to think about food differently? Here's an example: My husband got excited about the grab-and-go meal prep craze. To "meal prep," you make a lot of a meal and divide it into portion-sized containers to take to work and have for lunch. He showed me picture after picture of meals online, like pork chops and rice divided into a dozen small containers, each with a stylish line of broccoli separating the two.

I asked, "How is meal prepping any different from eating leftovers?"

"It's totally different!" he said, aghast.

"Really? Because the way I see it, you're making food one day and eating it on a different day. The only difference is the cute containers."

This is proof that people eat with their pride, not with their stomachs. Eating yesterday's dinner for lunch is totally lame, but prepping a meal that was *meant* to be eaten on a different day is trendy and way cool?

I'll admit: Reheating leftovers takes knowledge and skill. The food might be soggy, dry, overcooked, or you don't know how to heat it evenly. There is an art to it, and no one's going to like leftovers that are reheated badly. Friends have complained to me that reheating leftovers correctly or converting them into a new dish is too much work. Maybe, but it's a lot less work than making a meal all over again. Plus, it saves you money.

You might think you're doing well if you eat leftovers every night, but that doesn't guarantee that your food won't go bad. The order of the leftovers is important, too. Food that will go bad first should be eaten first. Don't dish yourself up pasta from the restaurant you went to yesterday when there's shredded pork in your fridge from five days ago. Below are a few tips to help you out.

Leftover Tips:

- The microwave can only heat one inch into a dish. This is why you have to stir your food in the middle of cooking. For food you can't stir, like lasagna and enchiladas, cut it into one-inch strips before reheating.
- If the food was fried, it needs to be toasted in the oven, put in the air fryer, or refried to get crispy again. French fries need to either be refried or liberally coated in oil before being toasted.
- To re-steam rice, put a tablespoon or two in a bowl or container, seal the top, and microwave for two minutes. Let it sit so the rice can soak up the steam. If it's too dry, add a bit more water and reseal the lid to let it steam longer. If it's too wet, remove the lid and let the rice air out a bit.
- Reheating pizza can be done many different ways . . . in the oven, in a toaster oven, in an air fryer, in a skillet . . . but never in the microwave. Microwaves heat liquid, and since the bread has less liquid than the cheese, it'll get hot and chewy before the cheese is melted Or you can always eat it cold for breakfast, like Andrew does. To do the skillet method, toast the crust for two-dish minutes, then add a bit of water away from the pizza, cover, and cook for a minute until the cheese gets gooey.
- When you cook bird meat like chicken and turkey, the molecules constrict and squeeze out moisture. That's why overcooked chicken is dry even if it's in broth or is covered in sauce. Keep this in mind when reheating bird meat and make sure you don't heat it any more than necessary.

No matter how well I plan out a meal, we often end up with odds and ends of a dish, or there might be enough left for only one person, so once a week, we empty out every leftover meal in our fridge and each family member reheats only what they want. Other families call this a smorgasbord, potpourri, or late-night buffet, or they uncreatively call it leftovers night. We call it Scrap Day.

I love Scrap Day. There are always too many delicious foods to choose from. Rose liked to turn it into a restaurant game. I'd read her all the choices we had and write down her order like a waitress, and she and Adalyn would hang out at the table with their dad like they do at restaurants while I reheated their orders.

If no matter what you do, you still end up with leftovers only you will eat, then I say embrace your situation by planning ahead. Make meals you don't mind finishing yourself. If your kids complain that you only serve food you like and not food they like, maybe they should cook dinner next time.

Stock Up on Staples

Most of us have odds and ends in the fridge with no plans for how to eat them. Luckily, there are plenty of versatile dishes where you can just throw together whatever you have.

It might sound counterintuitive to combat waste by buying more food, but stocking up on nonperishable staples is a powerful tool. If you have half a bell pepper, a tomato, cheese, and mushrooms, there's not much you can do with that, but if you also have the right staples, you could put that mixture in an omelet, in a quesadilla, over pasta, or on a baked potato. Some staples to keep on hand include:

- Rice. You can cook any meat and most vegetables in a sauce like teriyaki, bulgogi, sweet and sour, and so on, or make a stir-fry and serve it over rice. I also like breakfast bowls where you put an egg (either soft boiled or fried) over rice with whatever assortment of toppings you have on hand, plus hot sauce.

- Bread. Most foods can go on a sandwich. Have fun experimenting with different meats, cheeses, vegetables, and sauces. Grilling a sandwich can give it a whole new spin. Bread can be refrigerated or frozen, and if it's stale, you might be able to fix it by toasting it or grilling it.
- Eggs. You can put many things in scrambled eggs, quiche, frittata, or an omelet—meats, cheeses, and vegetables. You can also top most food with a fried egg to give it new life.
- Potatoes. This is probably the most versatile of all the staples. You can make baked potatoes and top them with just about anything—cheese and broccoli, chili, or sloppy joes, for instance. You can cut them into cubes and roast them with other vegetables. You can make hash browns or French fries and load them up with other foods and sauces. You can use them with meat and vegetables in stews and soups. You can mash them up and bake them on top of casseroles with cheddar cheese. And so on and so on.
- Pasta. You can pour on ready-made sauce, like marinara, alfredo, or pesto, with other things you have on hand, or you can make your own sauce based on the food you have. There's lots of room to think outside the box, too; you can make jambalaya pasta, pizza pasta, chicken fajita pasta, cheeseburger pasta, cheesy chili pasta, taco pasta, not to mention unusual sauces like pumpkin (which is surprisingly delicious), carbonara, lemon dill, and creamy sun-dried tomato. The sky is the limit when it comes to pasta.

- Piecrust. I always have piecrust on hand for savory meals like potpie and quiche, or when I have a sweet tooth and all the fruit in my freezer looks appealing.
- Couscous. I've never tried quinoa because it's pricey, but I do occasionally splurge on couscous. It's great mixed with roasted vegetables or served cold as a salad with a bunch of other ingredients. You can also serve it seasoned as a side to just about anything.
- Chicken and ground beef. These two staples can add protein to almost anything.
- Cheddar cheese. We use cheese in sandwiches, quesadillas, casseroles, soups, pasta dishes, Mexican food, with crackers and deli meat, and I even like to broil it until it's bubbly and eat it plain.

Maybe for some people, stocking up on staples doesn't help because they don't know how to just look in the fridge and whip up a pie. It's a skill that takes practice. I'll teach you how, but that's all the way in Step 9: Be Smart When You Cook and When You Shop.

Chapter 4:

Keeping Track of It All

When newbies first go waste-free, they typically think of one meal at a time. That won't work. You aren't planning the leftover of this one dinner or cleaning out the pantry and calling it good. You are directing a kitchen full of a rotating supply of food, all of which won't last forever, and everything connects to each other.

Being waste-free doesn't have to be hard, but you have to look at the big picture to be successful, and it can be overwhelming—especially at first as you're getting used to this big change.

That's why this chapter is all about keeping track of everything in your kitchen, all at once, all the time, without getting burned out.

Step 4: Be Aware of What You Toss

You've cleaned your kitchen, gotten rid of everything you don't want to eat, and eaten most of what you did want. You're practically an expert already. The next step is to analyze your progress.

You might think you already don't throw away much food, especially after following Step 2: Clean and Organize Everything and Step 3: Eat What You Have. I used to think that, too. Then I started keeping a list of everything I tossed.

It was an eye-opener. No matter what I tried or how hard I tried it, there would be between nine and twelve items on my list by the end of the month. I wonder how long the list would have been before I avoided food waste.

If you're skeptical about whether reducing waste is necessary for you, I suggest writing down everything you toss. You might be surprised.

A list can also track progress. It helps you see how much you're improving (or maybe not improving) by comparing the lists you make month to month.

Once you keep the list, you might notice patterns. Is most of your waste from Tupperware containers that got shoved to the back of your fridge? Do you leave food sitting out too long? Do you burn your food or mess up recipes? Do you make so much that you're sick of it before you can eat it all? This will help you improve even more.

I definitely noticed themes that helped me make changes. My most common mistakes were:

- I didn't freeze the food in time. This was a big one for me, which was embarrassing. I would think to myself, *I should probably freeze that soon because it's about to go bad*, and then not do it. There's just something about opening both the fridge and the freezer doors and lifting that food *all the way* from the fridge to the freezer.
- The kids destroyed it until even the dog wouldn't eat it. I developed tricks that helped with this. (See the next section—"Kids, AKA the Ultimate Food Wasters.")

- My fridge was kind of kooky, and the back was significantly colder than the front. Sometimes things ended up in the back that ought not to be there, like lettuce and celery, and they froze.
- I shopped at Sam's Club. For months, I tried to use my mad resource skills on bulk food, but my list kept telling me the same thing: when I shopped at Sam's Club, I wasted more.

Writing things down wasn't the most effective way to track waste because it was hard to visualize how it all added up. I decided to go by weight.

My original goal was to waste zero food for at least a year. After eight months of stubborn struggle (and wishing I owned a hungry Rottweiler instead of my picky Border collie), I admitted that zero wasn't quite as feasible for me as I had hoped. Maybe it would have been easier if I was living by myself, or I owned a pig, but we were a family of four that included a young kid and a toddler.

I would have to set an easier goal for myself before I could work my way to zero.

If zero wasn't reasonable right now, what should my goal be, and how well was I accomplishing it? I looked over what I had wasted in the past and picked a reasonable number for the time being: five pounds per month.

Most people aren't impressed by that number, but you might be surprised by how quickly the pounds add up.

Have you ever bought a ten-pound bag of potatoes from Sam's Club and let it go bad? That's more food than I throw out in two months. An average watermelon weighs twenty pounds. That's more than I waste in four months.

Once when I went on a trip, my husband let a whole head of cauliflower go bad. A whole head! That was three pounds—more than half of my monthly allotment—on one mistake.

Remember, the average family of four wastes sixty pounds of food a month. I threw out 92 percent less than the average American.

I decided to take things a step further. Instead of weighing or writing down every single item—which was a pain—I put an empty Tupperware container in the freezer and made a goal to fill it only once a month. I'll admit to occasionally stuffing waste in to get it to fit, but there were other months when the container didn't even get full.

I suggested this to an online group. They all guffawed at it. There was no way they could put a whole month of food waste in their freezer. I assumed this meant their freezers were packed to the brim. Nope. They just wasted too much food for it all to fit.

Going waste-free is a journey. It's a completely different lifestyle for most of us, and it takes adjustments and tweaks. Don't beat yourself up if your list is longer than you had hoped, or the weight is too heavy, or if you need to put a bigger container in your freezer. Remember Rule #5: No Guilt! Do your best today, and tomorrow, try a little harder. Each month is a new month when you get to start over.

Kids, AKA the Ultimate Food Wasters

I got asked a lot of questions about leftovers, but by far the most commonly asked question was what to do about kids.

Past generations taught their kids to finish what was on their plates. This made sense at different times and in different places. Depression-era families didn't have enough to eat, and they certainly didn't have enough to waste. Anyone without a refrigerator would be a loyal member of the clean plate club because there would be no "later" for their food.

But we live in a strange time when our food is nourishing us, but it's also killing us. There's too much of it. A lot of what we buy shouldn't be eaten in the first place because it's unhealthy. When diabetes and childhood obesity are on the rise and the food on your child's plate is high in fat, carbs, or sugar, it doesn't feel right to make children eat when they don't want to.

Families that only eat healthy food are more justified in finishing their plates, but let's face it: Most of our kitchens aren't full of perfectly nutritious food. Instead, parents are stuck in this balancing act of teaching kids not to eat too much, but also not to waste food when often the only way not to waste it is to eat too much of it.

Parents don't have to stay stuck in this balancing act between eating everything and not eating too much. A few changes can make a big difference. Granted, every family is different, and every child is different, not to mention that every age is different, but still, there is common ground to cover.

Let's start with babies. I like to organize things chronologically.

Babies destroying food. These little buggers throw food on the ground, pour juice over their plates, smash everything together, and otherwise render things inedible. It's like playdough for them. I was about to say, "It's like playdough you eat," but they eat playdough and don't eat their food.

The most effective technique is also the easiest: Don't dish baby up as much food. The less you serve, the less you have to worry about.

Also, try to give your kid only one thing at a time. My little ones got juice before or after they ate, but food and drink wouldn't be on the same tray together. (Unless you don't mind meatloaf drenched in orange juice.) You can try sippy cups with closed lids, but my kids learned how to get the juice out by turning the cups upside down and shaking them vigorously.

If your kid is prone to mixing her corn in with her mashed potatoes, dish her up corn first, then mashed potatoes when she's done with the corn.

If one of my kids threw food on the floor, I scooped it right up and plopped it back on her plate. It only took a few dog hairs in her mouth to learn her lesson. That might sound harsh, but I've seen them lick every toy they own; I've seen them suck on rocks; once they ate part of a Pop-Tart they found on the playground before I could take it away; and when Rose was three, she thought it was funny to bite my husband's toes. Not to mention all the food they found between couch cushions, under car seats, and under the kitchen table. If they could survive all that, they certainly could survive whatever was on the kitchen floor.

Besides, I don't want them to learn that acting up by throwing food on the ground is a way to escape their problems. No matter what they do to their food, they still have to eat it.

Pickiness. Many families follow the three-bite rule: The kid has to take three bites of a dish because that's how long it takes to decide if they like it. If they don't want more after three bites, they get to eat something else.

"What do I do with the rest of their food?" the parents ask.

The three-bite rule makes me squirm. I understand throwing together a peanut butter sandwich for a two-year-old who literally won't eat otherwise, especially if you have a gaggle of other children and you can only deal with so much at once. But if a child is old enough to count to three, I believe the child is old enough to eat food she doesn't like. Who says we have to like everything, anyway? What are we teaching our children when we throw out food that we worked hard to buy and worked hard to prepare, just because they didn't like it? Then they go out in the world, and nothing is the way they like it because everything sucks.

My parents taught me that picky eating is a sign of weakness. If I ever were to date a guy and found out he was a picky eater, that would have been a deal-breaker. No joke. Also, I'm constantly preoccupied with world hunger, so reminding my family there are starving children in Africa is a frequent occurrence. The three-bite rule doesn't quite match my lifestyle.

My children and I have an understanding; I try not to make food I know they won't like. If I mistakenly give them something they don't like, they still have to eat what I give them, but I likely won't make it for them again.

If the three-bite rule is a part of your home, the answer is simple: Don't dish your child up more than three bites. Then, there's nothing to throw away.

Portion Control. Little children need help with portion control. That's why when Rose told me she was full, I listened . . . but didn't always trust her. I could generally tell when my four-year-old daughter wasn't eating because she was distracted and wanted to do something else versus actually being full. If she said, "Can I watch TV?" and I said, "Eat your potatoes first," and then she said, "I'm full," it was pretty likely that she was just saying that to watch TV. But the goal is for them to regulate how much they eat instead of relying on us.

Sometimes I'd let Rose leave the table and she'd realize that she spoke too soon and she was still hungry. She'd ask for a snack. Her "snack" would be the rest of her dinner.

Also, it helps to give them tiny servings so they have to ask for more. Not only will this cut down on waste, but it gives them the opportunity to evaluate their hunger level and decide for themselves how much they want.

At some point, it's better for children to dish up themselves. They need to learn how to listen to their body's hunger cues so they can become responsible eaters. If we decide for them how much they want, they lose the opportunity to learn that lesson.

Besides, if I'm the one dishing up their plates, making them eat all of it isn't fair. I have no idea how much they want.

I talked about portion control in Myth 4 ("It'll make me fat.") so there's not much left to say, except that when I had young children who weren't old enough to dish up their own food, what they left on their plates was usually half my dinner. I'd purposefully dish myself up less than I wanted knowing that I was going to finish what they left.

This caused problems with Rose, though, when Daddy told her to finish her dinner and she said, "Don't worry. Mommy will eat it."

It's a work in progress. But that, my friends, is how our dinner-time food waste reached zero.

Snacks Before Dinner. Your family sits at the dinner table. The kids say they don't want to eat, and you don't want to force them. What do you do?

I scratched my head over this until a blog article suggested not letting kids snack before dinner. Duh! Rose rarely snacked, and she has always been good about eating what we give her. It seemed like Adalyn was pickier than Rose, but I realized that pickiness wasn't the reason she didn't want her dinner. It was because Adalyn is a compulsive snacker. For the entire thirty minutes to an hour that I would prepare dinner, she begged, pleaded, and coerced me into giving her snacks. I was so desperate to be left alone that I pretty much fed her whatever she wanted. Of course she didn't want dinner!

I read about a mom who always put cut-up vegetables and a bowl of ranch on her table when she prepared dinner. The vegetables were healthier than dinner would be anyway, so it didn't matter if her kids filled up on them. If they said they didn't want vegetables, they must not have been all that hungry.

My advice: Limit premeal snacking so that kids are actually hungry when they sit down to eat, and if that's unbearable for them, maybe serve dinner earlier. Hopefully once dinner is served, they'll be hungry enough to eat it.

Life Lessons at the Dinner Table. Dinnertime is an important part of child-rearing. Ideally, it's when the family has to sit together with no toys or electronics and talk to each other, possibly for the only time all day.

I also believe dinner is a teaching opportunity. A lot of children's behavior and attitude problems can be fixed at the table. For instance:

- *Patience.* Eating as a group means waiting your turn, especially if your family blesses their food and the kids have to stare at their steaming hot plates until the prayer is finished. They also have to wait their turn to speak during a group conversation and have to ask to be excused before they can run off.
- *Etiquette.* The dinner table is where children learn to act like human beings and not animals.
- *Consideration.* When a parent goes to a lot of work to make something and the child doesn't like it, this is a good opportunity for them to learn not to hurt Mom or Dad's feelings. They also need to be considerate when there isn't enough for everyone to have seconds, or when their behavior is annoying.
- *Gratitude.* This is a big one for me. We didn't go to all the work to feed them just so they could complain while so many children are going hungry. We can teach them to express gratitude at the dinner table.

- *Authority.* Often with young kids, getting them to eat is a battle. They will use everything in their arsenal to get out of eating certain foods. If Mom and Dad remain firm—if the kid never "wins"—that teaches them that they can't manipulate their parents in other situations, too.

Lunch Boxes. Regarding lunch boxes: Even though this hurts, I never pack food for my kids' lunch that I know they won't eat. I might be tempted to put broccoli or carrots in there for nutrition, but the fact of the matter is, they will not eat broccoli unless I'm there to make them finish it.

For years, Rose wouldn't eat crust. She was so adamant about avoiding the crust that she would leave a good half inch of sandwich around the edge—wasting almost half the sandwich—as if she wouldn't take any chances. I never thought I'd be one of those mothers who cuts the crust off my kid's sandwiches, but if the goal was zero waste, this was the only way.

I would grit my teeth, cut the crust off her school sandwiches, and save the crust in a Ziploc bag in the fridge. When I had enough, I made bread pudding. The irony is that Rose had a big serving of it, so she ate her crust in the end.

Even after using wisdom instead of pride to pack lunches, there would usually be leftovers. As soon as Rose got home from school and the girls wanted a snack, guess what their snack would be? Whatever was left in Rose's lunch bin. Throwing away leftovers from packed lunches was pretty rare in my house.

As for what Rose threw away at school, I didn't count it as my waste. I couldn't because I didn't know how much got thrown out, but also because the food wasn't my responsibility anymore. (See Rule #6.) When the kids left my house, they had to make their own choices. But I was confident—at least, I was fairly confident—that they would make the right choices.

It's the Responsibility That Matters

What really matters, perhaps more than anything else in this book, is that we are training future adults. The next generation will either dump trucks of produce into landfills, or they will pass laws against grocery stores wasting edible food. Will your grown-up children whine about being broke while they throw out 25 percent of the food they buy? Or will they brag to you about a new recipe they discovered because they were being resourceful?

For kids to be food-waste warriors, they need to (a) become aware of what food is and why we don't waste it, and (b) take pride in what happens to the food in their house.

Kids don't know how to be responsible with their food. It's up to us to teach them—and they can be taught.

One day, I picked up Rose from school and she was frowning.

"What's wrong, hon?" I asked.

"Mommy, my teacher said I could throw away my lunch." Rose had that upset look kids get when a grown-up does something wrong.

I had never talked to my girls about my resolve not to waste. They were five and three at this point, and it seemed too much of a burden at such a young age. It was almost too much of a burden for my husband! Rose was just following my example.

I told Rose, "I don't know if your teacher was right or wrong because I wasn't there. You are the one who decides whether to bring your lunch home or put it in the trash."

This might have been too much to say to a kindergartner, but I feel it's better to teach too much than too little. You never know what will sink in.

Children imitate what they see, and they learn from what we do without being told. Being a good example had a strong influence on my daughter when she was only five years old—such a strong influence, in fact, that one time when Rose had not even half a bite left of bibimbap in her bowl, she said, "I'm done. I will save the rest for later." She placed a hot pad on top and put the bowl in the fridge. Later when she ate only half a banana, she put the other half in a Ziploc bag all by herself.

I read about a woman who made her children pay for food they wasted. They paid for things they broke, too. When her son left a bag of chips open overnight, he had to replace the 99-cent bag with his own money.[1] In my family, we still would have eaten the stale chips, but it makes a valuable point.

Teaching kids how you feel about food, and how to have a relationship with it, can change their attitude about it. Below are some fun and easy teaching activities that can help foster a sustainable relationship with food.

Plant Plants. At gardening schools, the environment plays a key role in their curriculum. They plant their own garden, eat food they grew, compost, and take care of animals.

You don't have to build an entire garden to send the same message. It only takes one plant to give kids the magical thrill of creating life and to have respect for it.

My husband planted ten buckets of tomatoes on our deck one year. Rose took it upon herself to be his official tomato helper. They went outside every day to water the plants and harvest the tomatoes. Instead of snubbing her nose at the tomatoes like she used to, she was excited to eat a vegetable she had grown herself.

If you have enough, let kids give extra produce to friends and family. They'll be so proud to share.

Take Them Grocery Shopping. Rose was disappointed when her cousins went to a church activity she couldn't go to because she was too young.

We needed to go to the grocery store before going home. To cheer her up, I said she could buy anything she wanted.

Her face lit up. "*Anything* I want?"

I meant that she could buy one treat and expected her to pick a sucker or a pack of Oreos. Instead, she said, "Can I buy *all* the groceries?"

Curious to see where this would go, I said, "Sure."

She did pick one treat. Andrew and I usually get something sweet when we shop, so that was no surprise. Then she started planning meals.

"Can we get pasta?" she asked.

"Sure. What should we put on it?"

"Can I have meatballs?"

"Absolutely. You pick out the pasta you want, and then we'll get sauce and meat."

At the sauce aisle, her eyes widened. There were so many red jars. "Which one should I get?"

"You see these numbers?" I said, pointing to the price tags. "They say how much we have to pay to get the sauce. This one is the cheapest, and the others are more expensive. Some people think the expensive ones taste better. I think they're the same. But the more money we spend on the sauce, the fewer things we can buy. Which one do you think we should get?"

She picked the cheaper sauce.

Rose decided we needed bread (she picked out English muffins) and fruit (she got cherries and watermelon).

TIP: Some people are finicky about eating bread heels. If you flip the heel of your bread over when you make a sandwich, no one can tell the difference.

"Do we need a vegetable?" she asked.

"We have cauliflower at home, but you like cucumbers for snacks."

"Oh, yeah! Can you help me find them?"

Soon we had a modest load of mostly healthy groceries that she had selected all by herself. I let her scan all the items in the self-checkout, which she loved.

Rose bragged to Andrew about how she got to do all the grocery shopping herself. At home, she helped me make the meatballs.

Let Them Meal Plan. I was flipping through a cookbook on a day when nothing looked good. My rule of thumb is to meal plan when you're hungry and grocery shop when you're full, but Andrew was going to leave work soon and I needed to get him a grocery list before he got to the store, even though meals were the last thing I wanted to think about.

Rose was begging me to talk to her, and Adalyn was crawling all over me. I couldn't handle it all at once, so I pushed the cookbook over and said, "Here. *You* pick out what we eat."

She was surprised at first, then shrugged and pulled the binder to her. Rose couldn't read yet, but she could see the pictures, so she flipped through the pages and picked out what she wanted. Whenever we made one of her meals, Rose would announce to her dad,

"This was the meal *I* picked out." Not only does this teach them life skills, but it makes dinnertime easier. They'll only pick food they like, so there will be fewer struggles about finishing their dinner.

Let Them Cook. Imagine this scenario: After buying the pasta and meatballs Rose had picked out, she helps to make them, and we have meatballs for dinner. We tell Rose how good they are. Then we tip the pan over and throw all the remaining meatballs in the trash. I don't think that would go over well. Children might not care about the food we work hard to make, but they will care about their own hard work.

The girls are always begging to help me cook. I used to tell them no. Like I said earlier, dinnertime is the hardest time of the day, and I'm not in the mood to do enriching activities when everyone is hungry, tired, and angry over the fact that one sister looked at her too long and the other poked her just to be mischievous.

After hearing a kid say, "Can I help, can I help?" a thousand times, I would finally give in just to make the sound stop. I made an interesting discovery. The young girls had low attention spans, so they rarely stuck around for the whole meal. They would stir a bowl for a minute or two, then run away. It took less effort to let them help than it took to refuse them.

Once Rose reached five years old, I started letting her help out with meals from beginning to end. She and her cousin made Adalyn's birthday cake and frosting with me telling them what to do, but I didn't touch anything except the hot stove. They were very proud of that cake.

Rose likes playing with fruit and raw vegetables, too. I often found her arranging cut-up vegetables in the shape of faces or dinosaurs. Letting her do that was the best way to get her to eat vegetables.

When you let kids cook, you run the risk of food getting ruined and wasted. It's worth the risk. A few dinners might not turn out, but the child is learning, and those lessons will bring about change in the long run.

TIP: If you have too much cucumber, you can soak the slices in old pickle juice. They'll stay fresh for ages. You can do this with other vegetables too, like carrots, squash, okra, turnips, red onions, and green tomatoes.

The first meal Rose made mostly by herself was biryani, an Indian rice dish. The first time we had it, she loved it and had three helpings. The second time, I made it by myself. She didn't like biryani anymore.

Pride makes food taste better.

Teach Them to Compost. Kids get excited about composting, and keeping a bin will teach them the cycle of food production and the environment. The most important lesson compost will teach children is this: Every scrap of food has value. Even the peels, the cores, and the moldy stuff. When it comes to organic material, nothing is garbage.

Upcycle Leftovers Together. Everyone loves being clever in the kitchen. Making kitchen scraps into a casserole or a soup is fun for all of us, even kids. If you give children the opportunity to be creative with food, they'll learn to see it in a new way. Show them leftover chicken butter sauce from an Indian restaurant and see if they come up with naan pizza, or curry hand pies. Ask them what to do with the blueberry pie no one wants to finish and help them decide between milkshakes, oatmeal, or some dish they create on their own.

It's definitely an activity for older children, if not for teenagers, but if you let your children brainstorm creative ways to use leftovers, maybe they won't dislike them so much.

Step 5: Don't Buy Too Much Food

Five days before my birthday, my husband told me that my daughter's new backpack and my birthday present would be coming in the mail.

"Don't open either package," he said. "I don't want you to accidentally open your present."

The mail lady handed me two boxes that afternoon. One was a plain brown box closed with Amazon Prime tape. The other was a FoodSaver box, with a bright picture of a vacuum food sealer on the front, instead of a brown box. Oops.

Countertop vacuums suck all the air from bags of food to help the food last longer. A frozen steak in a Ziploc bag might last only six months (or so I've heard), but a steak that's been vacuum-sealed will last two years.

There were two issues at work here. Problem #1: I needed to make my husband believe his surprise hadn't been ruined. The FoodSaver box perfectly fit in the other box with the backpack, so I put my present in the empty box, fit the torn Amazon Prime tape together like puzzle pieces, and covered it with clear tape to keep it all together. Problem solved.

Problem #2: There wasn't even a small part of me that wanted a FoodSaver.

You'd think this would be a perfect present. In fact, it was one of the most considerate gifts anyone had ever given me.

But why would I keep a steak in the freezer for two years? Why would I keep it for six months, for that matter? Better yet, why would I put a steak in the freezer in the first place when I could just buy it and eat it?

My birthday was in five days. The only plan I could think of was to research FoodSavers and hopefully learn enough uses for them to drum up enthusiasm, and then I could act thrilled when Andrew gave it to me. Unfortunately, he was so excited that he had me open it as soon as he got home.

I'm a terrible liar. He figured out pretty quickly that I didn't want it and we took it back.

TIP: Freezer burn is caused by air getting to the food. You can wrap it in plastic wrap, then aluminum foil to keep the plastic wrap in place. Put it in a Ziploc bag with as little air in it as possible, and then write the name of the food on the bag so you know what on earth you wrapped in aluminum foil months ago. If you put food in a container, place plastic wrap on top of the food so that it's touching the surface before sealing the lid on.

After months of lowering my waste, I didn't keep food long enough to need a vacuum sealer. I didn't let food go bad, get stale, or get freezer burn. I just ate it. No matter how long you make your food taste fresh, you still have to eat it eventually, so you might as well eat it now before you buy more food.

Besides, the longer you hold onto it, the more likely you are to forget you even own it. I once found a bag of pecans in our cupboards that someone vacuum sealed and gave to us four years ago. They were rancid, of course. We would have eaten them if they hadn't been sealed.

I can see owning a vacuum sealer if you end up with a massive surplus of food, like if you garden or hunt. But if you buy food at the store and wait two years to eat it, you should wait two years to buy it.

Dan Nickey, associate director of the Iowa Waste Reduction Center, phrased it perfectly: "If you're in your kitchen and a water pipe burst, you're not going to stop and think, 'How can I use this water in a socially and environmentally responsible manner?' No, you're going to stop and turn the water off. And that's what we need to do first."[2]

Step 5: Don't Buy Too Much Food is the most powerful way to prevent food waste. Nevertheless, *everyone* hates it. Every time I tell people they have too much food, they resist me. Adamantly. No one wants to let go of their abundance. I don't know why. It seems like common sense to me. The more food you own, the harder it is to keep track of it. Imagine never having to check the expiration dates on your food ever again. Buy food. Eat it. Repeat. Problem solved.

TIP: When you limit how much you buy and eat what you have, there is no reason for food to reach its expiration date.

This step isn't only the most powerful, but also the easiest.

Let's say you discover a pear in your kitchen that you forgot about, and now it's too soft to eat raw. Not all of us can spend an hour making oatmeal pear sauce muffins to save one measly pear on our windowsill. We all have enough time to buy fewer pears.

Those huge bags of delicious produce at Sam's Club are tempting, but I resist with great effort. My family cannot finish ten pounds of potatoes.

I heard talk of someone inventing a fridge that keeps track of all the food inside so you don't forget about anything. It would even connect to smartphones so you can know at the store what you have at home.

If you need a smart refrigerator to keep track of what you have, you bought too much. You can't eat it all before it goes bad. I'd even go so far as to say that if you can't remember most of what's in your fridge without looking, you've bought too much. As much as 44 percent of Americans often find an item in their fridge in the past month that they didn't realize was there.[3]

Online, I kept seeing a tip to put sticky notes on food that needs to be eaten up so you're sure not to forget about it. I like the idea of a "leftovers shelf" where all the food that needs to be eaten up is grouped together, but if sticky notes seem necessary, that's a sign that there's too much food in the fridge.

TIP: Fluctuating temperatures can also cause freezer burn, so it's best not to keep the freezer door open too long or to allow the food to slightly thaw and then put it back in the freezer. Do not put warm food in the freezer or it will warm everything else.

I like to take one shelf out of my fridge to keep me from buying too much. Andrew *hates* it when I do this. He has a pack-rat mentality, including when it comes to food, and getting our kitchen to go bare against his will is a constant struggle for me.

His argument: We should have food on hand in case we need it. My argument: If we had to ride a horse half a day to get into town, I'd understand stocking up on groceries, but we can go to the store every day. I typically don't buy food unless I have a plan for it. If a recipe calls for two carrots, I don't buy the whole bag until I decide what to do with the remaining carrots.

Shopping Small

"I hardly ever waste food," said a friend who read my Facebook updates.

This came as a surprise. Most of my friends didn't realize how much they were wasting until they heard what I was doing and put real thought into it. This was the first time someone had put real thought into it and felt good about their food habits.

"How do you do it?" I asked.

"I hardly ever cook, so we don't have leftovers. Dinner is usually grilled cheese with a steamed vegetable or a can of soup." She laughed. "Eventually, I need to become an adult and learn how to cook."

When she went shopping, she only bought enough for one week, and by the end of the week, her kitchen was completely bare.

This reminded me of a lifestyle I had dismissed months earlier: "shopping like the French." From what I hear, French folk go to the store once a day and only buy what they need until tomorrow.

This was the polar opposite of how I used to shop, back when I bought so much that I couldn't fit it in my fridge without clearing space.

You might think, *If you go to the store every single day, you're going to splurge on useless stuff and waste a ton of money!*

I tried buying food only one day at a time as an experiment, and that wasn't the case at all. When you shop one day at a time, you can indulge in as many impulse purchases as you want—but only if you plan on eating it the same day. Before, I often found myself buying treats and snacks not because I wanted them, but because I might want them later. Now if I didn't plan on making a chocolate cake, I didn't buy the mix. If I wasn't in the mood for ice cream, I didn't buy the carton. This is especially important for produce, which often goes bad before people get around to eating it.

TIP: Bagged produce, like lettuce and spinach, are kept fresh with Modified Atmosphere Packaging (MAP). It'll stay fresh longer than unbagged produce, but once you open the bag and oxygen gets inside, the food will start to go bad at the same rate as other produce.

Not going on big grocery trips can be a hard habit to break. It's been drilled into most of us that stocking up on sale items and going to the store less often is the best way to shop. But in our family, not buying massive amounts of food reduced our waste—not to mention it was nice having so much space in my fridge and my freezer.

Of course, getting to the store every day wasn't always an option because I had young kids. Sometimes, I just needed to grab a box of mac and cheese and get the monsters fed before I collapsed from exhaustion. Even though the shop-every-day concept works, in the end, I loosened up a bit and bought enough for two days at a time, maybe three, plus some spur-of-the-moment twenty-minute meals.

Shop small, shop often, and only buy what you'll eat in the next few days. That's my advice.

The Magic of Freezing

You have a powerful tool at your disposal. When used properly, it can solve nearly all your food-waste problems: the freezer. Many people don't use the freezer as an essential part of their daily lives. It's more of a time capsule for past foods.

Imagine what you could do with your freezer if you put your mind to it. Bananas are getting mushy on your windowsill: freeze them and make smoothies later. The watermelon you bought is too big to finish: make popsicles. Half a casserole is sitting in the fridge: freeze it and there's a delicious meal ready for later.

Once at a church activity, I brought a small chocolate cake that I surrounded with cupcakes. Everyone ate all the cupcakes and didn't touch the cake in the center, probably because no one wanted to cut into it.

At home, Andrew was about to get a slice of cake when I stopped him and explained that if we didn't cut into it, we could freeze the cake and use it for something else.

This worked out because the next Father's Day, I was too sick to cook or plan anything special. I had a lovely, untouched cake in the freezer. It only needed to sit out overnight to defrost.

Waste not, want not.

TIP: Check the fridge every day to see if anything needs to be frozen.

If you're not sure what you can freeze, walk down the freezer section of the grocery store. They freeze just about every food you can imagine. Yet despite there being frozen lasagna, a person might make lasagna from scratch and throw it out before finishing it. Use your freezer!

The only downside to the freezer is that it doesn't help with the food you don't want to eat, since it's just delaying the inevitable. Step 8: Don't Make Too Much Food and Step 9: Be Smart When You Cook and When You Shop will help with that.

There are lots of things you can freeze that you might not have thought of: milk, cream cheese, bread, uncooked pies, cake, cookies, cheesecake, brownies, fudge, roux, chips, and crackers . . . to name a few.

I highly recommend labeling and dating everything you put in the freezer. It's surprising how many times I used to pull something out of the freezer with no earthly clue what it was or how long it had been in there. Occasionally I would thaw something out and still have no idea what it was.

Don't throw food in a container or a single bag unless you plan to defrost the whole thing. I often made this mistake when buying three pounds of chicken and freezing it all together in one, heavy lump. You can either freeze individual portions, or you can lay the food out on a baking sheet, so everything freezes separately—like fruit or vegetables—and then put it all in a Ziploc bag or a container. Now when I buy a large packet of chicken breasts, I wrap each breast in plastic wrap before putting them in a bag in the freezer so I can easily use one at a time.

Food in the freezer will be safe indefinitely, but the process will change some foods more than others. Water expands as it freezes, leading cells to expand and often burst. Defrosted produce is less firm, and plants with high water content will be downright mushy. Once you cook the foods that can be cooked, the fact that it was frozen no longer matters.

It's all a matter of what you plan on doing with the food you froze. Celery, for instance, will get soft. You can't defrost it and dip the sticks in ranch. You can chop celery, freeze it, and add it to soup later. You can also use frozen spinach in dishes like saag and quiche, but you can no longer add it to a salad.

TIP: Once you defrost food, it's best not to refreeze it. The food will still be safe, but more cells will burst, possibly causing it to get mushier each time it's frozen.

The way you prepare the food before freezing matters, too. Cheese needs to be grated or it will be crumbly. Mushrooms should be sautéed in butter first. Potatoes should be cubed, sliced, or grated.

Some foods will not taste good after freezing no matter how you prepare them beforehand or cook them afterward. Melon, cucumber, lettuce, radishes, mayonnaise, sauces with corn starch, and pears are all foods I would never freeze.

Before freezing vegetables, blanche them. "Blanche" means dipping food in boiling water for anywhere from thirty seconds to a minute and a half and then putting it in an ice bath. The hot water will kill bacteria, mold, and fungi and stop enzymes from making the food lose color, flavor, and vitamins.

A note on thawing: The best way to thaw food is to put it in the refrigerator for twenty-four hours. Thawing food on a counter or in a bowl of warm water could increase the temperature too much and give bacteria the opportunity to grow. Defrosting with the microwave doesn't heat all parts of food at the same rate. Not to mention defrosting is a pain, and you have to babysit the food. Thawing in the fridge is just better.

Below is a list of how to freeze different foods. Hopefully, this basic guide will show you the enormous possibilities of your freezer.

Food	How to freeze	How the food changes
Avocado	Mash before freezing.	It will turn brown, but this doesn't affect the flavor. Adding lemon juice beforehand helps the color.
Berries	Lay out on a cookie sheet to freeze and then put in a Ziploc bag or a container.	They will be mushy, which is good in recipes like pie and jam.
Bread dough	Instead of letting the dough rise twice, only rise it once. Shape It the way you want it, freeze it on a baking sheet, and then wrap it.	When you're ready to eat it, put the bread on a baking tray, cover with a towel or oiled plastic wrap, and allow to rise until it has doubled in size. Bake as usual.
Cabbage	Shred or cut into quarters.	It will be limp, so you'll want to eat it cooked.
Celery	Chop first, freeze on a cookie sheet, put in a bag or container.	It will be soft when raw but will taste the same when cooked.
Cheese	Grate first.	Cheese will get crumbly when frozen, but if you grate the cheese, it won't be any different.

Food	How to freeze	How the food changes
Cream	Either freeze as is or whip the cream first.	If the cream separates, whisk it until all ingredients are incorporated. Frozen cream won't whip up as well, but it can be frozen after being whipped. Freeze in the shape you plan to serve it and let it defrost in the fridge.
Eggs	Do not freeze in the shell. When freezing whole eggs, beat them first. When freezing egg yolks, beat and then sprinkle with salt or sugar to keep them from getting too gelatinous. Egg whites can be frozen as is. You can place each egg / egg yolk / egg white in an ice cube tray so it's easy to get the right amount for recipes.	The egg won't taste different when thawed.
Grapes	Freeze the whole bunch or remove from stem and freeze on a baking sheet.	Eat when they're still frozen unless you plan on juicing them or using them in a recipe.
Green onions	Chop first.	Won't be crisp but will still be good in recipes.
Greens (kale, spinach, turnip greens, collard greens, etc.)	Freeze as is.	Leaves will be limp but will taste the same when cooked.

Food	How to freeze	How the food changes
Ground beef	You can freeze it raw separated into portions (1/2 pound, 1 pound), and you can freeze it after it's cooked. You can also freeze ground beef after it has been prepared but before it has been cooked, e.g., meatloaf or meatballs.	No difference when thawed.
Herbs	Remove from stems and chop. You can freeze on a baking sheet as is, or you can pack them into an ice cube tray with oil, water, or broth.	The herbs will be limp.
Lemon zest	Zest the citrus by grating it with a cheese grater. Freeze measured amounts in an ice cube tray to use for recipes later.	No difference.
Milk	Milk will expand as it freezes, so don't fill the container to the top.	The milk will separate, so you have to shake it up after thawing, and it might turn yellow. It's fine to drink even if the color has changed.
Mush-rooms	Sauté in butter, freeze on a cookie sheet, put in a bag or container.	No difference.
Nuts	Freeze on a cookie sheet, put in a bag or container.	Toast after thawing.
Onions	Dice, divide into portions, and freeze in a bag.	Onions will not be crisp anymore, but they will taste the same once cooked.

Food	How to freeze	How the food changes
Pasta	It's best to freeze pasta that is slightly undercooked. Freeze flat if you plan to microwave it so the heat can get to the middle. Freeze sauce separately.	The pasta will be softer than when it was frozen, which is why it's a good idea to freeze it when it's undercooked.
Peppers	Remove stems and seeds and dice.	Peppers will get softer but will taste the same when cooked.
Potatoes	Parcook the potatoes first; do not cook them all the way. You can freeze them as hash browns (just shred partially boiled potatoes with a cheese grater), cubed potatoes, French fries, or mashed potatoes.	Potatoes will be mushy if they are not parcooked first. Otherwise, they will taste the same. Mashed potatoes will need to be fluffed in a mixer once thawed.
Pumpkin	Roast the flesh first, puree it, drain in a colander, and freeze in a container.	No difference.
Rice	Separate into portions and freeze. To defrost, place it in a bowl with a little water, cover in plastic wrap and microwave for 2 to 3 minutes. Allow to sit for an additional minute to absorb the steam.	No difference.
Sour cream	Freeze as is.	Will likely separate and become grainy, which is fine if it's cooked in a recipe.
Summer squash	Cut raw squash into cubes or shred.	No difference when cooked.
Sweet potatoes	Roast the potatoes either whole or cubed. Freeze either whole, in cubes on a cookie sheet, or mashed.	No difference.

Food	How to freeze	How the food changes
Tomatoes	Freeze raw or cooked, whole with the core cut out, diced, or pureed.	The texture will be mushier, but will be the same once cooked.
Tortillas	Separate individual tortillas with wax paper.	Corn tortillas might be dry and brittle but will soften up once heated on a skillet.
Watermelon	Cut into cubes or puree.	The watermelon will be mushy, but it's very good in smoothies, sorbet, or popsicles.
Winter squash	Cook until soft and mash.	No difference.
Yogurt	Freeze as is.	Will likely separate and become grainy.

Step 6: Focus on Your Motivation

I'm not proud of this, but there came a point in that first year when I almost gave up being a food-waste warrior.

Remember that I stopped wasting food at a particularly restless time of my life. The same month I began my waste-free quest, I also decided to get a master's degree in creative writing.

That was not a fun conversation with my husband. We had paid off my undergrad loans literally the month before. Then I asked to accumulate more debt for what is frankly a useless degree. He was still getting used to saving egg yolks and putting brown avocados in the fridge, and now I wanted to go back to school!

TIP: To keep an avocado from turning brown, store it in a bag or container with part of an onion. The sulfur in the onion slows the oxidation process.

Grad school started three months after going waste-free. Three months in was the hardest part of being waste-free because I still had no idea what I was doing, and now I had less time than before. I had built some good habits. It wasn't hard to keep my food waste down. But any effort isn't the same without passion, and one day after grocery shopping, I had to pull out a stack of uneaten food to throw away.

It was a painful low.

I was confused and disappointed. What was wrong with me? My reasons to stop wasting food were perfectly pure . . . or were they? Was not wasting food still important, or was it all just a way to burn off creative energy, just something to do when I was bored, and once I started school, I wasn't bored anymore? It was hard to remember why I stopped wasting food in the first place.

One day while trying to figure this out, I went to my favorite used bookstore and came across a book titled *Dancing Skeletons*. The name appealed to me, so I picked it up. It was about an American woman living in Africa and navigating its social problems.

I wish I could do that, I thought. It sounded like quite the adventure.

I plopped into a big, cushioned armchair and flipped through pages and came across a graphic description of one of the most heinous practices currently happening in Africa. I would tell you about it, but it would make this book too dark. Let's just say it disturbed me to my core. I shoved the book back on the shelf as if it had bitten me, but for days afterward, I felt squirmy and gross. The world was an ugly place, and no amount of beauty could make up for it.

I needed to do what I usually do: feel sad for a while and move on. To do this, I started to emotionally shut down through a series of rationalizations. *It isn't* my *country*, I thought. *There isn't anything I can do. It isn't my responsibility. It isn't my fault. . . .*

Fault? Huh.

It was a strange word to use. No one could possibly think, or even suggest, that I had any fault in the suffering on the other side of the world. It had been going on since long before I was born. Yet for some reason, I felt guilty.

Privilege is an interesting thing. Those who have it didn't earn it, didn't ask for it, and can't give it back. I can sell everything I own and live in a shack in a developing country, but I can't get rid of my supportive family, my education, my job experience, my race, or my American citizenship.

It wasn't my fault that people were hungry. It wasn't my fault that children were dying. It wasn't my fault that there was cruelty and selfishness and pain. So why did I feel so bad?

That's when I remembered the real reason I stopped wasting food. It wasn't because I liked the attention from my friends or to save money or because it kept my mind busy. It wasn't even because I thought I could make a difference in the world.

The real reason I stopped wasting food was that some villages in Nigeria had lost all their toddlers. Throwing away food that could have saved those children's lives is a slap in their mothers' faces. I decided then and there to dedicate my book to every mother who has lost a child to hunger.

Saving my own food is not going to help a single hungry child. Not in the Middle East, not in Africa, and not here in the States. My decision to stop wasting food is more like a tribute. It's a message that says, "I cannot help you, but I hear you."

When I don't waste food, I feel lighter, cleaner, and happier. Like I've rinsed gunk out of me. The guilt and helplessness aren't gone, but they're soothed.

Your task is to figure out why *you* want to stop wasting food and to not lose your focus. Perhaps put a reminder on your fridge. That's what I did. If you're rescuing food to save money, you could post a picture of what you want to buy with the money you save. Put up an image of the house you're saving up for, a vacation, or a car. If you want to get out of debt, you could post a picture of a person leaping for joy to represent the freedom of being debt-free.

Perhaps you want to save the environment. You could put up a picture of environmental devastation, like a landfill or a beach covered in plastic debris. Or if you're more motivated by positivity, you could look at a picture of trees or a waterfall to remind you of the beautiful world you're trying to save. You could look at a picture of an animal that's endangered because its habitat was destroyed by fields that farm food you eat, but that might be laying the guilt on too thick.

Animals Endangered by Food Production

- African wild dogs
- Cheetahs
- Chimpanzees
- Dolphins
- Giant armadillos
- Giant pandas
- Giraffes
- Gorillas
- Indian and Asian elephants
- Jaguars
- Lemurs
- Leopards
- Lions
- Orangutans
- Otters
- Pangolins
- Red pandas
- Rhinoceroses
- Sea turtles
- Tigers
- Whales

Maybe you just get a kick out of being resourceful. That's cool. You could put up a picture that inspires you to be resourceful in some way. Maybe it's a picture of your grandma because she lived through the Depression and taught you her tricks. The important thing is that it sparks the same burst of inspiration that made you pick up this book in the first place.

For me, I posted a print of my favorite painting. It's called *Worth of a Soul* by Liz Lemon Swindle. In the picture, Jesus is holding a small African child with the savannah in the background. Jesus is fiercely protective, like nothing matters as much as the safety of this little boy. The boy in the painting looks right at you. It feels like a challenge, saying you are just as responsible for taking care of him as Jesus is.

If a picture on your fridge doesn't help you focus, something else can work. This is your journey. Do what's right for you.

Chapter 5:

Exercising Wisdom

Too many of us don't put enough thought into our food to prevent wasting it. We're not too dumb, or too lazy; we just aren't utilizing our talents. This chapter will help you use your creativity and intelligence to the fullest . . . and it will help you avoid the stupid mistakes we all make.

Step 7: Make a Meal Plan and a Cookbook

Before I stopped wasting food, our evenings would often go like this:

"I'm hungry," said Andrew. "What are we having for dinner?"

"Dunno. Let me check." I looked in the fridge and couldn't think of anything from what I saw. A few leftovers and vegetables had gone bad, which I would either throw out or ignore because I didn't want to deal with them.

"Nothing in here looks good to me," I said. We had some leftover fresh basil, and I vaguely remembered a recipe that called for a lot of basil. Shoot, what was it?

"We could roast potatoes, though that would take an hour or two. I might be able to figure out a casserole or something," I said.

Andrew said, "I don't want to wait that long. We'll be starving before you're done."

"Let's just eat out."

It's hard to believe I used to live like that. We rarely ate meals that took a long time to make because we didn't think about dinner until after we were hungry. We got stuck eating the same things over and over because there were only so many spur-of-the-moment meals to make. Food went bad because we had no plan for everything we bought. We couldn't remember meals we liked because we didn't write them down.

When I stopped wasting food, I started meal planning ahead of time. Now I'm convinced that the secret to happiness is meal planning. It took away so much stress! I woke up in the morning and already knew what we would have for dinner. Many of the easiest meals to make take a long time, like roasted vegetables, baked potatoes, and anything in the Crock-Pot. I could get started in the late afternoon and kick my feet back until it was done. We weren't starving every evening because I didn't wait until late to get started. We also wasted less food.

Meal plan, meal plan, meal plan. I cannot emphasize this enough.

TIP: Keep a visible list of all the meals you plan to make, and don't erase the name of the meal until you've finished eating it. This will help you keep track of what leftovers you have.

Ways to Meal Plan

There's no one right way to plan your meals, but there are a few things to think about. When you plan meals, keep in mind how often you eat out. Don't buy a week's worth of dinners if your family eats tacos on Tuesday, pizza on Thursday, and goes out to a restaurant on Fridays.

There are a few different ways you might go about it. Here's a list of methods you can experiment with to find what's best for you.

The Rotation System: I went to a friend's house and saw a calendar on her fridge, and each day had the name of a meal scribbled in pencil.

"Do you plan your meals for an entire month?" I asked in amazement.

"That's the Three-Week Rotation System," she explained. "You make the same thing every three weeks. No one asks what we're having for dinner because they can just look at the calendar, and you don't have to stress about what to buy or what to make because you just go down the list. You don't get into a funk of making the same thing all the time because you only eat a certain food once in the rotation."

It blew my mind that anyone could be so organized. How easy dinnertime must be for them!

Except I couldn't limit myself to so few meals. Another way to do it is not to rotate through a list of twenty-one specific meals but to rotate through a list of meal types. Just as an example, you could have Casserole Monday, Mexican Tuesday, Sandwich Wednesday, Rice Thursday, Leftovers Friday, Pasta Saturday, and Breakfast Sunday. Or, if you want more variety, you can plan a category for every day of the month: the first could be soup, the second pork chops, the third homemade pizza, and so on. Lunches could be what you had the night before. It would require more thought than the Three-Week Rotation System, and I admit that putting next to no thought into our meals is appealing.

Still, the system wouldn't have worked for our family. Somedays I had more time or energy than others, and it was impossible to predict which days I'd have it in me to cook. I couldn't just up and decide to make butter chicken on the third Saturday of the month; maybe we'd prefer to have eggs, toast, and bacon that day because it was easy. Maybe I could do no more than heat up canned soup. If I had to make spaghetti and meatballs whether I wanted to or not, I'd get burned out on meal planning pretty quickly.

We also couldn't account for all the dinner invitations, impulse takeouts, or late nights out when we needed to grab fast food.

Most importantly, I couldn't always predict ahead of time how many dinners each meal would make. (Step 8: Don't Make Too Much Food can help with this.) My friend could have had a random leftovers night every week, but maybe we'd need to do it more than once a week, or maybe we'd get to leftovers night and not have enough for everyone.

It seemed like the only way this system would work would be if you threw away the leftovers every night so you could start over the next day. To me, cooking every night feels like a huge waste of time.

Maybe you can adjust the three-week system to work perfectly for your family. If not, there are other methods you can try.

Online Tools: Many websites, apps, and online worksheets can help you with your meal planning. Each one is different. Almost all of them automatically generate a grocery list off the digital recipes you picked.

Some programs do the entire meal plan, complete with a grocery list, so that you don't even have to decide what you will eat.

Everything is decided for you. That's nice if you have a tendency to fall down the Pinterest rabbit hole looking for recipes.

Then there are delivery services that drop off the ingredients and instructions for recipes. You don't have to do anything except cook what they give you.

I haven't tried any of those services because they seemed like more work than doing it myself. If you're having trouble figuring everything out, an online tool might be just the right thing for you.

The Once-a-Week Method: A friend of mine invited me over to her house on a Sunday. She'd recently had a baby, so I offered to bring dinner. She said not to worry about it because Sunday was when they made all their meals for the week.

It took me a minute to process this. They cooked all their meals for the whole week in one day?

This opened a world of possibilities. I would only have to cook once. I would only have to clean all the cooking dishes once. There would also be fewer dishes to clean because I could use the same dish for multiple recipes, like a chopping knife or a sautéing pan. I could chop and cook enough chicken for three meals all at once and clean the cutting board once. Going out to eat would be less of a temptation because reheating food was less work than loading the kids into the car to go to a restaurant. For meals that wouldn't reheat well, I could just do the prepping ahead of time. I could assemble a casserole and not bake it or chop up a lot of vegetables but not roast them until we were ready for it.

The once-a-week method was my favorite. The difference in the time I spent in the kitchen every day was dramatic. But there are downsides. Number 1: It took a lot of planning, and even though doing this saved me a lot of time during the week, I was still tempted to cop out and make just one meal for the day instead of all seven.

Downside number 2: Finding room in your fridge might be a problem. People usually only put leftovers in their fridge, which is half the food they made for dinner or less. With the weekly method, you put entire untouched meals in the fridge, and that takes up a lot more space.

It's very important that you do not buy too much food and you keep the kitchen organized if you plan on storing a week's worth of meals.

Downside number 3: Once you make a meal, the clock starts ticking. My friend's husband is Indian, and cooking Indian food ahead of time makes a lot of sense. They make stews and sauces that are easy to reheat and usually taste better the next day anyway. They also use spices that keep the food fresh longer.

For most American foods, the clock ticks faster. Dried beans have been cooked, canned foods have been opened, frozen meat has been thawed, vegetables have been chopped up. If you aren't careful to eat all your meals, you could end up with more food waste than if you had made the meals one at a time.

Don't forget: if you make more than you can eat, there's always the freezer!

To make a week's worth of meals, start with a clean kitchen. Making one meal in a messy kitchen is a pain, but making a week's worth of meals in a messy kitchen is impossible.

If anything needs to be defrosted, start on that first. Next, get out all the ingredients for all the meals all at once. That way, you aren't running back and forth to the pantry and the fridge.

Get out all the dishes you'll need. Knives, cutting boards, pots, spoons. Go ahead and get out all the measuring utensils in your drawer; you'll probably need all of them.

Instead of cooking the meals one at a time, I like to do the steps one at a time. I chop up everything that needs to be chopped, sauté everything that needs to be sautéed, assemble it all . . . you get the idea.

Store everything in containers for the fridge, or, if you've made more than you can eat in a week, put some in the freezer.

Finally, clean the kitchen and bask in the knowledge that you won't have to do so much cleaning for the rest of the week.

If you like the idea of doing all your cooking at once, you might also like the Freezer Method.

TIP: Some food is best stored in a glass or a vase full of water, just like flowers. Green onions, asparagus, celery, and herbs are examples.

The Freezer Method: A friend of mine swore by this method. She went to culinary school and was a very good cook. Many of the meals she liked making were pretty labor intensive: cheese soufflé, chicken potstickers, curry chicken buns, saag paneer.

Instead of spending an eternity in the kitchen every night, she'd spend a few days each month making mass quantities of food and put it all in the freezer. Every evening for the rest of the month, all she had to do was reheat and dinner was ready. She didn't have to eat the same food over and over because she had food in the freezer from the month before, or even two or three months before.

It's brilliant, but it does come with challenges. Preparing so much food takes a lot of planning. You have to have enough money to buy it all on one paycheck. And you have to be good at what you're making because if your meal doesn't turn out, you have a lot of it to eat through. My biggest issue, which is the smallest issue for everyone else, is that I hate defrosting.

If you don't want to do all your cooking in a day or two, you could stock your freezer one meal at a time. Double or triple the recipe every night, and put half of it in the freezer for another night. Eventually, you'll have a freezer full of prepared meals.

TIP: Some foods can be frozen in water, like shrimp or chicken. The ice keeps air away so there's no freezer burn.

The Loose Method: While the once-a-week method was my favorite, I would often default to the loose method.

I would buy enough groceries for one week and no more. Since I only cooked three times a week, I only bought three meals, along with breakfast, snacks, and lunches (keeping in mind that leftovers would often be for lunch). I would shop my pantry aggressively, leaning on meals that used as many ingredients I already had as possible. There would also be at least one meal in the freezer and a few "emergency staples" like Top Ramen and pancake mix.

Instead of a calendar, I used a chalkboard. I didn't decide what I would make until the morning of, but I knew what meals we had on hand, and deciding in the morning what I would make gave me plenty of time to get started on daylong dinners, like slow cooked meals and baked potatoes. Sometimes when Adalyn was napping, I'd prep the meals in the afternoon but not finish cooking them, so I didn't have so much chaos to deal with in the evening. I didn't erase a meal from the chalkboard once I made it; I waited until all the leftovers were eaten so we'd know what was in the fridge. And I didn't just plan meals; I planned portions, too.

This process worked, but only because I had already made a family cookbook. We'll get to that in a second.

Meal Planning Pitfalls

Maybe you've already tried meal planning, but it didn't go well. Here are some pitfalls to avoid:

- Planning too many recipes that are time-consuming
- Buying too much food (see Step 5: Don't Buy Too Much Food)
- Not having backup meals for when you don't want to cook
- Not writing the plan down
- Planning meals you want instead of shopping your pantry
- Not planning for leftovers
- Not checking the calendar for special occasions or when you won't be home
- Not keeping track of your recipes

Speaking of not keeping track of recipes, this leads me to my favorite section of this book.

Make Your Own Cookbook

The secret to happiness is meal planning, and the secret to meal planning is keeping a family cookbook.

The hardest part of meal planning was figuring out what I wanted to eat. I'd skim through Pinterest, our Betty Crocker cookbook, and a folder of recipes scribbled onto notebook paper. I constantly had to make dishes we had never tried before because I didn't know what else to make.

Before I stopped wasting food—back when my kitchen was basically a dysfunctional bombshell—I would occasionally find a recipe I liked and make it a bunch of times. When we got tired of it, I'd never make it again. It's not because I didn't want it anymore. It's because I forgot I even liked it.

When your only option is to commit to memory the names and locations of all your recipes, you aren't going to remember very many. Often this means making the same stuff over and over until you can't take it anymore and you get yourself stuck in a rut.

There was a point in our marriage when it seemed like every meal I made called for sun-dried tomatoes. I must have gone through a jar every month. Now I can't remember a single meal I ever made with sun-dried tomatoes.

I once spent a lot of time perfecting a recipe for frozen hot chocolate, but I never wrote it down. We only recently remembered that I used to make it, and I no longer remember how.

Then the cookbook came along.

I stumbled upon the rewards of a family cookbook by accident. After I got married, my parents took in a foster teenager who liked to cook. For Christmas, I compiled all our family recipes into a Word document and put them in a binder as a sort of welcome-to-our-family gift. I went ahead and put in all the recipes I liked to make, too, not just the ones my parents made for us growing up, and ended up including seventy-five recipes. It only made sense to print one off for myself.

The cookbook changed my life.

Sure, it took time to make it—a lot of time. I had to remember everything we liked, and then I had to track all the recipes down so I could type them up and print them out. I called relatives, I raided my Pinterest boards, and I skimmed through all my cookbooks.

It. Was. *Worth* it.

Now, whenever I need to make a grocery list, I just pull out my binder and I have everything I need right in front of me. When I'm ready to make the meal, out comes the binder again. Simple.

My husband said that once the cookbook came into our lives, he had never had so much good food.

I made a table of contents that includes meal ideas that don't need a recipe, like pancakes and salad wraps. The meals were organized into groups, like Asian, Korean, Creole, and so on. We rotated through the different groups randomly.

I still made new recipes, but only when I wanted to and not because I needed to. If my family liked a meal enough, they'd say, "Put that one in the cookbook!"

Did I seriously once have recipes strewn all over the house and the Internet? Was there really a time when I would make something delicious and then forget where I found it, or worse, that I had ever made it? What a bleak time that must have been!

The cookbook isn't just a tool to help you, but a sentimental gift for others. Your family members will treasure your cookbook. Imagine your child is about to move out, and as a present, you hand them a gift-wrapped book of every recipe your child loved growing up. Now imagine you've passed on, and your family is at your home after the funeral, leafing through your cookbook saying, "Remember when Grandma used to make that?" You can put that cookbook together *now* and build on it over time. It will be of great importance later.

Making the same meals over and over, instead of making a meal once and never having it again, has benefits besides maintaining your sanity. It improves the dish, for instance. Every time you make a recipe, you get better at it. You can also scribble notes in the margins of the recipes. I used to cook meals that didn't taste as good as last time, only to remember I had changed the recipe but didn't write it down. So frustrating! Now I can keep track of my changes, and the recipes keep getting better.

Making the same meal repeatedly saves time. The first time you make a dish takes the longest. You aren't entirely sure how it's supposed to turn out, and you check the recipe twice at each step to make sure you're getting it right. But if you make the same meal more than once, you get faster at it each time. You might even commit recipes to memory.

Believe it or not, it saves money. I used to pass up on recipes that sounded good because they called for a spice or a sauce that I didn't have, and I didn't want to buy a bottle of something I would never use again. It would have been too expensive. If you rotate through the same meals again and again, you use the same condiments, spices, and sauces until they're all gone.

For instance, I have one recipe that calls for dill weed. We don't use dill weed for anything else, but after ten years of making this recipe on a regular basis, we finally ran out and I had to buy another jar. We also recently ran out of garam masala and sriracha sauce. That's what happens when you repeat recipes!

My kids complained a lot less once I started using the cookbook —and let's face it: My husband complained less, too. Making a new recipe is always a crapshoot. At least when you repeat recipes, you know how your family will react to them.

Shopping your kitchen becomes a breeze. It's easy to flip through the pages to find a meal that uses ingredients you already have. I could see chicken in the fridge and pick a recipe we like that called for chicken.

Finally, you're less likely to waste food when you're organized.

If you're feeling inspired to make your own cookbook, let's get started!

How to Make a Cookbook

It can be daunting to remember all the meals you like, much less how to cook them, and then to track them all down and compile them in one place. At least you don't have a deadline to finish it. Unless you make it as a Christmas present, in which case, maybe a deadline is helpful. Take baby steps. You'll keep adding things as you try them, so the cookbook will never be finished, which means you don't need to pressure yourself to get it all done in one go.

There are many ways to keep a cookbook, and you can utilize whatever method(s) fits your preference. It doesn't matter how you do it. All that matters is that everything is in one place.

Ways to Compile Recipes

1. You can put notecards in a shoebox or one of those tiny plastic file cabinets.
2. You can put newspaper and magazine clippings, Xeroxed cookbook pages, printed blog recipes, and handwritten recipes in a binder with sheet protectors.
3. You can keep a board on Pinterest or use an app like Recipe Keeper. If a recipe you like isn't already online, you can take a picture and make a new pin or enter it manually into Recipe Keeper.
4. If all your recipes come from cookbooks and you don't want to copy them, you can save time by putting bookmarks or sticky notes on the pages you like. Write the name of the recipe on the sticky note so you don't have to open the book

to see what's inside. Make a list in a binder or document of all the recipes you've bookmarked and where to find them.

5. You can create a document and either pull it up on a device when you need it or print it out. Include a table of contents so you don't have to flip through pages. To do this automatically, make the title of each recipe a heading instead of regular text, go to insert, and add the table of contents. This will also create links to click on that will take you directly to the recipe.

For me, I put all my "keeper" recipes in a Word document.

Once you've picked your method, it's time to remember every meal you've ever liked. This worksheet will help. Take your time, think it out, and your list will likely grow faster than you think.

Cookbook Worksheet

What I had for dinner tonight: ______________________________

Last night: ______________________________

The night before: ______________________________

Etc. ______________________________

____

____

____

My favorite meals are ______________________________

____

____

____

My family's favorite meals are______________________________

When we go to a restaurant, we always order ____________________

Meals my parents and in-laws make: ____________________

Meals my grandparents make: ____________________

Meals my friends make: ____________________

When I'm in a hurry, I make: ____________________

When I want to impress company, I make: ____________________

____

____

____

Food I want to learn to make: ____________________

____

____

____

____

Frozen meals we often buy: ____________________

____

____

____

Meals I make in the slow cooker or pressure cooker: ____________________

____

____

____

My favorite desserts: ____________________

____

____

____

Desserts I'm good at making: ____________________

____

____

____

Categories of Meals

Mexican: ____________________

____

Rice dishes: ____________________

____

Pasta dishes: ____________________

____

Breakfast: ____________________

____

Chicken: ____________________

____

Pork: ____________________

____

Beef: ____________________

____

Fish: ____________________

____

Soups: ____________________

____

Casseroles: ____________________

____

Sandwiches: ____________________

____

Holiday Foods

Christmas: ____________________

____

____

Birthdays: ____________________

____

____

Easter: ____________________

____

____

Anniversary: ____________________

____

____

Mother's Day: ____________________

____

____

Father's Day: ____________________

____

____

Halloween: ____________________

____

____

Valentine's Day: ____________________

____

____

Fourth of July: ______________________________________

____

____

Thanksgiving: ______________________________________

____

____

Anything else you can think of: ______________________________________

____

____

____

____

____

Good luck, and happy cooking!

Step 8: Don't Make Too Much Food

Twenty-five percent of the food consumers throw away is due to having cooked, served, or prepared too much.[4] We don't put enough thought into serving sizes and leftovers before we get cooking. Then, we're left scrambling with an abundance of food.

I used to just cook whatever the recipe called for, even if that meant eating leftovers until we were sick of them and threw the rest out. Then I stopped wasting food, and when my husband and kids got tired of a meal, I'd have to finish it myself.

It was not a good system.

Three to four times a year, I would make a huge pot roast. The recipe called for four pounds of meat, so without thinking, I cooked four pounds of meat with loads of onions, carrots, and potatoes. It made enough to feed an army. We would happily eat the roast for one meal, but roasts aren't the same the next day. Even if they were just as good, no one wanted to eat *anything* as many times as was necessary to finish what I had made. I don't think we've ever finished a four-pound roast.

One day I was about to put another roast on, and I thought, *Maybe I shouldn't make so much.*

Uh, *duh!* It's weird how we get stuck in little destructive habits that are so easy to step out of. Cooking only one pound of roast at a time—maybe even less—just made sense. It's not like they take a lot of work to make. If hypothetically we wanted more after the one pound was gone, I could just throw another pound in the pressure cooker.

When I put real thought into it, the meat was good the next day if I used it for other things besides reheating as is. Homemade roast beef sandwiches are amazing. The potatoes were good once mashed, too. Upcycling to the rescue!

Step 8: Don't Make Too Much Food goes hand in hand with Step 5: Don't Buy Too Much Food, but it's important enough to get its own section. You can buy very little and still throw out a lot if you cook too much.

This is why I'm not a huge fan of scrap cookbooks. It's fun to make vinegar out of apple scraps and pesto out of carrot tops, but if you don't eat all the pesto you made, you end up wasting more food than if you hadn't bothered.

When I cook, I consider how much each member of my family eats and try to only make enough food for two meals. It's hard to get my family to eat it more than twice. Anything left after two meals goes in the freezer. Using your family cookbook will make this easier because you already know how much your family likes it and how much of it they'll eat.

If you don't like leftovers, don't make more than one meal. If you do like leftovers, plan out beforehand what you're going to do with them. I don't make small lasagnas. They're a lot of work! But they aren't nearly as good in the microwave as when they come steaming out of the oven, with the cheese gooey and the sauce bubbling. The solution is simple; I assemble as much lasagna as the recipe calls for, but only cook enough for one meal. The rest is separated into other casserole dishes in the fridge for me to bake in the oven on another day. A 4x8 bread pan is the perfect size to feed my family one meal.

Sometimes planning out portions meant my family got a little less of one food than they had hoped. If I were to buy a pound of green beans, I might only cook half and cook the other half in the next day or two or freeze it. Otherwise, if I cooked a whole pound and my family ate three-quarters of it, the remaining quarter pound wouldn't be enough to go with a meal and it would probably be forgotten and go uneaten. My kids might ask for more green beans, and I'd tell them sorry, they would have to wait until I made it again.

When I make biscuits, I only make enough batter for dinner and breakfast the next day regardless of what the recipe tells me to do. When I make cookie dough, I only bake two cookies for each person at a time and put the rest of the dough in the fridge or the freezer, or I make freezer cookies. (See Chapter 2.)

You get the idea.

I once bought eight hot dogs because they were on sale. (They ended up being more expensive than when they weren't on sale. That grocery store is tricky.) I also bought two cans of chili and a pack of eight hot dog buns. The number of hot dogs matched the number of buns. . . . When does that ever happen?

Dinner #1 was two hot dogs for my husband, one for me, half a hot dog for each of the girls, and one can of chili to be dumped on top of them all, with cheese. It was exactly half of what I bought, leaving just the right amount for Dinner #2. There was some chili left over from Dinner #1, which my youngest had for lunch the next day.

TIP: If you made a big pot of chili you don't want to finish, time to get creative. You can put it in a skillet, pour cornbread on top, and bake it, pour it on a baked potato with cheese and sour cream, pour it over Fritos and top with cheese (aka Frito Pie), or mix it into mac and cheese.

If someone had wanted more hot dogs, tough. I had a bag of potato chips and a platter of raw vegetables with ranch dip that they could help themselves to, but they couldn't have more hot dogs because they'd eat into Dinner #2. They didn't want more, though, because I correctly predicted how much they would want.

Imagine my annoyance when, the next day, I found my two daughters gnawing on the hot dog buns as a snack, even though there was a perfectly good loaf of bread right next to them. That evening, the girls were served hot dogs on partially eaten buns. We ate every scrap of everything because of my mad meal-planning skills, and I felt like a genius.

Don't expect me to say anything coy and stupid like "I guess it doesn't take much to make me happy, lol," because perfect meal planning isn't a little thing. I work hard on it and I'm proud of myself. You should be proud of your accomplishments, too.

The temptation is to cook more to save yourself time in the kitchen, but unless you make a solid plan for the leftovers, it doesn't save enough time to be worth the risk of wasting it. My pressure cooker only takes twenty minutes to cook dried beans. It's no skin off my back to make half a pound of beans now and half a pound later. That's better than cooking a whole pound and freezing half of it, as many blogs suggest, since that takes up precious freezer space. Plus you have to defrost and reheat it, which takes about as long as making it fresh.

Buy less, cook less, and waste less. You will save more.

TIP: Need more freezer space? Instead of putting boxes of food in your freezer, which don't get smaller as you eat through the food, take the bags out of the boxes. If the food came with cooking instructions, cut the instructions off the box and tape it to the bag.

Step 9: Be Smart When You Cook and When You Shop

None of what I've said in this chapter matters—*none* of it—if you suck at cooking. You can buy and store and portion everything exactly right, but if the end result sucks, it'll still go in the trash.

I like experimenting with new recipes, but in 2017, I hardly tried anything new. There was too much risk involved. The recipe might not have turned out, or it might have turned out, but we still didn't like it, or we did like it but not enough to finish it. We depended on our family cookbook in those days.

You can avoid common mistakes that might ruin a meal. Here are five tips:

Anticipate the End Result

When I did try something new, I learned to put more thought into the recipe before making it. Anticipating how it will actually turn out will prevent mistakes. Take cherry almond Dutch babies, for instance. The recipe called for fresh cherries, but I used canned tart berries, not anticipating that the sour cherries would taste like Warheads and make the pancake soggy.

One idea I keep seeing over and over again online is making vegetable broth out of scraps. Think: onion skins, carrot heads, celery leaves. Obviously, that idea is a home run for me. To think that I could turn vegetable scraps into something useful and delicious . . . brilliant!

At least, it *sounded* brilliant.

The lady in the video used onion, carrot, celery, garlic, parsley, mushrooms, and potato peels.

Boiled potato peels? That sounded repugnant. But far be it from me to question the wisdom of the Internet.

I kept a gallon-sized Ziploc bag in the freezer to toss vegetable scraps into, and when it was full, I boiled the scraps in water. It had onion, bell pepper, carrot, celery, potato peels, and probably some other things, but I can't remember. Really, only one memorable detail stands out in my mind: potato peels make stock taste *terrible.*

I feel a little ridiculous, because honestly, it tasted exactly how you would expect boiled potato peels to taste: like dirt. My gut told me this recipe wasn't going to work. I did it anyway, and a quart of toilet water broth got dumped down the drain. Did the woman in that video actually drink her potato water? It seems unlikely.

Still, I loved the concept, and I didn't want to give up. Potato peels were a bust, but what if I listened to my instincts this time and only used vegetables that I thought would taste good together?

This time, my broth was made up of red onion skin, sweet potato peel, carrot peel and heads, celery leaves, bok choy, romaine lettuce, bell pepper seeds and stem, tomato stems, green onion ends, and cucumber ends.

Voilà. Six cups of yummy vegetable broth that I later used to make black bean soup—although you could really only taste the onion, carrot, and celery. That explains why those are typically the only vegetables used to make stock. Maybe the other vegetables added nutrients.

People have asked me what to do with the remains of the boiled vegetables. Sorry to disappoint you, but those scraps have reached the end of their usefulness and are finally destined for the compost bin.

Once at someone's house, my hostess was so excited to make a breakfast scramble in the slow cooker. All you do is pour raw scrambled eggs over chopped sausage and frozen hash browns and turn the slow cooker on low, and breakfast is ready the next morning.

The woman in question is a good cook, but she had never made hash browns before. I knew that in order for shredded potatoes to be hash browns, they have to be cooked in a skillet of oil until they turn brown and crispy. A slow cooker would steam them, and they'd be mushy. There was no polite way to tell her that the food she was making would be awful, so I said nothing. I try not to be a jerk, and I'm occasionally successful. The next morning, we cringed over a huge pot of egg-flavored mashed potatoes. No one wanted to eat it, and I couldn't think of a single thing to do to salvage it.

"Are you going to take it home?" Andrew asked, his face filled with dread.

"Heck, no," I answered. "That was her mistake, not mine."

Here's a similar logic fail, although this time, I was at fault: shredded beef tacos with avocado lime sauce. The picture was exquisite, with each taco perfectly assembled and avocado sauce lusciously drizzled over the top.

The picture gave me complete faith that the blogger knew what she was doing. I should have known better because it was a paleo website. I can't vouch for the health of the paleo diet—or the logic of its premise—but when bloggers follow a restrictive diet, they aren't primarily concerned with taste.

I followed the recipe to a T. Even when it told me to cook the meat with a quarter cup of lime juice, which made it taste like hot, meaty limeade. Then the recipe called for a quarter cup of lime juice to be blended with *one* avocado. That was obviously going to be a fail, regardless of how good the picture was. The avocado did nothing but thicken up the tart lime, which I poured over my meaty limeade without tasting either the meat or the sauce first. If I had, my family wouldn't have had to eat dinner with painfully puckered faces.

Besides anticipating how a dish would taste and how to portion it out, I learned to anticipate the time I would put into it.

Once I had to make a large quantity of food for people I despised. I'll cycle back to this story later, but for now, all you need to know is that the thought of feeding them filled me with rage. I didn't want to put much effort into the dish. So I decided to give them deviled eggs.

I *always* do this. Every time there's a potluck, I think, *I'll just make deviled eggs. Those are easy.*

They aren't easy at all! I have to peel every single egg. Sometimes the yolk is crooked, so the white is thick on one side and thin on the other and the thin side breaks. Then I have to pipe the yolk into every single egg white. Not to mention it always makes a mess.

It's the same with candy corn. Every Halloween, I eat candy corn thinking this will be the year I like it, but it's just as bad every year.

I had yet to wise up to the difficulty of deviled eggs, so I boiled thirty-six of them and got to work peeling—except I couldn't peel them. The shells stuck to the eggs so tightly that huge chunks of the white came off in my hand. To make matters even more fun, my daughters had never eaten hard-boiled eggs before, and they wanted nothing more in the whole world. I had to keep smacking their hands away as they reached over the table to swipe one. It was like playing Whac-A-Mole.

As I mutilated egg after egg, I fumed, not only because it had been so stupid to choose deviled eggs yet again, but also because I was putting so much effort into feeding people I hated. By the time I finished the last egg (or more accurately, destroyed the last egg), I was mad enough to punch a puppy.

I posted a picture of the egg massacre on Facebook and wrote, "Time to make deviled eggs!" with an angry face. One of my friends responded with, "Dems was fresh eggs, weren't they?"

Turns out, the secret to peeling a hard-boiled egg is not to boil them when they're fresh. There's a thin membrane between the shell and the white, and ideally when you slide your finger between the membrane and the white, it'll slide right off. When the egg is fresh, the membrane isn't loose enough to do this. Lesson learned.

I shoved the tray away and told my daughters to have at it. They pounced on the tray and happily shoved the ruined eggs in their mouths. We had many egg salad sandwiches over the next two weeks.

I still had to make a dish, but this time, I decided to be smart for once and really think about how much work I would put in. I boiled a few pounds of spaghetti, dumped marinara sauce on top, and called it good.

Sample Food at Every Stage

When I stopped wasting food and properly used up all my leftovers, I had to cook a lot less often. At one point, I had an itch to cook but absolutely zero need for it. The fridge was full of delicious meals. Making more would only put them at risk of going bad.

I loved making fancy desserts, but rarely did I have the time or the energy for it. For the first time in ages—probably since I became a mom—I had all the time and energy I needed to create something sweet and beautiful. Thus, a chocolate crumble pie was made.

I chose this particular dessert because all the ingredients happened to already be in my kitchen. Shop your kitchen! The only ingredient I was missing was amaretti cookies, and I didn't know what those were, so I used a box of Nilla wafer cookies and hoped it was close to the same thing.

Do you remember the vacuum-sealed pecans from Chapter 4? There was a bag of pecans in our pantry that someone gave us years ago. Like . . . four or five years ago. Maybe six. I thought, *Yay! Pecans for my pie!*

Meanwhile, a quiet voice in my head said, "Maybe those pecans aren't good anymore." But I never listen to the little voice in my head because she is obnoxious. I chopped up the nuts, mixed them with cocoa and crushed wafers, and piled them high on the pie. Into the oven it went.

The pie tasted rancid. Surprise, surprise.

My annoying little voice could have prevented me from a *lot* of trouble over the years, including with food. I make an effort to listen to her now.

Luckily, only the crumble on the top of the pie was bad. I scraped it off and made a new crumble, this time with almonds. Rest assured, I tasted the almonds first to make sure they were still good.

Consider Your Family's Preferences

When you plan meals, consider what your family will actually eat. For years early in our marriage, I would cook what I wanted without giving any thought to whether my husband would like it, and then be shocked and hurt when he got up from the table and made himself something else. I felt that I shouldn't have to change my diet to work around his pickiness. Meanwhile, he felt that he shouldn't have to eat things I knew he wouldn't enjoy when he could easily make a sandwich.

Then we became parents and had even more preferences to navigate. My girls had trouble chewing hard vegetables like raw carrots, Andrew wouldn't eat soft vegetables like squash and eggplant, and I wouldn't eat any vegetable that had the word "greens" in the name. Turnip greens, collard greens, mustard greens. Yuck. They look like prison mush you see sweaty cafeteria workers plop onto trays with a huge ladle. Also, I won't eat okra: the vegetable of slime. Unless you fancy eating slugs, I do not recommend okra.

I refused to raise picky eaters. Still, there are some battles not worth bringing to the table. I learned to live without eggplant, and Andrew only cooks turnip greens for himself.

Buy Good Food

This is a no-brainer: if you buy bad food, your recipes won't taste as good and you won't want to finish them.

Produce can be a gamble. You buy peaches for a tart, and they have no flavor. You buy strawberries for shortcake, but they grow mold the day after you buy them.

I thought about making a chart of how to only buy ripe produce, but there were too many myths to test. Some say pineapple is ripe when it's yellow and the middle stem comes out easily. Others say not to look for yellow in the husk but green in the stem and that pulling the stem out tells you nothing. Everyone says to pick watermelon that sounds hollow, but they all sound the same to me.

Check if the produce is soft, firm, or crisp (depending on what it is), that it's colorful, and that it smells good. Best of luck to you.

TIP: Ethylene gas ripens produce, and some produce emits it as it ripens. Releasing that gas can make other produce ripen too quickly. It's best to keep the following foods separate from things you don't want to be ripened: apples, apricots, avocados, cantaloupe, figs, honeydew, bananas, nectarines, peaches, pears, plums, onions, and tomatoes.

I got myself into yet another tricky situation at a Thanksgiving dinner when I broke every rule for smart cooking, including buying yucky food. I thought it would be a fun tradition to make these *adorable* treats that look like acorns. They're so easy. You just use melted chocolate to glue a chocolate kiss on one side of a Nilla wafer and a chocolate chip on the other.

I went to the grocery store the day before Thanksgiving, and there wasn't a single box of regular Nilla wafers left. Not even the off-brand. Southerners often make banana pudding on Thanksgiving, so there was a big, gaping hole of empty space on the shelf where the boxes used to be.

The reduced-fat wafers, on the other hand, were untouched. Next to them were a few boxes of mini wafers—I didn't even know they *made* mini wafers.

How bad could reduced-fat Nilla wafers really be?

The girls and I settled around the table and got to work on the acorns. Three acorns into it, Andrew picked up one of them and turned it around with a puzzled expression.

"Is this what they're supposed to look like?" he asked.

"Oh, *no!*" I gasped.

I had only skimmed the recipe and missed that the wafers needed to be mini-sized. The "acorns" we made looked like sombreros on Mexicans with tiny necks.

We'd just have to find another use for them. Only there was one problem:

They were *abysmal.*

The taste was mostly okay at first, but the aftertaste had a chemical flavor like if I had licked a beaker at a high school science lab. Even my daughters wouldn't eat them. I declared on Facebook that the cookies had defeated me.

"It's okay to waste reduced-fat Nilla wafers," I wrote. "They are an abomination, and we should kill them with fire."

Some of my helpful readers suggested ways to improve them, like crumbling them up into a piecrust, which likely would have made a terrible pie. I wrote back, "You underestimate the horror of these cookies. They are unsalvageable."

Despite my decision to wash my hands of these lab-made Frankenstein cookies, I didn't throw them out right away. This failure didn't sit well with me.

I sampled an acorn just for kicks and discovered that if you eat one with a chocolate kiss, it's not so bad. Thus did I create chocolate-covered Nilla wafers.

I did not want to eat an entire box of cookies dipped in chocolate, so I brought them to church the next day and passed them around. They appreciated the treat and chuckled over the story that came with it.

Another scrap saved!

Upcycle Food That Needs Help

Just because you cooked food one way doesn't mean you have to eat it that way. A Sunday pot roast can become Monday's roast beef sandwiches, Tuesday's beef stew, and Wednesday's potpie.

Before I stopped wasting food, I often threw away leftover rotisserie chicken. Reheated rotisserie chicken is just not as good as the first day. I might make an effort to keep eating it, but could never muster enough enthusiasm to finish it.

Why did I think the chicken had to be reheated and eaten plain? I could have sliced it for sandwiches, cubed it for salad, shredded it for pasta, or chopped it for enchiladas. It could have gone into soup, casseroles, and pies.

TIP: Meat from rotisserie chicken and whole turkeys can be used in any recipe that calls for chopped or shredded poultry.

Even big businesses, which we often associate with selfishness and waste, know how to upcycle. Take tater tots, for example. These fried potato balls of deliciousness were invented when French fry–makers didn't know what to do with leftover pieces of cut-up potatoes. They simply mashed and fried their waste and sold it.[5]

That is upcycling. The phrase was originally used for art created from trash, like a cutting board out of salvaged wood or paper roses out of discarded library books. The basic premise applies to food: Unwanted Thing + Creativity = An Awesome Thing.

I love upcycling not only because it makes me feel clever, but because it makes my life easier. Making a meal where half the ingredients are already cooked saves me a ton of time in the kitchen.

For instance, I used to make fried rice from scratch whenever I was in the mood for it. That meant cooking the rice, waiting for it to cool in the fridge, chopping and cooking the vegetables and the meat, frying the eggs, frying the rice, and mixing it all together. . . . It was one of the most time-consuming recipes I made. But if the rice was left over from a different meal, and I used frozen vegetables and meat we had already cooked, suddenly, fried rice was one of the easiest recipes I made. And it tastes the same.

TIP: Rice often gets stuck to the bottom of the pan. To fix this, stir up the rice the moment it's done, add a couple tablespoons of water, and close the lid for 5 to 10 minutes. This will loosen up the stuck rice.

One more example: We love fondue at our house, but leftover fondue isn't great. The cheese will never reach that same wonderfully gooey consistency again. Instead, I like to turn the cheese into soup by thinning it with chicken broth. I toss in all the dippers—broccoli, cauliflower, sausage, mushrooms, and potatoes—which are already cooked—and toast the leftover cubed baguette to make croutons as a topping. It would have taken me an hour to make a soup like that from scratch. Upcycling it took maybe ten minutes.

Upcycling is great for leftovers, but it can also fix food that didn't turn out so well. I once made an Indian rice dish that ended up being too spicy for the kids. There was way too much for Andrew and me to willingly finish on our own.

"What if we added sour cream to calm down the spice?" asked Andrew.

I raised an eyebrow. "We do that with Mexican food, but Indian?"

"Why not? They marinate their meat in yogurt. That's basically the same thing."

I decided to upcycle the dish by making it into a casserole. (See the next section on concept cooking to learn more about winging it with casseroles.) I spread the rice on the bottom of the pan, smeared on a layer of sour cream, added leftover roasted cauliflower, and topped it with mozzarella cheese. Would this new dish horrify an Indian chef? Probably. At least it was tamed down enough for the kids to enjoy.

Another scrap saved!

The moral of the chapter is that every time we cook—especially when we try new recipes—we run the risk of making a mistake and destroying the food. Sometimes there's not much we can do to keep it from happening. Goodness knows I made more than a few inedible meals when I moved out of my parents' house. The more you know about food and grow to understand it, the more you know its rhythms and the rules you can and can't break. But regardless of your cooking skill, anticipating problems and tasting the food in stages will make a big difference.

Logic, knowledge, planning, and tasting. Those are the keys to preventing a bad recipe.

And for heaven's sake, don't burn your food. Use a timer.

Concept Cooking

"Concept cooking" is a phrase I coined myself. Well . . . I don't know if it counts as "coined" if no one else uses it. Maybe it'll catch on. Here's how it works:

There are certain foods you don't need a recipe to make. Take cereal, for instance. No one looks up how much milk to pour for the right ratio of liquid and cereal. You don't need a recipe for a sandwich, either. It can be helpful to hear ideas of what to put on a sandwich, but you'll never hear someone say, "How many grams of tomato should I use? Do I spread on a tablespoon of mayonnaise, or is that too much?" A recipe isn't necessary because you know how sandwiches work. You understand the "concept" of a sandwich.

Imagine if you had a grasp on a bunch of different dishes. Knowledge frees up creativity. You could see a hodgepodge of ingredients and assemble a soup or a casserole, just like that.

Concept cooking can be risky. Some of your recipes will be better than others. If your experiment turns out badly, you might end up not finishing it or throwing the whole thing away. The only advice I have is to proceed with caution. I recommend making a recipe several times to get the "concept" of it before venturing out on your own.

Here are some ideas that will get you going. Remember to add salt and pepper to everything and cooked onion to most things.

TIP: If you find yourself with extra yummy fluid, like a flavored broth, meat juice, or soup, you can cook rice, couscous, quinoa, or beans in the fluid. This will give it extra flavor.

Soup

Soups are a good way to use up pasta, rice, beans, barley, lentils, just about any kind of meat, and just about any kind of vegetable. I'd be very surprised if you didn't have enough ingredients in your kitchen to make a good soup right now. In this section, I've included recipes for the base of different soups, and you can assemble the rest from there.

The broth base can become chicken or turkey noodle soup, chicken rice soup, pesto chicken soup, udon soup, ramen, pho, hot pots (and lots of other Asian-inspired soups), French onion soup, Italian wedding soup, tortilla soup, cabbage and kielbasa soup, matzo ball soup, chicken and dumplings, and orzo soup. The tomato and broth base is great for vegetable medleys, minestrone, and taco soup.

The soups with slurry or roux become thick and can make clam chowder, corn chowder, cauliflower and ham chowder, blended broccoli and cheese, or blended potato and cheese.

The creamy broth base can become tomato soup or zuppa Toscana. (That's the soup from Olive Garden everyone seems to be obsessed with.) I came up with my own recipe using sausage, zucchini, cauliflower, and wild rice. Yum!

TIP: When fat is released from the food you make, such as bacon grease and the film on top of broth, you can cook with it. The fat is great for sautéing, greasing pans, or even replacing oil in recipes. If the bacon grease is full of food debris, microwave it until it becomes liquid and the debris will float to the bottom.

To make a blended soup out of the creamy broth base, you can mix in butternut squash, potatoes and leeks, sweet potatoes, pumpkin, roasted carrots, roasted bell peppers and tomatoes, cauliflower, spinach and potatoes, black beans with Mexican spices, roasted corn, or peas. And almost all these soups will need spices and other flavorings. Sorry, I can't help you with that—the possibilities are too many!

Creamy Soup with Slurry

Butter, oil, or bacon fat
Onion (optional)
Vegetables
Meat
½ cup flour or cornstarch
1 cup water or broth
2 cups half-and-half
Salt and pepper to taste

1. Sauté in fat all the vegetables you plan to add to the soup. Add meat if you want and sauté until done.
2. Whisk flour or cornstarch into cold or room-temperature water or broth.
3. Add all ingredients together and boil until thick.
4. If you want it thicker, whisk more flour or cornstarch in a bowl of cold water and add it to the pot. This is important because hot liquid will cook the flour or cornstarch before it's mixed in and this will cause lumps. If you want it thinner, add more liquid.

Creamy Soup with Roux

2 tablespoons fat (butter, oil, bacon grease)
2–3 tablespoons flour
Milk to desired consistency, about 3 cups or more
Vegetables
Meat
Spices

1. Melt the butter or heat the oil. Slowly whisk in flour and continue whisking until it's been bubbling for 3 minutes.
2. Whisk in milk a little at a time until it's the desired consistency.
3. Simmer for 10 minutes to thicken. Add milk if it gets too thick.
4. Add cooked meat, vegetables, and spices.

Creamy Soup with Broth

2 tablespoons fat (butter, oil, or bacon grease)
1 onion, chopped
Minced garlic (optional)
6 cups chicken broth or stock
3 tablespoons cornstarch
¼ cup heavy cream (or more if you want it creamier)
Salt and pepper to taste

1. Cook whatever you plan to add to the soup. You can either sauté it in butter/bacon fat or boil it in broth/water.
2. Add all liquids.
3. If making a blended soup, blend all ingredients together. Take care that the soup is not too hot so you don't burn yourself or damage the blender.

Broth Soup or Tomato-Based Soup

1. For the broth: You can buy broth or boil bones for four hours and drain the liquid. Salt and pepper to taste.
2. Add vegetables and boil until soft.
3. Consider boiling vegetables that take a long time to cook (like carrots) before vegetables that will be done faster (like yellow squash) so that they finish cooking at the same time.
4. Add cooked meat.
5. To make this soup tomato based, you can add diced tomatoes or V8 juice. Some people add a tablespoon or more of tomato paste.

"Cream of" Soup

1 cup chicken broth
Vegetables
1 cup half-and-half or evaporated milk
1 can "cream of" soup
¼ cup water
2 tablespoons cornstarch or flour
Meat
Cheddar cheese (optional)

1. Boil vegetables in broth until softer but still firm—for 5 to 10 minutes.
2. In a bowl, stir half-and-half, canned soup, water, and cornstarch together.
3. Stir mixture into the broth and simmer until thick. Add cooked meat, or boil raw meat in the soup.
4. Add ½ cup of cheddar cheese if desired.

TIP: Most recipes that use tomato paste only call for a tablespoon or two. For the rest of the can, measure out tablespoon-sized blobs, put them on a cookie sheet lined in wax paper, and freeze them. Once they're frozen, place in a Ziploc bag or a Tupperware container.

Pasta

Almost all meat and vegetables can be used on pasta. Make sure you add sun-dried tomatoes to your list of possibilities. They're delicious on pasta! Plus, you can use the leftover oil in your cooking to add extra flavor to your dishes.

First, you'll need a sauce. Marinara is an easy option to have on hand. I love vegetable marinara as a way to use up vegetables: You cook the meat, then chop the vegetables into tiny chunks and sauté until soft. Cutting them up small and making them soft will disguise the fact that you're eating so many vegetables. Then add the marinara sauce. I've used onion, carrots, zucchini, squash, spinach, celery, and mushrooms, all in one dish.

You can do variations of the white roux sauce I mentioned in the soup section—like for mac and cheese, stroganoff, or alfredo—by using less liquid and adding cheese or sour cream, depending on the sauce. Or you can skip the flour and use just cream, perhaps adding Parmesan cheese to thicken it. This is called pasta primavera. It's more or less equal parts cream, broth, and Parmesan.

I keep a jar of pesto in my fridge. It tastes good by itself on pasta or with chicken, but also with other green vegetables, especially green beans and asparagus. Pesto is also very easy to make from scratch, and basil plants are easy to grow.

I often use nothing more than a can of diced tomatoes as my sauce. I cook it until it's a bit thickened, add vegetables, and toss with pasta and Parmesan cheese.

Then again, you don't necessarily need more than just butter or olive oil with Parmesan cheese to make yummy pasta. Sauté the vegetables, add garlic and flavoring like basil or lemon zest, toss with pasta, meat, and vegetables, and top with Parmesan cheese.

Depending on the sauce, good meats for pasta are shrimp, chicken, shredded chicken, kielbasa, ground turkey, ground beef, bacon, and Italian sausage. I don't think there is a vegetable that doesn't taste good on pasta when paired with the right sauce.

Creamy Sauce Without Roux (aka Pasta Primavera)

Meat
Vegetables
Butter
Garlic
½ cup broth
½ cup cream
½ cup Parmesan cheese
1 pound of pasta

1. Sauté meat and vegetables in butter with a clove of garlic.
2. In a saucepan, bring broth to a boil.
3. Add cream and heat.
4. Stir in cheese.
5. Add meat and vegetables.
6. Toss with pasta.

Creamy Sauce with Roux

2 tablespoons fat (butter, oil, bacon grease)

3 tablespoons flour

Milk for desired consistency, between 1 and 2 cups. (It will thicken as you cook it.)

½ pound pasta

1. Melt the butter or heat the oil. Slowly whisk in flour and continue whisking until it's bubbling for 5 minutes.
2. Whisk in milk until it's the desired consistency.
3. Simmer for 10 minutes to thicken. Add more milk if it gets too thick.

For mac and cheese, add cheddar and then stir in pasta. For stroganoff, use broth instead of milk and add sour cream and cream cheese until creamy, then add cooked beef, onion, and mushrooms. For alfredo, add a cup or more of Parmesan.

Casseroles

The basic components of a casserole are pieces of meat or another protein, chopped vegetables, and a starch like chunked potatoes, rice, or pasta. Casseroles are often topped with cheese, or you can smear mashed potatoes on top, and sometimes topped with something crunchy like fried onions, bacon bits, cornflakes, croutons, or breadcrumbs.

You'll need a cream or sauce to bind it all together. "Cream of" soup is easy, though you'll probably want to add some liquid to loosen it up. A thicker version of the creamy soup base would work. You can also mix cheese into the casserole before adding more cheese on top.

Breakfast casseroles (see recipe below) use egg, milk, and cheese as a binder. They just about always have some kind of potato (tater tots, hash browns, cubed potatoes), meat, and possibly vegetables.

All the ingredients are typically cooked before adding them to the casserole. If you cook them all beforehand, you don't need to worry about when the casserole is "done" because it's safe to eat at any point; you just have to heat it. If anything in the casserole is uncooked before baking, I highly recommend following a recipe unless you're a pro at this. It's not easy to plan it just right so that everything is done at the same time.

Cook the casserole at 350 degrees Fahrenheit until it's heated all the way through. The cheese will be gooey, and the sauce will be bubbling. Depending on the size of the casserole and whether the ingredients are already hot, this can take between twenty and forty-five minutes. Lasagna takes an hour or more.

The cheese on top can burn, so some people cover the casserole until the last five minutes, then uncover it so the cheese melts and caramelizes. Other people don't even add the cheese until the last five minutes.

How do you know what ingredients will go together? A good rule of thumb is that if a mix of food tastes good together in another capacity, it'll likely taste good as a casserole. My family likes "pizza casserole," which is spiral pasta tossed with pepperoni, bell peppers, mushrooms, and marinara sauce, topped with mozzarella cheese.

Almost every soup recipe can be converted into a casserole—except for the blended soups, obviously. I have a recipe for chicken noodle soup casserole. It's just the ingredients of the soup but without the "soup" part. You make a white sauce by sautéing the vegetables in butter, adding flour, and then adding milk and cooking it until it's thick. Add thyme, basil, salt, and pepper, mix in the noodles and cooked chicken, stir in a cup of cheese, put in a casserole dish, and top with more cheese. Voilà: a soup casserole.

I rarely have the confidence to wing it with casseroles. They make so much food! If I screw up the recipe, that's a lot that'll get wasted. A type of casserole I do love to make, however, is upcycled dinners.

Sometimes for a meal, I make a lot of separate ingredients that need to be assembled at the dinner table. Take tacos, for instance. Eating leftover tacos is a challenge. I might run out of meat before I run out of beans, and then I'm stuck with a cup or two of beans that I have to find a use for. Or maybe I don't have enough shells to eat up all the leftovers, and we're stuck with all the taco fillings, unless we buy more shells, but then we'll have too many shells once we run out of filling . . . and the cycle continues. It's not an easy meal when you're waste-free.

Instead, I assemble everything that's left from the first meal into a casserole. The taco filling becomes layers of rice, beans, meat, and cheese, topped with broken-up tortilla shells. I bake it until it's hot all the way through and the cheese is bubbly, take it out of the oven, and top it with tomatoes, avocados, and sour cream. Individual servings might get a drizzle of hot sauce.

TIP: Tortillas that are old and cracking can be deep-fried to make tortilla chips. They're good with dips and salsas or rolled in cinnamon and sugar.

Thanksgiving leftovers can make a good casserole, too. Smear the mashed potatoes on the bottom of a casserole dish, mix your leftovers—turkey, green beans, sweet potatoes, and so on—with left-over gravy that's been thinned with milk. Or, if you have no gravy, make a cream sauce. Pour the sauce mixture over the mashed potatoes and top with stuffing. The stuffing will crisp in the oven so be careful not to let it dry out or burn. If you want to omit the stuffing, you can put the mashed potatoes on top like shepherd's pie and bake it with or without cheese on top.

I sometimes turn leftover beans (like chili or black-eyed peas) into a casserole by pouring savory cornbread batter on top and baking it.

It's also fun to convert leftover dishes into enchiladas. That's basically a kind of casserole. Just wrap tortillas around what you have left, assemble them into a pan, and pour sauce on the top. Enchilada sauce is an obvious choice, but mole sauce is great, too. Top with cheese. A friend of mine got stuck with an obscene amount of crepes once, so she made two pans of enchiladas with them and put one pan in the freezer.

TIP: When you freeze food in a pan, you don't have to keep the pan in the freezer. Put plastic wrap at the bottom of the pan before adding the food, wait for the food to freeze, then take it out. Wrap it up to prevent freezer burn.

Again, you will want to add spices, peppers, possibly toppings, and other flavorings, but what you use is up to you.

Breakfast Casserole

1 cup vegetables
1 pound meat
8 eggs
½ cup milk
20 ounces of hashbrowns, tater tots, or potatoes that are cubed and cooked
½ cup onion
2 cups cheddar

1. Cook vegetables if you plan to add any. Cook meat.
2. Whisk eggs and milk.
3. Lay potatoes and onions down on a 9x13 baking dish. Add meat and vegetables and top with cheese.
4. Pour egg mixture into the dish.
5. Bake at 350 degrees Fahrenheit for 50 minutes.

Meats you can use include sausage, chorizo, ham, and bacon. The cheese could be cheddar, mozzarella, Colby, pepper jack, or Swiss. Vegetables you can use include mushrooms, steamed broccoli, zucchini, bell pepper, and spinach.

Braids, Breads, Pies, and Hand Pies

Wrapping leftovers in a delicious carb will give it new life.

Pies are a great way to use leftover ingredients. When it seems like there's nothing in the kitchen to eat, I can almost always make a pie.

A potpie traditionally uses chicken, onion, carrots, celery, and peas, but you can use other meats and most vegetables. Mushrooms are common. I made a delicious vegetarian pie with potatoes, cauliflower, and broccoli. It might seem like the potatoes with crust would be carb redundant, but it was good. To save time, you can use a frozen vegetable mix. You'll want to make a cream base out of slurry that's thicker than you'd use for soup, and you'll want enough for it to bubble through the crust when it's hot. You can also cheat and mix a cream of soup with half a cup of milk.

Another savory pie is quiche. It's eggs and cheese with a crust, and every recipe I've seen uses only two add-ins. Often it's one meat and one vegetable. Bacon is an exception. Every recipe seems to agree that bacon and cheddar need no vegetables to be great. Add in what you want . . . go nuts! These are the ingredients I've seen recipes use in various combinations: ham, bacon, crab, green onions, spinach, onion, mushrooms, sausage, tomatoes, asparagus, kale, peppers, sun-dried tomatoes, and broccoli.

For cheese, I've seen cheddar, feta, brie, goat cheese, gruyere, white cheddar, and Swiss.

Frittata is just quiche without the crust. I've never made a frittata. Omitting delicious flaky crust makes me sad.

Hand pies are a fun way to use up smaller portions of leftovers, and they go with most things. My favorite hand pies are with Indian dishes like tikka masala or butter chicken. Meatballs with marinara and mozzarella would go well in hand pies, too. You'll definitely want to add cream or sauce if the leftovers aren't saucy already.

To make a hand pie, roll out piecrust, wrap leftovers into hand-sized portions, cut slits so they don't explode, and bake at 375 degrees Fahrenheit for twenty to twenty-five minutes or until the crust is browned.

Fruit pies use a *ton* of fruit, which could come in handy for gardeners who end up with more produce than they can handle. Of all the uses of fruit (besides eating them plain), this is the most efficient. Plus, unbaked fruit pies can be frozen, pie filling can be canned, and fruit pies make great gifts.

TIP: For fruit past its prime, mix into pancakes or Dutch babies (aka German pancakes), or mix with sugar and serve as a topping. Apples should be cooked.

A braid starts with dough rolled out into one big sheet. I use crescent dough from a can. Spread ingredients down the middle. The mixture you use would be the kind of thing you'd put in a casserole, for instance, but without a carb or starch, and with cheese mixed in. I've seen recipes like buffalo chicken braids, BLT, ham and Swiss, chicken and broccoli, pepperoni and cheese, potpie, ham and egg, and many dessert braids.

Next, you cut the dough on each side into strips and lay each strip on top of the other in a pattern, which might look like a braid. Cook on 375 degrees Fahrenheit for twenty-five minutes or until the crust is golden brown.

You can also spoon leftovers into calzones, empanadas, and tamales.

I saw the idea to bake stuffed bread on a food-waste website. I can't for the life of me find it now, but the gist of it is that you wrap bread dough around your leftovers and bake like you would normally.

Hot Fruit Pie

Sugar: 1 cup for peaches, ½ cup for blueberries, 1 cup for other berries, and ¾ cup for apples

⅓ cup flour

¼ to ½ teaspoon cinnamon, if desired (good with blueberry or apple)

6 cups of fruit

Two 9-inch piecrusts

1 tablespoon lemon juice if the fruit needs more tartness

2 tablespoons butter, cubed

1. Mix sugar and flour. Add cinnamon, if using.
2. Sprinkle over fruit and stir until evenly coated.
3. Turn into pastry-lined pie plate.
4. Sprinkle with juice and top with chunks of butter.

5. Cover with piecrust and cut slits into crust or use a crumble topping.
6. Bake at 425 degrees Fahrenheit for 35 to 45 minutes, or until crust is brown and fruit is bubbling.

Potpie

About 4 cups of meat and vegetables
¼ cup butter
⅓ cup flour
1½ cups broth
¾ cup milk
Two 9-inch piecrusts

1. Cook meat. Set aside.
2. Sauté vegetables in butter.
3. Sprinkle flour on vegetables and stir until well combined.
4. Slowly add broth, stirring constantly to avoid lumps. Add milk.
5. Cook until thickened. Add meat.
6. Pour onto prepared piecrust and top with crust.
7. Bake 350 degrees Fahrenheit for 30 to 45 minutes, or until crust is browned and gravy is bubbling.

Quiche

9-inch piecrust
1 cup cheese
1–2 cups of add-ins
6 eggs
¾ cup milk, cream, or half-and-half
¼ teaspoon each of salt and pepper

1. Line a pie pan with crust. Place add-ins on the crust and top with cheese.
2. Beat eggs and milk with salt and pepper. Pour over pie.

3. Bake quiche at 375 degrees Fahrenheit for 35 to 40 minutes or until egg is set in the center.

Welp, that's all I got. Hopefully, you feel inspired. Again, I encourage you to find recipes for this stuff at first if concept cooking is new to you. You'll soon become an expert. Then, no food will stand between you and a great meal.

Part 3:

Keeping It Going

Chapter 6:

One Year Passed, but I Wasn't Done

On February 2018, I passed the one-year mark of my food-waste lifestyle, and that month, my family only wasted two pounds and six ounces of food.

I told a friend we had reached the one-year anniversary of going waste-free. That was what I had publicly committed to. She grinned and asked, "Are you just so ready to throw out everything in your fridge?"

Many of my friends asked me the same thing, but I had no answer for them. I had yet to decide what we would do once the first year was over. My goal was to get my food waste to zero, then decide how I would live the rest of my life—if I would keep it at zero or give our family more flexibility—and while it's true that I could fit a month's worth of food waste in a small container, that wasn't zero. The year had ended, and I didn't feel relieved at all. I didn't have the sense of completion I had expected.

Instead, I felt like I was just getting started.

It had taken nearly a year to figure out how to do everything I've taught you. I was months into it before I properly organized my pantry; ten months into it before I made my cookbook; I was doing research the whole time; I'd barely gotten a handle on portioning out meals; and even though my food waste was minuscule, it wasn't zero.

I made a lot of mistakes that year, and I could have done better. I wanted to run a waste-free kitchen without all those mistakes. I had learned how to do it. Now I wanted to actually *do* it.

I felt apprehensive as I approached Andrew. "Hey," I said. "It's been a year since I decided to stop wasting food, but . . . I think I want to do it at least another year."

Andrew was on his phone. He didn't even look up.

"Okay," he said.

When Food Waste Gets Complicated

Even once I had everything more or less figured out, I still got hit by hurdles that caught me off guard. I prevailed, and you can prevail over hurdles, too. As the great Tim Allen said in *Galaxy Quest:* "Never give up. Never surrender!"

Diet Transitions: My Biggest Challenge

Have you ever seen the show *This Is Us*? There's a character named Kate who is obese. In the first episode, she stands in front of a full fridge. All the food has labels to keep her from eating it. Some of the labels say how many calories are in the food. Others say "bad" and "throw this crap out."

She becomes committed to her weight loss goals, but her kitchen is still full of food labeled "bad." What does she do? She throws all of it in the garbage bin. Once it's all in the bin, she approaches a neighbor who is walking her dog, asks for the bag of dog poop, and dumps it over the food so she won't be tempted to go back for it.

You can guess how I felt about this scene. It's supposed to be this empowering moment, but . . . well, I'll save you the rant. Granted, she throws out food like soda and doughnuts, which may or may not pass the Hungry Kid Test. Still, the idea of celebrating food waste bothers me.

The scene brought up an interesting dilemma. How do you diet and go waste-free at the same time? Actually, I hate the word "diet." Let's use a different term. Restrictive dietary adjustments? Naw. Building healthy habits?

Weight loss isn't inclusive enough for what I want to say. A person might need to adjust their eating for reasons besides weight loss. Perhaps you've become a vegetarian or a vegan. Perhaps you've eliminated sugar. Health problems can require changes, too, like celiac disease and heart disease.

Instead of "going on a diet," let's call it a transition.

I don't want to call food "bad" either because there's no such thing as bad food. Even doughnuts have value because they make us happy. Also, food that's "bad" for one person might be fine for another. Let's say food that's off-limits or forbidden instead.

So, how do you transition with no waste when your kitchen is full of forbidden food?

This became a big problem when my husband dropped a bombshell on me. We were in the car on the way home from a friend's house when he said, "I've decided to get on the keto diet."

"No!" I cried. "Oh, no!"

"What?" he asked, perplexed.

"I knew this would happen someday," I said, shaking my head dramatically. "You keep talking about losing weight, and now there's a bacon-only diet. I saw it coming for me like an angel of death." I placed the back of my hand against my forehead. "I just thought I had more *time.*"

"Cut it out. What's the big deal?"

Serious now, I said, "The 'big deal' is that I have to eat keto now, too."

"This won't affect the family," he insisted. "I feel very strongly that you all should keep eating the way you have been."

I scoffed. "Yeah, right. We're not going to eat your favorite foods in front of you while you make carb-free-whatever stuff. Not to mention that you don't have the time to make your own dinner unless you eat just bacon and eggs. And, as if I need another reason, I don't want to spend an hour in the kitchen cooking a meal for just me and the kids when the kids don't want to eat dinner in the first place. We'd end up having mac and cheese every night." I shook my head. "If you want keto meals, that's what we'll all get."

A little bit of context: "ketosis" is a process your body goes into when you eliminate carbs. Since you have no glucose to give you energy, your body starts burning fat. They say the extra weight just melts off.

I tried the keto diet once. I stuck to it for ten hours.

That's not a typo. Everyone assumes I meant to say ten days or ten weeks. Seriously, ten hours was my limit. I thought I would just look at the food pyramid they show you in grade school and not eat anything on the bottom of the triangle. After a little research, I learned that this was way off. I needed to limit my onions, carrots, and bell peppers. Seriously? Bell peppers? Bananas and apples were off-limits entirely. I had eggs for breakfast and salad for lunch, but then my friends invited me to go out for tacos, which I wasn't supposed to have. I said, "Screw this. A diet without tacos is not the diet for me."

My support surprised Andrew, but I never wanted my husband to say, "I want to [insert aspiration here], but my wife won't let me." He had gone waste-free when I asked him to. I could cook keto meals for him.

Thus began our transition.

For the kids and I, breakfast and lunch were the same. I hid all the carbs in a drawer so he wouldn't see them and we didn't eat anything with carbs in front of him. That part was no problem. I'm a mom, so most of my treats are hidden and eaten in secret anyway.

Dinners were keto. My husband's lunches would be leftovers from our dinners, which is what he used to have for lunch anyway.

Sounds easy, right?

It was *not.*

Keto was new culinary territory. Carbs are everywhere, in everything, and we had to look stuff up every time we ate or shopped. I started to picture carb grams as evil little buggers that sneaked into our food when we weren't looking.

With practice, I got the hang of it. I learned to make zucchini noodle spaghetti, almond flour biscuits, Parmesan pizza crust, and cauliflower rice sushi. Cauliflower is the secret to a successful keto diet. You can make cauliflower taste like rice, mashed potatoes, pizza crust, tortillas, and alfredo sauce. It's a good meat substitute, too, if you roast or deep-fry it with low-carb batter. I loved cauliflower hot wings and fried cauliflower bulgogi over rice. I even found a recipe for popcorn cauliflower. It did not taste like popcorn.

You should have seen the look on people's faces whenever I loaded five heads of cauliflower into my shopping cart. One woman even stopped me to ask what on earth I was making.

In time, keto cooking became a fun game. Making meals carb-free was a puzzle to work out, and I enjoy challenges.

It seemed that everything was going well. That is, until I saw what this new lifestyle was doing to our food waste.

There are three problems with dietary transitions when you're also going waste-free:

Problem Number 1: Every recipe I made was new. Not all of them were good. I made a frozen chocolate whipped cream claiming to be an ice cream substitute, but it didn't fool anyone. Avocado chips will never happen again in my household. We discovered after a dreadful blueberry cake that using almond flour in desserts is never okay. Ever. Any food blog claiming that almond flour works in desserts is lying to you.

Step 9 is to be smart about what you cook. Making a dozen new meals back-to-back that are likely to taste bad—keto isn't exactly known for being delicious—is not smart.

Problem Number 2: Spontaneous cooking became a thing of the past. I could no longer just whip up a meal from whatever we had on hand because much of what we had on hand was off-limits. Meals took much more planning.

Problem Number 3: The kitchen was full of carbs.

Any transition starts with a kitchen full of food from your old lifestyle. What do you do with the meat, the gluten, or the carbs? And let's face it; once you get rid of forbidden food, it has a tendency to sneak its way back into your kitchen. Friends bring gifts without knowing your goals. Family members give in to weaknesses and bring home naughty indulgences. Sometimes it seems like little kitchen fairies sneak treats into your home in the night.

It felt like I was treading water until Andrew lost thirty pounds and quit the diet, but the problem came up again when a friend posted a picture of me in a swimsuit that displeased me. I was so over the postpregnancy version of my body.

I came up with a pattern that worked very well for me: Slim-Fast for breakfast, vegetables for lunch (I'd either have soup, salad, or roasted vegetables over cauliflower rice), low-carb snacks, a modest portion of a regular dinner, and one small treat at the end of the day.

This didn't fit with my old lifestyle at all. My focus had been to eat what was in our kitchen, regardless of calories, and suddenly I was portioning out off-limit food and running the risk of not being able to finish it in time.

You can trim your waste and still trim your waist. After trial and error, I learned some tricks:

1. Make healthy food in big batches and off-limit food in small batches. You'll feel pressured to eat up all the healthy stuff before it goes bad and won't feel pressured to eat the bad stuff.
2. When you buy impermissible food, don't buy too much of it. Face it: You're going to slip up and get food that's off-limits. When you buy more unwanted food than you can eat in one sitting, you've committed yourself to eating it more than once. Perhaps you buy a three-pound roast, only to feel guilty the next day because you had vowed not to eat animals. Don't buy three pounds of roast. A one-pound transgression is better. If you're diabetic and you give into a sugar craving, buy one cookie instead of a pack of twelve—and so on.

3. All your "cheat" food belongs in the freezer. Say you gave in and bought a dozen cookies. Eat one and freeze the rest. Now the pressure to finish them before they go stale is gone. They can be a periodic treat as opposed to a diet buster. Bread stays good in the freezer for the gluten-free, and certain dairy products can be frozen for the lactose intolerant.
4. Give food away. Just because you bought the food doesn't mean you have to be the one to eat it. Make sure the recipient wants your food before you hand it over, or else you'll just be making more waste.

Believe it or not, I lost eight pounds while going waste-free. I planned on losing more, but it was a lot of work, so I learned to love myself to save time. I never feel more beautiful than day three of a diet because that's when I try to talk myself out of needing to go on one.

If you're on one of those restrictive diets where you have to measure and log every single calorie, my recommendation is that you abandon your masochistic efforts and learn to love yourself. You are a beautiful goddess. Spread your wings and fly.

Vacationing with Zero Food Waste

While I was working on my master's, my program did a one-week residency in Dublin.

Vacations are not an easy time to go waste-free. Eating out means leftovers, and on vacation, putting food in the fridge isn't always an option. Not every hotel has one. Sometimes you won't go back to the hotel for hours, and you don't want to explore the town with a doggie bag in your hands. Even if you have a fridge in your hotel and your food makes it to the fridge, the people you're with might want to go out again instead of eating leftovers from the night before.

I experienced a perfect storm of food-waste hurdles in Dublin. My hotel room didn't have a fridge: strike one. We paid for our meals ahead of time, which compelled me to get my money's worth, and we ate breakfast, lunch, and dinner in restaurants as a group at specific times. That meant three full restaurant-sized meals whether or not I was hungry: strike two. Worst of all, it's tacky in Ireland to take food home, so many restaurants don't even have take-home boxes: strike three.

My first night, I woke up at 4:30 AM because of jet lag, and I was starving. It was long past dinnertime in America.

Nothing was open yet. I read a book in the semidarkness while my stomach rumbled until, finally, 6:00 AM rolled around and I could go to a convenience store.

I bought a pastry for breakfast and a baguette to eat for the next night, in case I woke up hungry again. It wasn't until after I left, munching on my cheese Danish, that I realized the baguette was not going to stay fresh long enough for me to eat the whole thing.

TIP: When your baguette is stale, rinse the baguette very briefly with water, wrap it in aluminum foil, and put it in a cold oven. Turn the oven on to 350 degrees Fahrenheit and set a timer for 10 to 12 minutes. Note: the bread will get stale again very quickly, so you'll want to eat it right away.

At home when a baguette went stale, I either ate it dipped in olive oil and balsamic vinegar, toasted slices with cheese, or toasted it to a cracker and topped it with tomatoes to make bruschetta. If it was stale enough, I'd do the bake-in-aluminum-foil trick. Bread pudding was also an option. But I couldn't do any of those things on my trip.

This vacation was going to be trouble.

One night, we went to an Irish pub for dinner. Our waitress was ditzy, busty, and believed shirt buttons were optional. When we asked for separate checks for the four of us, she handed us only two checks, and some of the drinks on our tab were for a different table. Judging from the way she was spilling out of her bra, I'm guessing they did not hire her for her waitressing skills.

I was not even the slightest bit hungry and didn't plan on ordering anything, but they had fish pie. It sounded absolutely terrible. In a British book I liked, a character was sulking in her room when her sister said there was fish pie downstairs. I thought, *All the more reason for her to stay in her room!* Instead, the pie compelled her to come downstairs.

Curiosity lured me in. I couldn't resist ordering it.

The three other students I sat with had been asking me a lot of questions about food waste. While we waited for our order, the four of us got into a surprisingly heated debate about composting.

"How is composting waste?" one of them argued. "Microorganisms have to eat, too, you know."

"It's so good for the environment," another added.

"I did not go to all the work to buy the food and cook it just so I could throw it in a bin in my backyard," I quipped back. "Microorganisms can find their own food."

The waitress came with our meals and handed out the plates at random. We switched the plates around until we all had the right orders.

Fish "pie" isn't pie at all, but fillets in a white cream sauce topped with mashed potatoes. It's delicious—I can see why that character likes it—but it's very filling, and the portion they gave me was huge.

Every meal I ate in front of people felt like a test. *Will she finish her food? Will she take some of it with her?* Mostly, it was a test of my pride, since the other students didn't care that much, but I had to prove I was as good as my word.

I gave it my best shot, but by the time I was full to the point of misery, half of it was left. I had to throw in the towel.

"Did it defeat you?" a student joked.

"I'll just take it back to the hotel," I said.

The waitress asked if we needed anything, and one of my friends asked for a dessert menu.

"You do *not* want to get dessert here," she said. "Trust me. They're terrible."

I asked, "Can I get a takeout box, please?"

She looked at me like I had asked to take home their garbage pail and mop bucket. "Do you mean a doggy bag?" she asked with a scrunched-up nose. "I don't think we have any. Let me check."

The busty waitress came back with an open cardboard bowl and a small bag that the bowl couldn't fit inside.

When the manager came back to sort out the tab our waitress had messed up, he saw my bowl of mashed potatoes and fish and looked puzzled.

"I'm taking it home," I explained.

"You need plastic wrap for that," he said, then left and never brought me any.

The waitress came back with the second check, which was correct this time, and saw my food in the bowl. It looked so ridiculous that she took the Lord's name in vain and rolled her eyes. I laid the bag on top of my bowl so that at least no one could see what I was carrying.

Later in my room, I ate the remains of the fish pie with my fingers when I still wasn't hungry and decided the way I was eating had gotten out of hand. People gain weight on vacations without shoveling in food long after they're full.

Lesson learned: Ordering the fish pie was a mistake. We want to try everything when we go on vacation, even if that means ordering more food than we can possibly eat. I've made the same mistake on other vacations. An appetizer looks so good, and I can't eat both the appetizer and a main course, but I can't resist and once again end up with too much food and nowhere to put my leftovers. The answer is to exercise constraint, no matter what delicious foods come my way.

The next day, I ordered fish and chips at yet another restaurant, which came with a side of either English peas or mushy peas. That confused me because all peas are mushy, but the waitress explained that they're mashed up, like mashed potatoes. I couldn't decide which sounded more horrible but eventually picked the unmashed peas. While stuffing down the huge serving they dished out for me, determined not to waste it, I realized I shouldn't have asked for peas at all. Just because my meal comes with a side doesn't mean I have to order it.

Five days in and I was still waste-free. I was finally defeated at breakfast.

Every morning, our hotel provided an Irish breakfast buffet: baked beans, toast, tomatoes, mushrooms, potatoes, sausage, and black pudding. It was the weirdest breakfast I'd ever had. The black pudding wasn't even pudding at all, but sausage patties. I like weird, so I enjoyed the breakfasts, including the delicious pudding-that-wasn't-pudding.

On day six, our program met with a group of Irish authors. The topic of breakfast came up, and one of them explained how black pudding is made, giving us a graphic description (complete with hand gestures) of slicing a pig's throat to drain out the blood, letting the blood coagulate, mixing it with oatmeal, and frying it up. I stared at him in horror.

I'm usually open about trying new foods. Blood, however . . . there may be no such thing as edible garbage, but blood . . . *ew. Just . . . ew*. Vampire love stories have always disgusted me because I would never kiss a man whose mouth had been full of blood, but now *my* mouth had been full of blood.

The next day at breakfast, I saw the black pudding in its heating tray and shuddered with disgust. The server asked me what I wanted before I was ready to order. Behind me was a line of loud and hungry people and I blurted out black pudding, not because I wanted it, but because it was the first thing that popped into my mind. Carrying my bizarre breakfast to a table, I groaned over the ridiculous situation I had gotten myself into.

If only black pudding passed the Hungry Kid Test.

No waste, I reminded myself.

It would only take four bites to finish my patty of cooked blood. After two, I just couldn't go on. All I could think was, *I have blood in my mouth*, and then, *I have blood in my stomach*. For the first time in two years, I willingly put edible food in the trash.

I know what all of you are thinking right now: What happened to the baguette?

Not surprisingly, I only ate half the baguette before it was too stale to continue. By the end of the trip, it was hard enough to club a cat to death. The black pudding was one thing, but there was no way I would waste so much bread. What could I do?

What I did was probably a little crazy.

After wrapping the bread in napkins, I packed it in my bag. Fitting the baguette wasn't easy; I had the genius idea to only bring a carry-on bag for my eight-day trip in order to save money, only to find out carry-ons cost the same forty-five dollars as checked bags. All my belongings + souvenirs + half a baguette = not a lot of room. But my maiden name is Packham, and I've always joked that our ancestors picked the name because we're great at packing. It all fit in the end.

Taking my rock-hard food through customs was awkward. If they saw inside my bag and wondered why on earth an American brought a baguette from Ireland, they didn't say anything.

It was the middle of the night in America, and I bought a salad at the only shop that was still open. After dining on meat and potatoes every day for over a week, I needed something green.

It wasn't just the worst salad I've ever had. It might be the worst *thing* I've ever had. The spinach was limp and soft like a T-shirt, and the dressing made it taste like a wet T-shirt. I stuffed down each mouthful. Three bites left of the salad, and I just couldn't do it. I had been up for twenty hours at this point, and I was too miserably tired to care. It went in the trash.

Still, in an eight-day trip, I only wasted two bites of bloody oatmeal and three bites of leaves. That's not bad.

At home, I faced the challenge of the rock-hard baguette.

My trick of getting it wet and baking it in aluminum foil didn't work. The water couldn't permeate it no matter how much water I used, so the outside was soggy, and the inside was still too hard to chew. I tried cutting the bread into slices to toast, but the knife couldn't slice through, and misshapen chunks snapped off as the knife pressed down. I couldn't even make croutons with that stuff, which was fine since we already had four gallon-sized bags of croutons after a sale on bread made me behave irrationally. I also had breadcrumbs running out my ears after an unfortunate incident with forgotten crackers. After years of saving Rose's bread crusts, my family was sick to death of bread pudding.

The baguette sat in the freezer for a month before I found a recipe that would solve my problem. Except it was . . . well . . . different:

Gazpacho.

It's a cold Spanish soup made with raw tomatoes, cucumber, onion, bell pepper, spices, and stale bread, all pureed together and topped with sour cream.

I mentioned before that going zero waste made me hesitant to try new recipes because they have to get eaten whether they're good or not. When I saw that recipe, I laughed and said, "I am never making that!"

Except it just so happened that I also had half a bell pepper and a cucumber with no plans for how to use them. I had onions. I had spices. All I needed were tomatoes.

Trying new recipes *is* fun even if it is risky, and everyone on Pinterest said their gazpacho recipes reminded them of Spain. Plus, I love raw vegetables. It was like I was meant to make this soup.

The dish called to me, whispering softly in my ear, "Do it, Teralyn. Do it. You know you want to." I steeled myself and puréed the ingredients in a blender.

That's how I made Spanish soup in America using French bread I bought in Ireland.

TIP: Some uses for old bread include French toast, bruschetta, bread pudding, French onion soup, stuffing, breadcrumbs, croutons, and recipes like gazpacho (a raw vegetable soup), stratas (layered casseroles, like breakfast casseroles), panzanella (a salad with bread soaked in dressing), and canederli (Italian dumplings).

The soup had to sit in the fridge overnight. When my husband saw it, his reaction was so predictable that I could have written the rest of this chapter before it happened. First, he made a face and asked, "What is this?"

I smirked and said, "You don't want to know."

"Come on," he said, rolling his eyes. "Tell me."

"It's cold Spanish soup."

"So? What's in it?"

"Are you sure you want to know?" I asked mischievously.

Annoyed now, he said, "Just tell me."

"Tomato, cucumber, bell pepper, and onions . . ."

"Okay." He waited for the rest.

". . . and stale bread."

He was so repulsed that I laughed out loud.

"*What?*" he said.

"Do you want to try it?" I teased.

He shuddered. "Absolutely not."

The soup smelled fantastic: flavorful and fresh like summer. It looked like vomit. It was the texture of paper pulp.

In all fairness, I might not have made it correctly. The recipe said to soak the stale bread before pureeing it, which I didn't do because it sounded stupid. I was adding it to soup. Is there not enough liquid in soup? It's always better to follow a new recipe exactly the first time, instead of finding out the hard way that you got it wrong, but I once again disobeyed Step 9: Be Smart When You Cook and When You Shop.

It took a while to finish the soup (I was the only one who would eat it), but against all odds, my gazpacho did start to grow on me. The texture was never my favorite, but I liked the vegetables and ate it all without having to freeze any.

Another scrap saved!

My Restaurant Policy

I like Panera Bread. A lot. Once in the fall, I saw a sandwich on the menu that was too outlandish to resist. It had roasted turkey breast, white cheddar, apple and cabbage slaw, arugula, and mustard horseradish sauce on cranberry walnut bread.

I thought, *Apple and cabbage slaw? With horseradish? That's madness! I must try it.*

I ordered a sinfully sticky pecan roll to go with my strange-but-probably-delicious sandwich and grew eager for my new adventure.

When they handed me my order, I saw avocado sticking out from the bread. It seemed a strange choice for an apple/cheddar/turkey sandwich. Still, I thought, *Yay, avocado!* because I've never said no to an avocado. When the question is, "To avocado, or not to avocado?" the answer is always to avocado. Then I saw bacon, plus a lack of cabbage slaw, and figured out what had happened. They had given me the Turkey and Avocado BLT.

Thinking back on it, I remembered telling the cashier, "I want the turkey one," wrongly assuming there was only one turkey sandwich on the menu. There were in fact three, and the employee just picked one at random. Strangely, he didn't choose the sandwich called "Turkey."

I could have easily traded it in for the sandwich I wanted, but then they would have thrown the BLT away.

This got into the fuzzy territory of when food waste counted as "mine." Food that I served to guests wasn't "mine" as soon as I dished it on their plates. If they didn't finish their food, I don't count it as my waste, even though I made it and it was served at my house. The scraps don't go in my freezer container to be weighed at the end of the month.

The question was whether returning the BLT counted as the restaurant's waste or mine. It was their mistake, and they would physically put the sandwich in the trash, not me.

My opinion is that the sandwich was transferred to my stewardship. I was the one to decide whether it would be eaten or wasted. That's when I made the rule that, as long as the dish was safe and edible, I would never return a meal at a restaurant. I ate that turkey sandwich with the intention of getting the apple one later. And I very much enjoyed it.

Panera Bread repeatedly tested my resolve. The next time I went, I once again ordered my curious apple turkey sandwich. They brought me a sandwich without turkey. It had cheese, apple slices, and coleslaw on cranberry bread, but no meat.

(Rather than this reflecting on the quality of Panera's service, I prefer to believe the sandwich itself is cursed.)

When the waiter came by, I showed her my incomplete sandwich, and she apologized profusely.

"What kind of cheese did you choose?" she asked as she reached for my plate. She was going to make me a new sandwich and throw the old one away.

"Wait!" I cried. Realizing this was an overreaction, I cleared my throat. "Actually, could you just bring me some turkey on a plate?"

"Sure, we can do that for you."

Whew. Another scrap saved.

Returning an order can't always be avoided. An Italian restaurant once served me a risotto that tasted like it had been scooped out of a mummy's skull. There's no telling how long it had sat on a shelf before they served it to me. There may be no such thing as edible garbage, but this wasn't edible. It was the restaurant that let the food become inedible, so it wasn't my fault that no one ate it. Off to the kitchen it went.

If, after reading so far into the book, you aren't yet convinced of my determination to not waste food, consider this: Once, I went to Panda Express and ordered the honey walnut shrimp. They served me orange chicken instead. The audacity! The injustice! Still, I stuck to my guns, even though it meant denying myself the honey walnut shrimp that I had paid for. If it had been broccoli beef, my will might not have been so strong.

Make Food Rescue Fun

In Chapter 3, I talked about a pantry swap party where a group of women brought unwanted food to my house to trade. I enjoyed the pantry swap party so much, it got me thinking: What other ways can food rescue be fun?

Everyone loves using food hacks, upcycling food, and coming up with their own recipes based on what's in their kitchens. Being resourceful is awesome! Besides that, there are food-waste activities that can be entertaining for kids and grown-ups.

Meals That Are Meant for Leftovers

First, I'm going to tell you a story that begins not fun in any way.

It was our first Mother's Day without my mom. (See? I told you this wouldn't be fun.) We were still reeling from the loss, and no one had planned much that day. My family showed up at her gravesite and just stood there feeling out of place while the kids played in the grass.

Letting everyone disperse didn't feel right. I wanted to invite everyone over to my house for dinner. Except . . . there wasn't anything to feed them. I didn't have the heart to ask my siblings and dad to run home and bring a dish to my house. Ordering takeout for fifteen people would take too much effort at a time when we felt like doing nothing.

Right as my family turned from the gravestone to their cars, I had an idea.

"Do you guys want to come over for okonomiyaki?" I asked.

My brother, who was on his way to spend the rest of Mother's Day with his in-laws, cried out, "You guys didn't tell me you were making okonomiyaki!"

"Yay!" said the others.

My younger brother is the one who introduced me to this Japanese dish. He was a missionary in Japan with little money who was eager to make his food stretch, and okonomiyaki is one of the cheapest and most resourceful meals he knew.

The only ingredients you need are cabbage, flour, eggs, mayonnaise, leftovers, and okonomiyaki sauce, which I knew my brother had. You combine the shredded cabbage, flour, eggs, and water together to make a pancake-like batter, mix in whatever you want, fry it like a pancake, smear mayonnaise on top, and drizzle on the sauce. We had to pick up cabbage on the way home and that's it.

All I had to do was get out all the meat, vegetables, cheese, and any leftovers that were in my fridge. Each family member mixed in what they wanted and fried the pancake themselves, so no one had to spend much time in the kitchen.

Recipes for okonomiyaki might call for scallions, carrots, bacon, yams, seafood, kimchi, and often a bunch of Japanese foods I've never heard of, but you can use just about anything. My brother likes "pepperoni pizza okonomiyaki," which I think is just wrong. The only constant in our family, although it isn't Japanese at all, is cheese. Preferably mozzarella.

The meal was cheap, easy, stress-free, required almost no shopping, and used up leftovers, and it was a fun activity.

A hot pot is another dish that works for leftovers. It's a Chinese broth that you simmer over a heat source in the middle of the table. You boil food in the broth, take it out, eat it, and repeat by boiling more food. I love ordering it at restaurants, but you can also throw a hot pot party where guests bring over food they have on hand that needs to be eaten: meat, noodles, dumplings, and vegetables like tarro, mushrooms, broccoli, and so on. A friend of mine who did a study abroad in China said that's what people in China do, though a dozen Chinese people on Reddit told me they've never heard of communal hot pots for leftovers. Whatever. It's still a good idea.

Another leftover-using recipe is Everything Cookies. You make chocolate chip cookie dough and then add as many random items as you can squish into the dough. There should be at least four things, though I've added as many as seven, and it should feel like there isn't enough dough to keep it all together, but it will bind it all just fine. You can use white chocolate chips, peanut butter chips, butterscotch chips, caramel, toffee, marshmallows, M&M's, candy bar chunks, pecans, walnuts, cashews, pistachios, graham crackers, shredded coconut, raisins, cranberries, oats, Rice Krispies, and chopped malt balls, to name a few. Just make sure you have a salty component like potato chips, salted nuts, crumbled bacon, popcorn, or pretzels. Otherwise, it will be too sweet. The salt makes them pop.

They're typically called Kitchen Sink Cookies because they're "everything but the kitchen sink," but that sounds gross. Everything Cookies are exciting because they're different every time and making them is a great activity for the kids. I just hand my girls a Pyrex measuring cup and let them fill it with whatever they want. This cookie isn't going to use up scraps because you only use a little of everything. Instead, it's a good teaching opportunity for the kids. They learn that you can make great things with the food you already have on hand.

See? Rescuing food doesn't have to be a chore, and when you turn it into a party, that's even better.

Events: Make a Plan for Leftovers Ahead of Time

If you throw a party and have too much food left over, you can either make a plan for the leftovers beforehand—at parties, I only serve food that we can finish ourselves, like single-serving bags of chips instead of big bags that will go stale—or give extra food to your guests before they leave. Just don't do that thing where you say, "Take home whatever you want," and then everyone stands around wanting to take more but not wanting to be rude, and they don't have a way to get it home anyway.

I was the president of my church's youth group while going waste-free. To raise money for summer camp, the girls hosted a taco buffet. Not *nearly* as many people showed up as the other leaders and I had expected. Tons of food was left over.

That was okay. I already had a plan for the leftovers. We poured the buffet remains into a pot: seasoned ground beef, beans, onions, salsa, and corn. Ta-da! Taco soup.

After simmering it for a bit, we poured the soup into plastic takeout containers I had saved from ordering soups and curries at restaurants. We divvied up the shredded cheese and tortilla shells in Ziploc bags and put sour cream in smaller containers. Every scrap of food was used.

Loaded with enough food to feed six families, the girls in our congregation and their parents delivered the meals to needy members. This taught the girls responsibility, resourcefulness, and compassion. Plus, it was fun.

TIP: Store food in clear containers and mason jars so that you can easily see what's in them. Containers that aren't clear, like those that come with Cool Whip and yogurt, are great for giving away food so you don't need to get your dish back.

Here's an example of what happens when you don't plan ahead. A friend of mine threw her own baby shower, and she made all the food for the party. She was an incredible chef. Everything she made was amazing, like she had culinary magic. I got angry whenever I ate her cake, because why can't everyone make cake that good?

She had spent all week prepping and baking leaf-shaped tarts, brie quiches, chocolate truffles, and more. My friend urged us to take some home. I wanted to pour every platter into my diaper bag. That would be frowned upon, so instead, the hostess and her guests did this little etiquette dance, saying things like "I don't want to take it from you, if you insist, I would love some but I'll just take a little," and so on. In the end, we each took home as many treats as would fit on a tiny paper plate. Mounds of gourmet works of art were left on the table, even though most of it would likely end up in the trash. What she should have done is dish the food out for us and put it in bags we could easily take home.

It just takes a little foresight. Once I hosted a book club meeting to discuss *The Night Circus,* and I baked a bunch of black-and-white treats to fit the theme. This was before I had kids, so I had enough time to go way overboard. Black-and-white cookies, dark-chocolate-dipped pretzels with white chocolate drizzle, shortbread dipped in chocolate, and even a cake with black and white stripes to look like a circus tent. (I can be a bit extra when it comes to books.) But no one wanted that much sugar. When I realized that they were going to leave me with a diabetic nightmare, I ran into my study where I kept plastic treat bags, filled them, and handed them out like party favors.

It works for large dinner gatherings, too. The first time I did this was at an Easter brunch. Everyone always brings too much food to a gathering . . . that's a given. We were each about to take home our surplus, which I knew everyone would eat until they were sick of it or it would go in the trash. Instead, I divided up the food evenly among our families. My sister didn't have to take home half a pan of high-calorie cinnamon rolls: she took home three cinnamon rolls, with German pancakes, potato egg scramble, six breakfast sausages, and four strips of bacon. It was enough for another meal.

A Group Food-Waste Challenge

Most of us love a good challenge. Telling myself I would "waste less" didn't work for the many years that I tried it. "Less" isn't a real goal, and it's not much of a challenge either. It wasn't until I set my sights on the number zero that things got interesting.

At the time, I fought the fight against food waste by myself. I posted my progress online while my interested friends watched, and their interest bolstered me forward. Imagine how different things would have been with a group of us doing it together.

Maybe you could have a family meeting and decide on a reward for reaching a food-waste goal. Maybe pick this as your book club's monthly read and set a goal as a group—while also doing a pantry swap party! Schools, offices, businesses, churches . . . wherever your influence lies, there's your potential for camaraderie.

If no one in your physical world is willing to join you in a food-waste challenge, there are always communities in the online world.

Chapter 7:

Looking at the Big Picture

Did you think food waste was about wasting food?

Think again.

Humans are complex, and all our decisions are interconnected. We also live in a big world, and what we do connects us to everyone else.

Every problem we see is deeply rooted in a problem we don't see. That's why problems are so difficult to solve. If your household is wasting food, my guess is that the problem didn't start in your kitchen. It didn't even start in your home. It started with the paradoxical nature of our culture: when abundance stopped being a joy and instead became a burden.

A Paradox of the Middle Class: The Burden of Abundance

Andrew and I had a yard sale when the girls grew out of their baby stuff. I combed through the house and found enough stuff for a sale and then some, and it barely made a dent in our belongings. You couldn't even tell anything was missing.

I'm fascinated by the *weight* of stuff. It's such a chore to own so many things, find a place for them, clean up after them, and pack them when you move, and then to be unable to make room for new things because you are weighed down by the old. Food is easier to throw away than things, so people don't feel the burden of excess—that is, not until they commit to not wasting it. Maybe it's easy for you to throw out things, and you buy stuff and throw stuff out all the time. Is that really any better?

I call it being "stuffocated." Suffocated by stuff. It perfectly described how I used to feel most of the time, in my kitchen and elsewhere. Yet despite the excess running out of my ears—despite my fridge and home stretching at the seams—I lived a lifestyle of *never having enough*. We couldn't pay off our medical debts, we couldn't meet financial goals, and we couldn't survive without a credit card to bail us out at the end of the month.

We put all the profits of the yard sale toward an exorbitant medical bill in an effort to transfer our surplus into our want, to balance things out. There's something very wrong about the middle class if we can have too much and not enough and suffer from both. *Minimalism: A Documentary About the Important Things* discusses how people seek joy in objects and for some reason find misery instead. Neuropsychologist Rick Hansen said, "At a time when people in the

West are experiencing the best standard of living in history, why is it that at the same time, there is such a longing for more?" They talked about the dopamine rush of new purchases becoming addictive. They also said the survival instinct to improve our lives is making us restless.

If you're biologically programmed to make your life better, and you have everything you need . . . what do you do? Too many of us soothe restlessness with purchases. The dopamine hit gives us the illusion of improvement, when in actuality, we are increasing our surplus and our want at the same time without making our lives better at all.

The limbic system of our brain is often called our "lizard brain." It's in charge of basic survival: food, safety, reproduction, and bodily functions. It's the reflex and instinct. Scientists call it "lizard brain" because that's the only part of the brain that a lizard has. Mammals have more complex emotions and are able to make complex decisions, which is why we have strong emotional bonds with others and a lizard does not.

I often ask myself whether my decisions are made with my mammal brain or my lizard brain. The lizard wants to accumulate resources to increase its chances of survival, like buying food storage or keeping scuba gear you'll never use, just in case. The mammal understands the consequences of accumulating instant-gratification resources versus long-lasting resources, and the mammal knows how to resist pleasure that will have consequences later. When you go to the grocery store, make sure you're shopping with your mammal brain and not your lizard brain.

Remember when I talked about shopping your pantry? You can shop your house, too. Often we feel the need to buy new things when we could just fix, paint, or patch what we already own. That's good for the environment, by the way. Repairing your stuff instead of buying more keeps it out of landfills.

My girls were both in grade school when we were planning out Christmas gifts, and I halfway considered regifting my kids some of their presents from previous years. There were so many things in our house the girls were too young to use before, or that broke right away and we never fixed, or that they forgot about because they were distracted by other toys.

That's how we came up with a new tradition: On the last day of school before Thanksgiving break, I take out all the toys that are broken, torn, stained, or out of batteries and I fix them. The toys are laid out for the girls when they get home from school. If there's a board game we never got around to playing, we play it, and if there's a gift card we never used, that's the day we cash in. Dinner is something special we have in the pantry or freezer that we just never got around to making. We call it pre-Christmas.

Pre-Christmas isn't just good for kids. You might feel like you need a new dress when you forgot about a fantastic one in your closet, or you just need to accessorize a dress differently. One Christmas, my mom got a large tin of fancy Ghirardelli chocolates. It seemed like a good treat for special occasions, so she put it in a closet to save for later.

Personally, I have more of a carpe diem attitude toward my stuff. I believe in using special things even at the risk of ruining them—"loving it to death" is what I call it—because if things sit on a shelf, they serve just as much purpose as if they were in the dump.

I convinced my mom to get the chocolates down, even though we were just in our pajamas watching a movie. That seemed like a special enough occasion to me. We opened the packets, and each square was covered in white wax. They were so old that we couldn't eat them.

There's a sad parallel to life in this story. How much do we miss out on because it never feels like the right time? Before you treat yourself to a shopping trip, try treating yourself to what you already own. Maybe you have things that would make you happier if you just used them.

This all ties into food. So many of us complain about the high cost of groceries and our exorbitant grocery bill. We clip coupons and join Ibotta. Meanwhile, we're writhing in agony under the weight of our debts.

And then we throw our food away.

Doesn't make much sense, does it?

It's time we changed our way of thinking. When we look at our food, we shouldn't think, *I wonder if I should throw this away?* Instead, we should think, *I can't* afford *to throw this away.* Because most of us can't, yet for some reason, we do it anyway.

Save yourselves! Stop buying stuff.

I'm going to take a tiny step back here and specify that I don't expect you to pinch pennies. It's not about being frugal; it's about filling your life with value.

One night, my husband and I watched a Netflix documentary about an expert sushi chef who is supposed to be the best in the world. Dinner at his restaurant is a performance and an experience. We would love to go to a restaurant like that . . . though it would cost $300 per person. I have no idea how much money we'd have to make to justify spending that much on one meal. If we ever decided to do it, though, I wouldn't count that as wasting money. It would be a memorable experience that would bring us joy.

On the other hand, I can't wrap my head around buying name-brand products. We all have one or two favorite brands we insist are better, but twenty-nine times out of thirty, the generic is just as good. What a silly way to waste money.

Paying interest on credit cards is also a waste of money, as is buying mined gemstones instead of synthetic . . . but I could do this all day, and I've made my point.

The *Minimalism* documentary showed a graph of how household expenditures exploded in the mid-'90s. This happened because products became so much cheaper once they shipped from China—a land of sweatshops and worker abuse.

What I'm about to suggest might be bogus—I can't decide if I believe it or not—but at least it's an interesting thought experiment.

Most of what we own and what we eat had to hurt someone in order to get to us. Many of our clothes and belongings were made in sweatshops overseas. Much of our food was picked, cooked, or served by workers who aren't earning a living wage. Foods like chocolate and coffee are tied to slavery, human trafficking, and child labor.[1, 2]

If a commodity isn't hurting humans, it is likely hurting animals or the environment. Consider how much of our meat, dairy, and eggs come from animals who are trapped in overcrowded cages. Palm oil, which has caused major deforestation and devastated animal populations, is in vegetable oil, mayonnaise, peanut butter, soap, lipstick, packaged bread, and biodiesel fuel. If you want *everything* you own and eat to be ethically produced, too bad. You can't even make a peanut butter and jelly sandwich or eat a candy bar without causing harm.

What if there's a cosmic, karmic, metaphysical reason we cannot enjoy the stuff we own?

I'm just spitballing here, but maybe when we cram our lives with food, treats, toys, gadgets, and clothes without finding any fulfillment in it, the real reason we feel pain instead of pleasure is because of the pain those objects carry with them.

Take sugar, for instance. More people have suffered and died producing sugar than any other product, from the early days of Western slavery down to child labor in the present day.[3] Now, we know sugar is toxic. Almost 9 percent of us are diagnosed with diabetes, and it causes high blood pressure, inflammation, weight gain, fatty liver disease, cancer,[4] and Alzheimer's, and I'm suspicious that sugar might be causing our mental health epidemic. It seems like sugar is cursed. Maybe it is.

This all makes me think of the quail in the Book of Exodus. When God brought the Israelites out of Egypt, He rained a bread called manna from the sky every morning for them to eat. Eventually, the Israelites got tired of the manna and murmured against God and Moses, even going so far as to say they wish they could be slaves in Egypt again to get better food. In response, God sent them quail. Masses and masses of quail. The Scriptures say, "And while the flesh was yet between their teeth, ere it was chewed, the wrath of the Lord was kindled against the people, and the Lord smote the people with a very great plague. And he called the name of that place Kibroth-hattaavah—the graves of lust—because there, they buried the people that lusted" (Numbers 11:33–34). We can buy and eat but never be satisfied. Perhaps the reason is the same for us as it was for ancient Israel: greed and gluttony are evil, especially at the expense of other people's happiness, and evil never tastes good.

No one can change all these problems that are so deeply rooted in our culture. I can't afford locally made clothes, even though I'd like to buy them. Perhaps instead, each of us can pick one issue we feel strongly about and attack it with everything we've got. The world can be changed by passionate individuals who tackle atrocities one at a time. I started out by eliminating my food waste. It was a good place to start. And even if I can't change how much food we waste, it feels good to look at this problem and say—honestly—that I had nothing to do with it.

My Experience with the Hungry

You and I have all this knowledge now about how food production works and how we can make the most of what we have. It seems only right that we *do something* with that knowledge. It was hunger and poverty that put me on this path. At the end of the road, I took what I had learned and asked myself, *How do we solve hunger?*

I wondered if food responsibility was enough to solve hunger, and if not, what it would take.

When I was in my early twenties and still relatively naive, I went to the park with my sister. A group of people there were giving away free lunches to children. My sister explained, "They found out that for some kids, free school lunches were the only meals they were getting, so they keep feeding them during the summer."

I was shocked. "What about welfare? Food stamps? Disability? WIC? Unemployment? Why would any child in America go hungry?"

My sister shrugged, accepting that this was a problem without needing answers. But I needed answers.

I grew up hearing the line, "Being middle class is harder than being poor because lower-income families have everything provided for them." Hungry Americans flew in the face of everything I had been taught.

I asked a friend of mine the same question when she told me the teachers at her school often loaded the children's backpacks with food on Fridays to make sure they had something to eat over the weekend.

"Why aren't they eating at home?" I asked.

"We don't ask questions," she said with a shrug.

"The sad truth is, not everyone takes care of their kids," another friend said when I told him this story. "A lot of people abuse the system and keep the money for themselves. That's how they can afford expensive cars."

"No, no, no," a friend said in response to this argument. "That is extremely rare. I'll bet you anything the *vast* majority of people on welfare desperately need it."

"Food stamps aren't enough to keep people from going hungry," said yet another friend when I brought this up again. "You can work three jobs, be on welfare, and still not have enough to get by."

"You can get up to $70,000 a year from the government if you work the system right," read the lead sentence of an article, "and here's how to do it."

The more I talked to my middle-class circles about this, the more I realized how many of us have no idea what's going on. And yet, we get to vote.

Rich people can be even more oblivious. Once during COVID, my husband came home from work fuming angry. He had picked up tacos at a food truck, and the man standing six feet in front of him was on an expensive new phone ranting about how all the restaurants were closed.

"It makes zero sense," the man said. "You can't shop and stay six feet away from everyone, but you can at a restaurant. They should close the *grocery stores* and keep the restaurants open." Then he got his food, climbed into his outrageously pricey truck, and drove away.

"This idiot just assumed we can all go out to eat three times a day," Andrew said. "It didn't occur to him that most of us can't do that. He has no idea how others live."

People with a low income are mysterious to many of us who are doing well. We wonder: *What went wrong? How did they end up this way? Why can't they fix their problems? Can they fix their problems, and they just don't? How can I help? Do they deserve my help? Do they even want my help?*

There's only one thing I knew with 100 percent certainty: Hunger is a problem in the United States, and if it were easy to fix, it wouldn't be a problem. Something complicated was going on.

I was eight months pregnant with Rose when the bishop of my church asked to meet with my husband and me. He said it was to "get to know us better." I actually believed him. We should have known he was going to give one of us a calling.

In the LDS church, everyone has an assignment. Some of us are teachers, some are leaders. There's a librarian, and even someone to make the pamphlets each Sunday. No one gets to pick their job, or "calling," as we call them. This is to make sure every job gets filled, including the less desirable ones, and to make sure no one fights over callings they do want. Even the prophet, who is the head of the church, doesn't volunteer. They go by which man has been an apostle the longest.

The auxiliary members pray about the people for each calling—the young women's president prays about her counselors, secretary, and teachers; the elder's quorum president does the same for the men; the primary president prays about the kids' teachers, and so forth. Once they feel like the right person has been revealed to them by God, they submit the name to the bishop, who also prays about it, and if he feels like it's right, the calling is issued, and the member prays and decides whether to accept it.

After a brief talk, the bishop turned to me and said, "I asked you here to issue you a calling. It's unusual because you're young and about to have a baby, but we all felt strongly that the Lord wants this for you. I'd like you to become Relief Society president."

Let me explain to you what that means and why I had to pick my jaw up off the floor.

The Relief Society president is in charge of all the women ages eighteen and up. By "in charge," I mean she's not only responsible for assigning lessons and activities but for the spiritual, physical, and emotional well-being of every adult female church member within her geographical area, including the ones who are on the roles but don't attend church. She has helpers, like her counselors, ministering sisters, and a compassionate service team, but it all falls under her umbrella.

If a woman is having family problems, the Relief Society president comforts her. If a woman is having health problems, she helps in any way she can, which might mean assigning visitors, finding volunteers for cleaning, scheduling meals, or driving her to doctor appointments. She has to know all the sisters in order to help them. Needless to say, being Relief Society president takes a lot of time and effort. That's why it's primarily given to older women who have more time. It's one of those callings where you accept it, and people don't know whether to congratulate you or console you.

Relief Society presidents are also responsible for handling hunger.

"Are you sure you want to accept this calling?" my bishop asked, and he glanced briefly at my pregnant belly.

"Sure!" I said, excited to serve because I had yet to learn how much work was ahead of me. "Sounds like an adventure!"

"Huh," he said. "I guess you don't know about food orders."

Our welfare system is different from other church programs. Unlike the food pantry close to my house, the LDS Church is more interested in long-term fixes. The bishop assesses the member's needs and helps him or her get as much assistance from the government as possible. If more help is needed, the Relief Society president steps in. She visits the home, assesses the need, helps the member plan a menu for the next two weeks, and places a food order.

A big truck of food comes once every two weeks, and the gymnasium is transformed into a grocery store. Everyone picks up the items from their list: nothing more, nothing less. I could only help so much with my pregnant belly, but I unloaded and bagged the groceries as best as I could. I helped many different kinds of people with many different kinds of problems. There was one woman, however, who had an impossible problem—and I only made it worse.

There was a lot of poverty in our area, but one of our elderly members lived in the worst circumstance of them all. These are the directions I gave to the missionaries when they went to her house: "First, you cross the train tracks and take a left. You'll see a house in terrible condition. Go past that. The next house will be even worse. Go past that. Then you'll get to a house that looks like you could blow it down with a single breath. That's the one."

She was old and disabled with heart problems and diabetes. I occasionally took her to the doctor, and she had so much trouble with mobility that I had to help her in and out of the car. All her income came from the Social Security of her deceased husband, which was piddles, but still too much to qualify for food stamps.

Not that food stamps would have helped her.

The woman could not read, so she couldn't pay her bills without help. Her sister paid her bills and met other needs, like bringing food on occasion. For her efforts, she took a $100 cut from every monthly paycheck.

We were willing to give this woman everything she asked for. Her situation was that dire. The first time I sent her food, we stocked that kitchen until it was full, and when we came back two weeks later, everything was gone. Everything.

"What happened to all your food?" I demanded.

"I ate it," she said.

"You ate a full jar of peanut butter in two weeks by yourself?" I asked. "A jar of jam? A jar of mayonnaise?"

"Yes," she insisted defensively, "I ate all of it." To change the subject, she told me about a party her family hosted at her house.

"Are they the ones who ate all your food?" I asked.

She frowned and didn't answer.

I understand now how ridiculous I must have seemed to the woman. There she was, old, sick, hungry, uneducated, and neglected when in walked a twenty-seven-year-old white girl she didn't know with a huge pregnant belly declaring that she was going to fix all her problems.

But her problems couldn't be fixed. Every time we delivered food to her house, her children and grandchildren came over like a plague of locusts and took everything. No matter how much food we delivered, every time I visited, there would only be a plate of butter in her fridge and a bag of beans in her pantry.

The more food we brought, the more often her vulture family hovered around her house. More and more people were there every time we visited. The woman got mad at me for giving her so much because she didn't want her family around, but then she'd call asking for food because she was diabetic, and because she couldn't take her heart medicine on an empty stomach.

I sometimes gave her cornbread when I visited, which was her favorite. Once she eagerly accepted the cornbread and said, "I'm going to hide this in my room so my kids can't find it."

A few minutes later, her kids walked in carrying buckets of Kentucky Fried Chicken.

I asked, "Why do you need me to deliver food when they're out buying fried chicken? If they can feed themselves, why can't they feed you?"

She got angry and didn't answer.

Her family needed to be reported for elder abuse, but she never would have ratted them out. She wouldn't even admit abuse to us.

Finally, I'd had enough, and I pulled aside one of her daughters.

"Do you know what keeps happening to her food?" I asked, even though everyone knew who was taking it. I just wanted to hold her accountable.

She got flustered and said the backdoor is never locked, so maybe someone was sneaking in and taking it.

A few days later, our sister missionaries found the woman on her bed in agony and her wrist swollen to twice its size. She said she had fallen and broken it but wouldn't answer us when we asked why no one had taken her to the hospital. Missionaries can't give people rides for liability reasons, so they called me asking what to do. I agreed to take her to the doctor.

I helped her in the car and buckled her seatbelt while my newborn slept in the backseat. Then the woman started shouting at me.

"You should not have talked to my daughter!" she yelled. "Now everyone is mad at me!"

It didn't occur to me until many, many years later that her daughter might have pushed her and that's how she broke her wrist.

This was a low moment in my life. I had spent so much time and effort trying to help this woman, only to screw everything up and get yelled at for reasons I didn't understand. I kept silent as she hurled her anger at me the entire drive.

We have a saying in our church that "charity never faileth." It seemed to have failed this time. All my energy was going into either my baby or my calling, and this was what I had accomplished? It made me wonder what I was doing with my life.

At the hospital, I helped the woman into a wheelchair, parked and got my baby out, then went inside to the front desk where a nurse had wheeled her. I checked her in and bounced my daughter on my knee in the waiting room while they set her wrist in a cast.

On the way home, the woman apologized to me for shouting. She said she was grumpy because she was in a lot of pain.

"It's okay," I said. "I understand."

I didn't really understand, even though I thought I did, but that only became clear to me later.

In my weekly meetings with the bishop, we talked about this woman often. Or rather, I often fumed about how frustrated I was.

"Why doesn't she call the police?" I asked.

"People like her don't trust the police. They don't use them to solve their problems," he said. "It's hard for us to imagine that their lives can be so hard, and it's hard for them to imagine that our lives can be so easy."

I put my hand on my forehead and sighed with exasperation. "I don't know what to do here. I spend more time working on this issue than all the other women combined, and nothing I do helps!"

Sternly, he said, "You need to have more compassion."

Compassion! No one has *ever* accused me of not being compassionate. I sat there stunned for a while until I realized what he meant. To me, she was a problem to solve. Not a human who needed a friend.

Calling the police wouldn't have done her any good anyway. For better or worse, she needed her family. Besides, elder abuse isn't a life sentence. The law might have locked up some of them for a year, if they even got convicted, and then they would have come back home bitter and vindictive.

You've probably assumed by now that this woman was an anomaly: a freakish set of horrific circumstances that are far from the norm. Actually, her name became a code word between the bishop and me. Let's pretend her last name was "Miller." The bishop would call me and say, "We have another Sister Miller situation."

I shifted my focus from feeding the woman to being kind. Trust grew between us, and she and I became friends.

"I used to think you were mean," the woman told me one day. "But now I like you."

Even after I was no longer Relief Society president, we kept in touch. Both my children were born and I had vowed to stop wasting food when I got the message that she had died.

The church put together her funeral, which irked my husband.

"This is her family's responsibility. Here we are, bailing them out again," he said.

"She deserves a nice funeral," I argued.

"I guess," he admitted reluctantly. "I just can't believe we're feeding her family *again*."

"At least this is the last time," I snorted.

"If I were you," he said, "I would bring something cheap that takes zero effort."

"I'll make deviled eggs," I said.

I should have handled that situation differently in so many ways. Instead of following a checklist and stocking her kitchen like I did for everyone else, I should have asked her what she needed and actually listened. I should have assigned members to bring her dinner every evening. We also could have hidden nonperishable food in her room so that she could control her diabetes and take her heart medicine every day, and with no food in the kitchen to steal, her family would have left her alone.

I have many regrets. Shame from hindsight weighs me down, but I have one emotion that is much stronger: gratitude. This woman taught me more about poverty than I ever could have learned without her. She also taught me that compassion isn't doing the work but rather feeling love. I am so thankful for the perspective she gave me and that I can carry it for the rest of my life.

Finding Solutions

While working for the Relief Society, I discovered a long list of reasons an American might go hungry—reasons I had never considered. We helped people who were between jobs, and it didn't make sense to get on food stamps when they would soon have an income. We helped people who had already applied for assistance and needed to eat while they waited to be approved. It takes three to five months to apply for disability, or longer, depending on how quickly the government can access medical records. It takes five months to receive benefits after disability assistance has been approved. I don't know how common this is, but a judge in our town made a habit of rejecting everyone's first application. He did this to test if they were disabled enough to try again.

Mentally disabled members often didn't have the capacity to navigate the complicated welfare system. A few times, I had to put together grocery lists for members who couldn't do it themselves.

We had hungry members who were looking for better jobs, or who were in the middle of job training or getting a degree. Some of our members were sabotaged by the government. One of them was on welfare when she started cleaning houses for a little extra money. The government found out and slashed her welfare check in half. She hurt her leg shortly after that and had to live with no income and half the food stamps she had before.

We did come across people who didn't want to work. Welfare benefits are often equal to what someone would make at a minimum-wage job. If the government will give you just as much money as McDonald's, why on earth would you spend eight hours on your feet in a sweaty, oily kitchen when you can just stay at home?

Sometimes, people just got stuck.

That baffled me for a long time. Being young and middle-class while also being fed a lifetime of rags-to-riches stories, it was difficult to fathom an unfixable problem. But many of them were. Even the fixable problems often felt insurmountable.

Abusing welfare and charities does happen. In *Hillbilly Elegy,* the narrator worked at a grocery store and often saw people buy nothing but soda with their welfare checks to sell to others, then use the money to buy alcohol and cigarettes.

While doing food orders, I occasionally had to do surprise drop-ins when we suspected abuse and would find cupboards, freezers, and fridges packed to the brim with food, but they still wanted more. A few people would order food, but when it was time to pick it up at the church building, they didn't show. That part puzzles me the most. I've never faced hunger, and I probably never will, but I still can't imagine turning down free groceries.

I had a little trick for figuring out who needed help and who didn't. Our church offers employment assistance, free self-reliance classes, and discounted education. If I referred an able-bodied member to the employment office and found out they didn't go, they likely weren't going to get assistance from me.

It is also true that people will lie about how much they earn or use welfare money for their own benefit while their kids go hungry, and the only way the kids can eat would be if their teachers fill their backpacks with food. How many people do that? Is it one in ten? One in a thousand? One in a million? Is it most of them, or very few of them?

How would I know? Everyone talks about welfare fraud, but no one can agree on how big a problem it is, or if it's even a problem worth worrying about. They know what they believe and act like that's the end of the argument, but belief should never trump truth. Instead of "I believe," more of us need to say "I don't know."

My opinion, if I have the right to voice an opinion with my limited knowledge, is that people who abuse welfare aren't passing up on a well-paying job. It's not like they have the resources to earn six figures and say, "Nah, I'd rather be unemployed or work someplace lousy." Cracking down on welfare fraud doesn't solve the problem of why people are on welfare in the first place.

For most of my life, I wondered why hungry people didn't just buy groceries with a credit card. The obvious answer is that if a person can't afford groceries one month, it's unlikely they'll be able to afford both groceries and a credit card payment the next. Never in my wildest dreams did it occur to me that not everyone can have a credit card. An article on CNBC claims that as many as one in four Americans who don't have a credit card don't qualify.[5]

It only takes a few failed paychecks for many Americans to end up on the street. The Federal Reserve reported that when faced with a hypothetical expense of $400, 61 percent of adults in 2018 said they would cover the expense using cash, savings, or a credit card that would be paid off at the next statement. Others said they would carry a balance on their credit card, borrow from family and friends, sell something, use a bank loan, line of credit, payday loan, or deposit advance, or they'd just overdraft. Twelve percent said they would be unable to pay the expense by any means.[6]

Jonathan Bloom, the author of *American Wasteland*, went to an elementary school in the poorest county in the United States and watched them eat lunch. Nearly all the students got their breakfast and lunch for free because they came from food-insecure homes. You'd think they would have stuffed their faces and poured thank-yous on all the teachers.

Wrong. Some of the kids barely touched their food, and a lot of it went in the trash.

One might take this to mean the children weren't needy in the first place. One could even use this as evidence to stop funding free meals. To Jonathan Bloom's credit, he dug deeper into the situation, and what he found is surprising.

The kids ate lunch in shifts. Some of the shifts were so early that kids were being fed lunch only two hours after eating breakfast. The cafeteria workers dished up the food, even if it was more than the kids wanted and even if it was food the kids didn't like. The school only gave kids fifteen minutes to eat, and the kids were eager to go to recess. I remember having this problem when I was a kid. Tired of shoveling down my lunch so quickly, I finally took as long as I wanted to eat lunch, even though it meant my friends went outside without me. I missed recess completely. After that experience, I went back to eating as fast as I could.

Bloom suggested schools have recess first. Not only will they finish their food instead of dashing out to recess, but they'll be hungrier after playing. That's brilliant.

The kids didn't like most of what was being served. I usually don't champion picky eating, but if we're going to go to all the work and expense of providing them food, we might as well serve something they like.

To summarize: The kids were given food they didn't like when they weren't hungry without enough time to eat it, and if they threw out their lunch, they were rewarded with recess.

Meanwhile, we rest easy thinking our tax dollars helped these children when we didn't help at all. Linda K. Burton, the Relief Society general president of the entire LDS Church, summed it up perfectly in the title of one of my favorite church talks: "First Observe, then Serve."

My college had an amazing event to spread awareness about international poverty. Everyone was given a card representing an income level. A small percentage were rich, and they were guided to fancy tables and served gourmet catered meals. The participants with middle-class cards were given chairs and served hot dogs. The vast majority of us—including Andrew and I—lived in poverty. We sat on cardboard boxes on the floor and were served beans and rice. A speaker gave a long speech about poverty, but he said only one thing I will never forget: If you give a blanket to someone who can get a blanket on their own, you take away that person's dignity.

Government programs like food stamps are never going to cure hunger because they don't know the people they serve. Some people get too much. Some get what they need. Some don't get enough.

That's where charity comes in. Actually, they don't have the resources to help everyone. That's where *friends* come in. The key to charity isn't just a soft heart and a fat wallet; the key is to get to know the people you're helping so that you can meet their needs, and when you can't meet their needs, you can give friendship. If we all had friends from different demographics with different challenges, we could understand these issues and be better equipped to solve them.

Maybe all this is too much for you right now. You might not have enough time, enough money, or enough food to help alleviate hunger. My advice: at least don't waste what you have!

Chapter 8:

Reaching the End, and How I Finally Achieved Zero Waste

Two years had passed since my experiment started, and I had taken things as far as I could. I had read countless books and articles, practiced my techniques month after month, and learned as much as I knew how to learn. For the entire second year, I wasted six cups of food or less each month. This number made me proud . . . but it wasn't my goal. No matter what I did, I could not achieve zero waste.

Feeding scraps to the dog got more complicated when we got a Dachshund. Unlike my Border collie, she would inhale as much food as she could find. She'd even sweep treats out from under the other dog's nose while the Border collie looked on helplessly. Making my tiny dog obese wasn't going to help anyone.

It was time to stop.

By "stop," I don't mean going back to my old ways. I still reduced my waste as much as possible, but I stopped stressing over the number zero. My husband and I stopped taking home pizza crusts at parties that our kids didn't eat. We didn't let our fridge get practically empty. I didn't weigh food that had gone bad or put it in the freezer, but instead sent it straight to the compost bin. Avoiding waste was no longer the center of my life.

The time had come to write this book, but when the first draft was done, I didn't feel the victory I had expected. The goal was to get to *zero.* I had wanted to know what it would take. Until I figured that out, the book would never feel finished.

Then, I was randomly given the answer:

Chickens.

When my mother passed away, I inherited the birds and their coop. We gave them only chicken feed at first because that's what my mom did until a fellow chicken keeper told me to give them my table scraps. This blew my mind. It was so simple, so efficient . . . could this be the answer?

I admitted to my dad that I was nervous about feeding scraps to the chickens. "What if I give them something they're not supposed to have?" I asked.

"Teralyn," he said flatly, "they eat rocks."

It's true. You're supposed to mix rocks into their feed to help with their digestion.

Chickens are such prolific eaters that gardeners will let them loose in their gardens at the end of the season to clear out plant scraps. I can't even keep a bed of hay in the coop because they eat all the hay.

When I say they'll eat anything, I do mean anything. One day when Andrew was gathering eggs, he only saw five of the six chickens. In the center of the coop, there was a bird carcass picked clean.

After a wave of horror passed, he found the sixth chicken in the coop, sitting on her eggs and perfectly healthy. We didn't know my brother and his wife were also tossing in scraps, and they had fed them the remains of a rotisserie chicken.

A good rule is that chickens can eat just about anything we can eat. Exceptions include avocados, chocolate, and citrus. Don't give them anything we can't have, like dried beans, uncooked rice, popcorn kernels, or raw potatoes. Moldy and rotten food is a no-no. People say not to give them onions or garlic, but that's just so the eggs don't taste funny.

There are more benefits to chickens than just feeding them scraps. Getting the eggs felt like recycling. I was still eating the scraps, which, when you think about it, were just inside an egg. Chickens even converted our food into compost. Making animal poop is much faster than waiting for food to decompose in a bin. Finally, I love that the chickens live in humane conditions. The cages that farm chickens live in make me sick. Plus, it's cute to hear their happy cooing noises when they go after the scraps I give them.

Backyard chickens seem like a win-win all around.

The only downside: We can't solely rely on backyard chickens if everyone keeps wasting the way we do. Imagine how many chickens we'd need!

If you live in an urban area with a tiny backyard, chickens might not seem like an option. The truth might surprise you. Some cities allow backyard chickens under certain conditions. There are rules about how many chickens you can have, how big the coop can be, how you must store the feed, and what you must do with the waste. If your town isn't chicken friendly now, it might not be that way forever. Rules change. Maybe you can be the one to help change them.

There's a company called Mill that can cure your chicken problem. For thirty dollars a month, they give you a bin that turns your scraps into dried, ground-up food. You ship the grounds to Mill, and they feed it to chickens.

Chickens could save the world. Who knew?

I'll admit to using the chickens as a crutch. I'll also admit that food in our house occasionally went bad before I could get it to the chickens, and it needed to be composted.

That's okay. I didn't want to be zero waste my whole life. The point is that I knew *how* to reach zero waste. It is possible, despite what others might tell you. The goal you shoot for is up to you. I just hope now that you've read my book, you'll be able to reach your goal, whatever it might be.

The No Scrap Left Behind Community

It had been two years since my food-waste journey began. By now, I had learned so much and felt ready to share what I knew.

The question was: How?

The typical paths to online stardom didn't appeal to me. Under no circumstances did I want to make an Instagram account or a YouTube channel where I just talked and talked and people left comments. I didn't want to spend time taking photos and videos and editing blog articles just so people could see them once and forget about them.

Instead, I wanted a community: a living, breathing thing built by others. A place where people could share their ideas and successes with each other instead of just listening to me. That was my vision. Luckily, a new platform came into my life—Reddit—and it was exactly what I needed.

If you're not familiar with Reddit, it's a website made up of communities where people are only allowed to share a very specific type of content on each community. R/turtleswearingstuff is, as you can easily guess, a group (otherwise known as a subreddit) for posting pictures of turtles wearing stuff. A picture of a naked turtle, or a picture of a hatted cow, would be deleted by moderators for being off topic. It was a perfect place for people to share videos, articles, pictures, questions, and ideas about food waste.

I created the subreddit, put up a few example posts with recipes and food hacks, and started letting people know about us. I posted in r/EatCheapandHealthy, r/ZeroWaste, r/LifeHacks, r/Environmentalism, and more. Posting in twenty-eight subreddits might have been overboard . . . but hey, I don't like to do things only halfway.

A hundred followers joined in the first hour. That exceeded my expectations! Then an hour later, there were two hundred. Five hundred. I checked my phone all day long, amazed as the numbers jumped higher.

A member of the r/ZeroWaste community left this comment in my post: "I went to No Scrap Left Behind this morning and it was 200, and now it's 700. What is happening? Why is this so big?"

The subreddit reached one thousand members in a single day. On the second day, it reached five thousand.

Soon, the forum was flooded with posts. They shared their success stories: turning sour milk into soda bread, stale doughnuts into French toast, and apple cores into syrup. Making broth was a rite of passage, and most of us tried Everything Cookies.

I had envisioned myself as being an adviser for others to turn to, but my food-waste warriors, as I would call them, didn't need my help. A woman posted asking what to do with leftover pickle juice even though it passed the Hungry Kid Test. Within four hours, she had dozens of suggestions like marinading chicken; brining fresh vegetables like celery and carrots; brining tofu; adding flavor to tuna salad, pasta salad, potato salad, egg salad, coleslaw, and homemade ranch; soaking potato slices before roasting them for chips; adding it to stew; using it in sourdough or rye bread; and, of course, "Just chug it." Someone even suggested using it as "pickleback," which is a shot of whiskey chased with a shot of pickle juice.

On the r/lifehacks forum, someone said this about us: "These people are intense. They're saving stuff like canned fruit juice!"

In a short period of time, I became a moderator overseeing tens of thousands of members. It was was my responsibility to build a culture around my subreddit and, frankly, to keep everyone in line. Some subreddits expect their members to be nice, like r/wholesome-memes, while others are magnets for snarkiness.

I knew right away what the tone of this subreddit should be. A tweet inspired me, actually. It said, "I love how Pinterest is the only place on the Internet where people get along. There's not much to argue about cheesecake recipes." The tweet spoke to so many people, it got tens of thousands of likes. Maybe I had a similar opportunity to create one of the few places online where people could get along.

Much like the cooks making cheesecake on Pinterest, the vast majority of members were enthusiastic and creative. But some people came in with their figurative fists raised, ready to argue. One user called me a "corporate shill" for "putting the blame of food waste entirely on individuals instead of looking critically at supply chain problems." Before banning him, I pointed out that a subreddit about supply chains would have been much less popular.

In those early days, people argued about which scraps were safe for dogs. Vegans and vegetarians criticized meat eaters. A member was even criticized for keeping chickens because buying chickens supported the meat industry, even if they weren't eaten. People argued about expiration dates, of course. If anyone posted unhealthy food, there would be the inevitable, "Just throw it out. You shouldn't be eating that anyway." A few were adamant about throwing away food made by Nestlé as if an evil corporation would care that you threw away their product after buying it.

There was even an argument over the best way to remove egg yolks from the whites. I kid you not. One member insisted that the only way to do it was to separate a single yolk into a small bowl, then add it to the rest of the yolks because that way if you crack open a bad egg, it won't spoil the rest of the batch. People went back and forth on this for a while and some feelings were hurt. Finally, a member wrote, "This is a weird thing to be so passionate about." The whole thing reminded me of the egg in Gulliver's Travels that satirized pointless arguments.

All these problems were easy to fix. Every subreddit gets to make its own rules, so I made these rules for mine: Be nice. No diet shaming. Don't tell people when to throw away food. Let the original poster name the dish. (I was so tired of people arguing about whether the original poster had made dumplings or empanadas!)

The negativity cleared up. Even when things got ugly, I handled it lightheartedly. Once when two members were arguing over something silly, I wrote, "You two be nice or I'll put you both in time-out." Embarrassed, one of the users deleted all her comments in the argument. I could have deleted the comments myself, but this was better.

A culture of kindness built itself up. I found people apologizing for things they didn't need to apologize for and then the other person apologizing for making them feel the need to apologize. It was like the Canada of Reddit.

I even had to depend on my food-waste warriors every now and then. Once Adalyn was excited to make cupcakes all by herself and we were out of vegetable oil, so I used olive oil. This was not the kind of olive oil I had used in baking before. It had a strong flavor that tasted terrible in cupcakes and no one in my family would eat them. Olive oil cake is a thing, but for some reason, it didn't work at all.

Desperate to save my daughter from disappointment, I made a post asking what to do. The other members pointed out that olive oil cake always has citrus because the two flavors work well together. We made orange frosting, and voilà! The cupcakes were so good that Adalyn proudly shared them with her aunts and uncles.

Our subreddit was a hub for resourcefulness and creativity. My proudest moment was when a member posted, "What part of food do you eat that most people toss?" The answers included kiwi and mango skin, apple core and seeds, the white part of the watermelon rind, watermelon seeds (roasted), strawberry tops, cilantro stems, potato skins, the cores of iceberg lettuce and cabbages, cauliflower leaves, and shrimp with the shell on.

TIP: You can roast pumpkin seeds on a cookie sheet for 45 minutes in a 300-degree Fahrenheit oven, stirring occasionally. Watermelon seeds can be roasted at 325 degrees Fahrenheit for 15 to 20 minutes.

It was also a good place to vent about waste. A user posted about needing to use twelve unsweet cantaloupes (I have no idea how he ended up with so many) and lamented that he didn't have enough freezer space for them because his freezer was full of rabbit pelts.

"You seem like an interesting person," posted a member.

The original poster explained that he raised rabbits and killed them for meat, even though it was gut-wrenching to do so. "These animals mean a LOT to me," he wrote. "I love the animals and I love watching them grow up." But he felt strongly about self-sustainability and raising food in healthy environments as opposed to the cruel meat industry. It was a lot of work, and frankly much more expensive than buying meat in the store.

He had zero support from friends and family. The only person who thought he wasn't a psychotic murderer was his neighbor, so he gave him two of his rabbits. The neighbor left them in the fridge too long and threw them out.

"I put lots of time and effort into each one, and their lives were wasted. I hate that more than anything and it still makes me upset," he said.

Everyone showered him with comments of support and sympathy.

Remember in Chapter 5 when I was drowning in hard-boiled eggs? A member had the same problem. Her post got 282 comments.

Granted, many of the comments were jokes about a Papa Roach song. Someone wrote, "Cut them into pieces and throw them in a salad." The next comments were: "Cut my egg into pieces / This is my chef salad / Starvation, no eating / Don't really care if I cut my hand peeling." I love the Internet.

There were so many good ideas. Ramen noodles, egg curry, tuna salad, chef salad, pasta salad, potato salad, potato soup, gribiche sauce, Korean mayak, creamed on toast, Scotch eggs, pudding (blend eggs with milk, sugar, and flavoring), tiger skin eggs, son-in-law eggs, pickled eggs, or pickled beet eggs on sandwiches, salads, and avocado toast. I am going to try all these ideas.

Plus, some British guy said he drops whole pickled eggs in a bag of potato chips and shakes them up. Someone wrote, "This is just crazy enough to be absolutely delicious."

Turns out, there are lots of fellow food-waste warriors out there. I just had to look for them.

Fixing a Broken World: We Can Do This

In the first chapter, I laid out a seemingly insurmountable problem. Using all the food we produce will be no easy feat.

But as awareness of food waste is building, laws are changing. In France, it's illegal for grocery stores to throw away food. They have to give it to nonprofits. Singapore requires shopping malls and hotels to separate organic waste from other waste. Austria passed a Waste Management Act. Because England doesn't have as much room for landfills, they've implemented a landfill tax to reduce waste and encourage recycling.

Citizens in Seoul and other South Korean cities have to weigh their food waste, and they're charged a small fee according to the weight, encouraging them to throw out less, and then that food becomes either animal feed or fertilizer. South Korea went from only recycling 2 percent of its food waste in 1995 to now recycling 95 percent of its food waste.[1] Han Sung Hyun, the Seoul Environmental Management Division, says that "about 10 to 15 percent of households don't produce any food waste at all."[2]

At the time I'm writing this, there are six states in the United States that prohibit sending food waste to landfills. San Francisco made composting mandatory for all households and businesses, and Seattle did the same for single-family homes.[3] California has passed a sweeping organic waste reduction law that requires residents and businesses to recycle organic waste.[4] They're still ironing out the kinks to make the bill effective,[5] but efforts are well underway. The United States announced in 2015 that by the year 2030, we would reduce our food loss by 50 percent.

Businesses are forming around this issue. Wtrmln Wtr is a drink made from "ugly" watermelons that were abandoned in the fields. Renewal Mill makes flour from the byproduct of tofu and soy milk. Coffee Cherry Company makes flour out of the fruit that holds the coffee bean, and Regrained makes flour out of the byproduct of beer. Barnana makes dehydrated banana snacks out of imperfect bananas. Sir Kensington's makes vegan mayo with aquafaba, which is the liquid left after cooking beans. The list goes on and on.

I was going to briefly write about some of the charities and awareness campaigns that fight food waste, but there are too many, and by the time this book gets to you, there will be many more. Instead, there's an appendix at the end with a list of food-waste resources that exist at the time I'm writing this. The list is long!

Yet there is still so much work to do. The United Kingdom announced a goal to reduce total waste by 50 percent by 2020. Not only did they not meet their goal, but food waste actually went up by 11 percent.[6] At least they are still committed to their goal.

The United States may want to cut its food waste in half by 2030, but by 2022, it had only reduced it by 2 percent.[7] We should give credit where credit is due; food waste was once increasing every year, so it is heartening to see the numbers mostly level off.[8] Still, we are a far cry from where we want to be.

My food-waste journey was over, and, with the help of my chickens, life had gone back to normal. I went to a deli to pick up a cheesecake for my husband's birthday right before the store closed. Behind the counter, there was a shopping cart piled high with packaged cakes and pastries.

"What's that?" I asked, which was kind of a jerk thing to ask since I already knew.

"That's the stuff that we throw out at the end of the day," she said.

"You don't donate it?" I asked.

She frowned and rang up my cheesecake.

For some bizarre reason, I felt emotional. As in *about to cry* emotional. I had to look up at the ceiling to keep tears in as I handed her my debit card. *Keep it together, keep it together,* I said to myself as I left the store. *You can shed a tear or two once you get in the car.*

When I was safe in the car, I didn't only shed a few tears. I started sobbing. My reaction bewildered me. It was just one shopping cart, and it's not like I didn't know every store in my town loaded up its dumpsters at the end of the day. There was just something about seeing it in person that shook me.

Stand-up comedian Julio Diaz has a joke about how the song "Fly Like an Eagle" by Seal makes no sense. The song says, "I want to feed the people who have nothing to eat. I want to shoe the people with no shoes on their feet. I want to house the people living on the street. There's a solution. Lemme fly like an eagle."

"How the hell is that a solution?" he asked. "Could you imagine? You ask somebody for help and they said that s*** to you, you would never ask for help again. 'Yo, bro, I'm desperate, I need you.' (and I be like) 'I gotchu bro. Caw! Caw!'"[9]

Diaz perfectly illustrates a pattern in our society. We have this tendency to get all revved up about an issue, inspire everyone into believing they can fix it, then tell them some affirmation that makes them feel good but doesn't help the problem and they go about their day without changing anything. We need to get mad, and we need to *stay* mad until food waste is over.

I dream of a world where all food-waste programs are unnecessary. There won't be compost companies because there won't be any uneaten food to compost. Someday, farmers will sell everything they grow, grocery stores will sell or give away everything they stock, and people will eat everything they buy.

I believe in my dream because not long ago, humans were different. Our grandparents didn't burn through their resources like this. Remember that in the 1970s, Americans wasted half as much as we do now.

We made this problem within the last few decades, and we can fix it just as fast. Our culture of waste will be a tiny blip in the history of mankind. Upcoming generations will learn about us in school, and they will be horrified by how we live now.

It will take all of us—you, me, and everyone else—to fix this problem.

Let's go change the world.

Appendix 1: Tips and Tricks

1. **Clear containers.** Store food in clear containers and mason jars so that you can easily see what's in your fridge. Containers that aren't clear, like those you buy with Cool Whip and yogurt, are great for giving away food so you don't need to get your dish back.
2. **Freeze baked goods to keep them fresh.** You can buy cupcakes, cookies, a pie, or a cheesecake, eat a serving or two, and freeze the rest to be eaten gradually over time.
3. **Toast stale food.** This works great for crackers, chips, and cereal. Spread the food over a baking sheet and bake on a low temperature for a few minutes. Keep a close eye on it so it doesn't burn.
4. **Prevent freezer burn with plastic wrap.** Freezer burn happens when frozen food is exposed to too much air. Lay plastic wrap over the top of frozen food to protect it.
5. **To keep cookies fresh:** Add a slice of bread to your container of cookies. The moisture from the bread will keep them soft.

6. **When cookies are stale:** To make stale cookies taste like they just came out of the oven, put them in the toaster. They'll fall apart if you try to pick them up, so tilt the toaster on its side and take the cookies out with a spatula. You can also reheat them in the oven.
7. **Tomato paste.** Most recipes that use tomato paste only call for a tablespoon or two. For the rest of the can, measure out one tablespoon blobs and put them on a cookie sheet lined in wax paper, then place in freezer. When they're frozen, place in a Ziploc bag or a Tupperware container for later.
8. **Chili.** If you made a big pot of chili you don't want to finish, time to get creative. You can put it in a skillet, pour corn-bread on top, and bake it, pour it on a baked potato with cheese and sour cream, pour it over Fritos and top with cheese (aka Frito Pie), or mix it into mac and cheese.
9. **Stale rice.** Rice seems to get stale the second you put it in the fridge. Pour a little bit of water in the plastic container with the rice—not much, maybe a tablespoon or two—seal the container but leave a corner up for ventilation (or else a hole will burst through the lid, as I learned from experience) and microwave for two minutes. Let the rice sit in the microwave for a few minutes more. If it's still too dry, add a teaspoon or two of water, close the lid completely, and let it sit a few more minutes. If it's too wet, open the lid and let the moisture evaporate.
10. **Microwaving leftovers.** The microwave can only heat one inch into a dish. For food you can't stir, like lasagna and enchiladas, cut it into one-inch strips before reheating.

11. **Toast fried food.** Fried food needs to be toasted in the oven to get crispy again. French fries need to be refried or liberally coated in oil before being toasted.
12. **Reheating pizza** can be done many different ways: in the oven, in a toaster oven, in a skillet . . . but never in the microwave. Or you can eat it cold. To do the skillet, toast the crust for two minutes, add a tablespoon of water away from the pizza, cover, and cook for a minute until the cheese gets gooey. I also like putting my pizza directly in the toaster oven, but you have to be wary of toppings falling in.
13. **Overcooking bird meat.** When you cook bird meat like chicken and turkey, the molecules constrict and squeeze out moisture. Overcooked chicken will be dry even if you smother it in sauce. Keep this in mind when cooking and reheating bird meat.
14. **Freezer Space.** Need more freezer space? Instead of putting boxes of food in your freezer, which take up a lot of space and don't get smaller as you eat through the food, take the bags out of the boxes. If the food came with cooking instructions, cut the instructions off the box and tape it to the bag.
15. **Freezer burn** is caused by air getting to the food. If you don't have a vacuum sealer for your food, wrap it in plastic wrap, then aluminum foil to keep the plastic wrap in place, put in a Ziploc bag with as little air in it as possible, and then write the name of the food on the bag so you know what on earth you wrapped in aluminum foil months ago. If you put food in a container, place plastic wrap on top so that it's touching the food before sealing the lid on.

16. **Freeze food in water.** Some foods can be frozen in water, like shrimp or chicken. The ice keeps air away so there's no freezer burn.
17. **Leftovers into breakfast.** Lots of leftover dishes can be eaten for breakfast or converted to breakfast food if you just add scrambled eggs or put a fried egg on top.
18. **Egg yolks.** If a recipe calls for egg whites only, you can save the egg yolks and add them to scrambled eggs (about one yolk per egg). It'll make them tastier, more vibrant, and more nutritious. You can also add an egg yolk to cookie recipes to make your cookies gooier.
19. **Potato peels.** Don't throw away potato peels! They're nutritious, and they are a yummy treat. Just deep-fry or toss with oil and salt and bake in a 400-degree Fahrenheit oven for fifteen minutes. It's a good snack for the kids when they can't wait for dinner to be done.
20. **Organize your kitchen.** There are a lot of products to help keep your kitchen organized. For instance, you can use pull-out drawers, sliding shelves, racks, baskets, lazy Susans, over-the-door organizers, drawer dividers, and lid racks.
21. **Evaluate fridge daily.** Check the fridge every day to see if anything needs to be frozen.
22. **Bone broth.** Anytime you have leftover bones, just boil it for four hours to make broth. Refrigerate, scoop off the fat, and then you can place one cup of broth in individual containers or bags to freeze and pull out for recipes.
23. **Stock** is basically just a flavored broth. You can make it by adding vegetables (typically carrots, onions, and celery) and herbs, boiling the bones and vegetables for four hours, and

straining out all the liquid to add to soup. To avoid wasting edible vegetables, you can use scraps like carrot peels, celery leaves, and onion ends.

24. **Vegetable broth.** Whenever you have vegetable scraps, save them in a bag or container in the freezer until you have a decent amount. Boil for four hours to make broth, then strain the fluid and throw the scraps away. At a minimum, vegetable broth has onions, carrots, and celery, but you can experiment with most vegetables. Do *not* use potato peels or your broth will taste like dirt.
25. **Tortillas** that are old and cracking can be deep-fried to make tortilla chips. Flour tortillas are good rolled in cinnamon and sugar.
26. **Shop in season.** Keep a table of when fruits and vegetables are in season in your kitchen. They're cheaper, and produce bought locally is fresher and will last longer.
27. **Blind baking.** When you make a tart or a pie shell, you have to weigh it down as it's cooking with heavier food like rice, beans, or quinoa. You can still soak and cook the "weights" after baking them in the oven.
28. **Find new uses for bird meat.** Rotisserie chicken and whole turkeys can be used in any dish that calls for chopped or shredded meat.
29. **Savory pies.** You can spoon leftovers into hand-held pies, empanadas, calzones, potpie, or shepherd's pie.
30. **Hosting food parties.** When you host parties and think you might have a lot left over, you can have containers, bags, or plates with tinfoil ready to hand out to your guests, or you can ask them to bring their own containers.

31. **Clips.** Using clips to keep bags closed will do wonders for keeping food fresh.
32. **Use pantry food.** If you want to clear out your pantry but still use all the food inside, plan to include one item in your pantry for every meal you make. You can do the same thing with your freezer.
33. **Sour milk** is safe to drink as long as it is pasteurized. It can be used in baking or turned into buttermilk.
34. **Overripe fruit.** For fruit past its prime, mix into pancakes or Dutch babies (aka German pancakes), or mix it with sugar and serve it as a topping.
35. **Frying oil.** After frying food, keep the used vegetable oil in an empty container to use later. You might want to strain out the gunk with cheesecloth, a paper towel, or even just a colander.
36. **Pickle juice.** If you have too much cucumber, you can soak cucumber slices in old pickle juice. It won't turn them into pickles, but they are delicious, and they'll stay fresh for ages. You can do this with other vegetables, too, like carrots, squash, okra, turnips, and green tomatoes.
37. **Stale baguettes.** Rinse the baguette with water, wrap it in aluminum foil, and put it in a cold oven. Turn the oven on to 350 degrees and set a timer for ten to twelve minutes. Note: the bread will get stale again very quickly, so you'll want to eat it right away.
38. **Peels.** Before throwing your apple cores, orange peels, or lemon peels in the compost, you can simmer them over the stove to make the house smell good. You can also use orange and lemon zest in recipes, boil apple peels and cores

in water for syrup and jelly, or use apple cores and peels to make apple cider vinegar.

39. **Freeze fruit.** Purée soon-to-expire fruit to make smoothies or fruit pops or chop it up and put it in the freezer to use in smoothies later. You can keep a gallon-sized bag in your freezer and pop scraps of fruit in whenever you don't think they'll get eaten.
40. **Yogurt.** If you're worried about yogurt that's getting old, you can make frozen yogurt pops or mix it into smoothies.
41. **Wilted vegetables.** If a vegetable is wilted and then cooked, it doesn't taste any different than if the vegetable hadn't been wilted.
42. **Leafy vegetables.** For vegetables like lettuce, celery, broccoli, and green onions, rinse them thoroughly in water and wrap them in aluminum foil when they're still dripping. This can keep vegetables crisp for longer than a month, and doing this often makes them taste better than when you bought them.
43. **Potatoes and onions.** Both onions and potatoes should be stored in a cool, dry place, but they shouldn't be stored together. Onions release ethylene gas that can make the potatoes ripen, sprout, and go bad faster.
44. **Keep freezer doors closed.** Fluctuating temperatures can cause freezer burn, so it's best not to keep the door open too long or to allow the food to slightly thaw before putting it in the freezer. Do not put warm food in the freezer or it will warm everything else. Wait for it to cool first.
45. **Pumpkin and watermelon seeds.** You can roast pumpkin seeds and watermelon seeds on a cookie sheet.

46. **Brown food.** When food turns brown, it is caused by oxidation, not decay. It's safe to eat food that has turned brown, including fruit, vegetables, and even raw meat. To prevent browning, you can keep food sealed and away from the air, and you can add lemon juice to some foods like apples, avocados, and pears.
47. **Mold.** Solid foods with mold on the outside, like bread, hard cheese, and fruit, are still good to eat after all the mold is cut off. Soft foods, including soft cheese, and liquids are not safe once they're moldy.
48. **Broccoli stalks.** If you peel off the woody exterior, the inside flesh is delicious. You can eat it raw, shred it for slaw, or cook it right alongside the florets.
49. **Vases.** Some food can best be stored in a glass or a vase full of water, just like flowers. Green onions, asparagus, and herbs like basil and cilantro are examples.
50. **Smoothies and milkshakes.** To save smoothies and milkshakes, pour them into ice cube trays and freeze. If it is difficult to remove the cubes, dip the bottom of the tray in hot water until they get loose. Store the cubes in a sealed bag or container. When you're ready, mix the cubes in a blender with just a little liquid.
51. **Avoid precut produce.** When fruit and vegetables are cut up, they go bad faster. Your food will stay fresh longer if you cut it up right before you eat it.
52. **Bagged produce.** Bagged produce, like lettuce and spinach, are kept fresh with Modified Atmosphere Packaging (MAP). It'll stay fresh longer than unbagged produce, but once you open the bag and oxygen gets inside, the food will start to go bad at the same rate as other produce.

53. **Put up an EAT ME FIRST sign in your fridge.** That's where your most perishable food should go.
54. **Popcorn as packaging material.** Use popcorn in a sealed bag as a biodegradable cushion for shipping . . . and then the receiver can eat it!
55. **Old bread.** You can use stale bread in French toast, bruschetta, bread pudding, French onion soup, stuffing, breadcrumbs, croutons, and recipes like gazpacho (a raw vegetable soup), stratas (layered casseroles, like breakfast casseroles), panzanella (a salad with bread soaked in dressing), and canederli (Italian dumplings).
56. **Bread heels.** Some people are finicky about eating bread heels. If you flip the heel of your bread over when you make a sandwich, no one can tell the difference.
57. **Ethylene gas** ripens produce, and some produce emits that gas as it ripens. It's best to keep the following foods separate from things you don't want to be ripened: apples, apricots, avocados, cantaloupe, figs, honeydew, bananas, nectarines, peaches, pears, plums, and tomatoes.
58. **Fresh avocados.** Before buying an avocado, feel for air bubbles where the peel has separated from the flesh. This means it is overripe.
59. **Organizing.** When organizing your pantry, put the stuff you know you'll use (i.e., flour, sugar, rice) in the back, and put the stuff you're likely to forget about in the front.
60. **Trade food.** If you have a lot of food in your kitchen that you don't want to eat, throw a pantry swap party.
61. **Freezer compost.** If you can't take your compost out to a bin immediately, keep it in a bowl in the freezer so it doesn't stink up your kitchen.

62. **Upcycling.** You can save a ton of time in the kitchen by repurposing into a new dish food you've already made.
63. **Overcrowded fridges.** Food will stay fresher longer if you don't overcrowd your fridge. This allows the cold air to circulate around the food.
64. **Pans in the freezer.** When you freeze food in a pan, you don't have to keep the pan in the freezer until you're ready to eat the food. Put plastic wrap at the bottom of the pan before adding the food, wait for the food to freeze, then take it out. Wrap it up so that no air gets to it to prevent freezer burn.
65. **Refrigerator temperatures.** How cold is your fridge? It should be no higher than 40 degrees Fahrenheit or 5 degrees Celsius, according to the Food Standards Agency. A warmer fridge will cause food to spoil faster. The temperature dial in fridges isn't always accurate, so they recommend using a fridge thermometer.
66. **Not pretty food.** While it may not look appetizing, food is still safe when it's brown, bruised, discolored, scarred, stale, and wilted, because bacteria doesn't cause those issues.
67. **Post a list of meals.** Keep a visible list of all the meals you can make with the ingredients in your kitchen. Don't erase the name of the meal until you've finished eating it so you can easily see what leftovers you have.
68. **Avocados and onions.** To keep an avocado from turning brown, store it in a bag or container with part of an onion. The sulfur in the onion slows the oxidation process.
69. **Salvaged fat.** When fat is released from the food you make, such as bacon grease and the film on top of broth, you can

cook with it. The fat is great for sautéing, frying, greasing pans, or even replacing oil in recipes. If the bacon grease is full of food debris, microwave it until liquid and the debris will float to the bottom.

70. **Keep dry food dry.** Water is one of the components that bacteria need to survive and multiply. Keeping your unrefrigerated food dry will help it last longer.
71. **Cook beans and grains in broths.** If you find yourself with extra yummy fluid, like a flavored broth, meat juice, or soup, you can cook beans and grains in the fluid instead of using water. This will give it extra flavor. Think: rice, couscous, quinoa, etc.
72. **Freezing dairy.** Most dairy products can be easily frozen, like butter, cottage cheese, cream cheese, milk, and ice cream. Cheese frozen as a solid brick will get crumbly, so it's best to shred it first. Cream will not whip as well after being defrosted. Sour cream, yogurt, and buttermilk will likely become grainy.
73. **Rice at the bottom of a pan.** Rice often gets stuck to the bottom of the pan. As soon as it's done cooking, stir it up, add a couple tablespoons of water, and close the lid for five to ten minutes. This will loosen up the stuck rice.

Appendix 2: Resources

Organizations and Charities

NOTE: The locations listed refer to the charity's headquarters, but many of them have multiple chapters, and some of them are looking to open more chapters.

Aloha Harvest (Honolulu, Hawaii, United States)
Amp Your Good (Mendham, New Jersey, United States)
Boston Area Gleaners (Boston, Massachusetts, United States)
Boston No Waste Coalition (Boston, Massachusetts, United States)
Boulder Food Rescue (Boulder, Colorado, United States)
Caritas (Vatican City, Italy)
Center for a Livable Future (Baltimore, Maryland, United States)
City Harvest (New York, New York, United States)
Community Food Rescue (Montgomery County, Maryland, United States)
Community Plates (Norwalk, Connecticut, United States)
Copia (San Francisco, California, United States)
Culinary Misfits (Berlin, Germany)
DC Central Kitchen (Washington, DC, United States)

Dreaming Out Loud (Washington, DC, United States)
Express NYC (New York City, New York, United States)
ExtraFood (San Rafael, California, United States)
Feedback (London, United Kingdom)
Feeding America (Chicago, Illinois, United States)
The Felix Project (London, United Kingdom)
Food Cowboy (Bethesda, Maryland, United States)
Food Cycle (London, England)
Food Forward (Los Angeles, California, United States)
Food Loop (Cologne, Germany)
Food Not Bombs (Santa Cruz, California, United States)
Food Policy Action (Washington, DC, United States)
Food Recovery Network (Washington, DC, United States)
Food Recovery Project (Fayetteville, Arkansas, United States)
Food Rescue Hero (Pittsburgh, Pennsylvania, United States)
Food Rescue US (Stamford, Connecticut, United States)
FoodSave London (London, England)
Food Share (Bloomfield, Connecticut, United States)
Food Shift (Oakland, California, United States)
Food Tank (New Orleans, Louisiana, United States)
Food Waste Reduction Alliance (Arlington, Virginia, United States)
Forgotten Harvest (Oak Park, Michigan, United States)
412 Food Rescue (Pittsburgh, Pennsylvania, United States)
Hands for Hunger (Nassau, Bahamas)
Iskashitaa Refugee Network (Tucson, Arizona, United States)
Island Grown Gleaning (Vineyard Haven, Massachusetts, United States)
L.A. Kitchen (Los Angeles, California, United States)
Last Minute Market (Bologna, Italy)
Lean Path (Portland, Oregon, United States)
Love Food Hate Waste (Banbury, England)
Lovin' Spoonfuls (Boston, Massachusetts, United States)

Markets Institute, WWF (Washington, DC, United States)
No Food Waste (Coimbatore, India)
OzHarvest (Sydney, Australia)
Portland Fruit Tree Project (Portland, Oregon, United States)
ProduceGood (San Diego, California, United States)
Produce to the People (Tasmania, Australia)
The Real Junk Food Project (York, United Kingdom)
ReFED (Long Island City, New York, United States)
REFRESH (Wageningen, Netherlands)
Rescuing Leftover Cuisine (New York City, New York, United States)
ReThink Food (New York City, New York, United States)
Salvation Farms (Morrisville, Vermont, United States)
Satisfeito (São Paulo, Brazil)
Save Food Asia-Pacific (China)
Save Food from the Fridge (Torino, Italy)
Second Bite (Melbourne, Australia)
Second Harvest (Toronto, Canada)
Sesc Mesa Brasil (Mato Grosso, Brazil)
Society of Saint Andrew (Big Island, Virginia, United States)
Stop Wasting Food (Copenhagen, Denmark)
Sustainable America (Stamford, Connecticut, United States)
Think.Eat.Save (Geneva, Switzerland)
Tkiyet Um Ali (Amman, Jordan)
Urban Gleaners (Portland, Oregon, United States)
Waste No Food (Silicon Valley, California, United States)
White Pony Express (Pleasant Hill, California, United States)
World Resources Institute (WRI) (Washington, DC, United States)
World Vegetable Center (Tainan City, Taiwan)
Zero Percent (Chicago, Illinois, United States)

Apps

Flash Food
Food for All
Food Hero
Food Rescue US
OILIO
Pantry Check
Plant Jammer
Ready, Set, Dinner
Share Waste
Too Good To Go
Transfernation
Your Local

Websites

Ample Harvest
Food Not Bombs
Food Print
Getty Steward
Going Zero Waste
Love Food, Hate Waste
Max la Mana on Instagram
My Sustainable Kitchen
Save the Food
Second Harvest
Second Helpings
Zero Hunger, Zero Waste
Zero Waste Chef
Zero Waste Chef on Instagram
Zut Gut

Companies

Hungry Harvest
Imperfect Foods
Misfit Market
Oddbox
Preserve Farm Kitchens
Rubys in the Rubble

Documentaries and Shows

Best Leftovers Ever
Dive! Living Off America's Waste
Expired? Food Waste in America
Just Eat It: A Food Waste Story
Sustainable
Ten Stories About Food Waste
Wasted: The Story of Food Waste

Books

The (Almost) Zero-Waste Guide: 100+ Tips for Reducing Your Waste Without Changing Your Life by Melanie Mannarino

An Almost Zero Waste Life: Learning How to Embrace Less to Live More by Megean Weldon

American Wasteland: How America Throws Away Nearly Half of Its Food (and What We Can Do About It) by Jonathan Bloom

Cooking Scrappy: 100 Recipes to Help You Stop Wasting Food, Save Money, and Love What You Eat by Joel Gamoran and Katie Couric

Cooking with Scraps: Turn Your Peels, Cores, Rinds, and Stems into Delicious Meals by Lindsay-Jean Hard

Cook More, Waste Less: Zero-Waste Recipes to Use Up Groceries, Tackle Food Scraps, and Transform Leftovers by Christine Tizzard

Eat It Up!: 150 Recipes to Use Every Bit and Enjoy Every Bite of the Food You Buy by Sherri Brooks Vinton

Food Foolish: The Hidden Connection Between Food Waste, Hunger, and Climate Change by John M. Mandyck

How to Go (Almost) Zero Waste: Over 150 Steps to More Sustainable Living at Home, School, Work, and Beyond by Rebecca Grace Andrews

The Leftovers Handbook: A–Z of Every Ingredient in Your Kitchen with Inspirational Ideas for Using Them by Suzy Bowler

More Plants Less Waste: Plant-Based Recipes + Zero Waste Life Hacks with Purpose by Max La Manna

My Zero-Waste Kitchen: Easy Ways to Eat Waste Free by Kate Turner

The No-Waste Meal Planner: Create Your Own Meal Chain That Won't Waste an Ingredient by Becky Thorn

One: Pot, Pan, Planet: A Greener Way to Cook for You and Your Family by Anna Jones

River Cottage Love Your Leftovers: Recipes for the Resourceful Cook by Hugh Fearnley-Whittingstall

Root-to-Stalk Cooking: The Art of Using the Whole Vegetable [A Cookbook] by Tara Duggan

Scraps, Wilt & Weeds: Turning Wasted Food into Plenty by Mads Refslund

Simply Sustainable: Moving Toward Plastic-Free, Low-Waste Living by Lily Cameron

Six Weeks to Zero Waste: A Simple Plan for Life by Kate Arnell

The Sustainable(ish) Living Guide: Everything You Need to Know to Make Small Changes That Make a Big Difference by Jen Gale

The Thrifty Cookbook: 476 Ways to Eat Well with Leftovers by Kate Colquhoun

Waste-Free Kitchen Handbook: A Guide to Eating Well and Saving Money by Wasting Less Food by Dana Gunders

Waste Not: How to Get the Most from Your Food by James Beard Foundation, Keirnan Monaghan, et al.

The Waste Not, Want Not Cookbook: Save Food, Save Money and Save the Planet by Cinda Chavich

The Zero-Waste Chef: Plant-Forward Recipes and Tips for a Sustainable Kitchen and Planet by Anne-Marie Bonneau

The Zero Waste Cookbook: 100 Recipes for Cooking Without Waste by Giovanna Torrico and Amelia Wasiliev

Newsletters

Food Waste Feast

Mother Earth News

Scrap Kitchen

Notes

Chapter 1

1. "World Faces Worst Humanitarian Crisis since 1945, Says UN Official," *The Guardian,* March 10, 2017, https://www.theguardian.com/world/2017/mar/11/world-faces-worst-humanitarian-crisis-since-1945-says-un-official.

2. Dana Gunders, "Wasted: How America Is Losing up to 40 Percent of Its Food from Farm to Fork to Landfill," Natural Resources Defense Council Issue Paper, August 16, 2017, https://www.nrdc.org/resources/wasted-how-america-losing-40-percent-its-food-farm-fork-landfill.

3. "Food Waste: Last Week Tonight with John Oliver," YouTube, July 19, 2015, https://www.youtube.com/watch?v=i8xwLWb0lLY&t=541s.

4. Rob Greenfield, "How to End the Food Waste Fiasco | Rob Greenfield | TedxTeen," YouTube, February 2, 2016, https://www.youtube.com/watch?v=w96osGZaS74&t=2s.

5. Jean Buzby and Jeffrey Hyman, "Total and Per Capita Value of Food Loss in the United States," *Food Policy* 37 (2012): 561–570, https://www.sciencedirect.com/science/article/abs/pii/S0306919212000693.
6. Gunders, "Wasted."
7. Dana Gunders, *Waste-Free Kitchen Handbook* (San Francisco: Chronicle Books, 2014).
8. Zach Conrad, "Daily Cost of Consumer Food Wasted, Inedible, and Consumed in the United States, 2001–2016," *Nutrition Journal* 19 (2020): art. 35, https://doi.org/10.1186/s12937-020-00552-w.
9. CEC, *Characterization and Management of Food Loss and Waste in North America* (Montreal: Commission for Environmental Cooperation, 2017).
10. Jean C. Buzby, Hodan F. Wells, and Jeffrey Hyman, "The Estimated Amount, Value, and Calories of Postharvest Food Losses at the Retail and Consumer Levels in the United States," US Department of Agriculture, Economic Research Service, Economic Information Bulletin 121, February 2014, chrome-extension://efaidnbmnnnibpcajpcglclefindmkaj/https://www.ers.usda.gov/webdocs/publications/43833/43680_eib121.pdf.
11. Food and Agriculture Organization of the United Nations, "Food Wastage Footprint & Climate Change," 2011, https://www.fao.org/documents/card/en?details=7338e109-45e8-42da-92f3-ceb8d92002b0.
12. Gunders, "Wasted."
13. Grant Gerlock, "To End Food Waste, Change Needs to Begin at Home," The Salt, *NPR*, November 17, 2014, https://www.npr.org/sections/thesalt/2014/11/17/364172105/to-end-food-waste-change-needs-to-begin-at-home.

14. Food and Agriculture Organization of the United Nations, “Food Wastage Footprint & Climate Change.”

15. Conrad, “Daily Cost of Consumer Food Wasted.”

16. Selina Juul, “Stop Wasting Food: Selina Juul at TEDxCopenhagen 2012,” YouTube, October 4, 2012, https://www.youtube.com/watch?v=dIIhbjY4s8A.

17. Food and Agriculture Organization of the United Nations, “Milan Urban Food Policy Pact Monitoring Framework,” 2021, https://www.fao.org/3/cb4181en/cb4181en.pdf.

18. Food and Agriculture Organization of the United Nations, “How to Feed the World in 2050: Database of Reports: Global Trends & Future Scenarios,” October 12, 2009, chrome-extension://efaidnbmnnnibpcajpcglclefindmkaj/https://www.fao.org/fileadmin/templates/wsfs/docs/expert_paper/How_to_Feed_the_World_in_2050.pdf.

19. R. K. Pachauri and L. A. Meyer, eds., “Climate Change 2014: Synthesis Report. Contribution of Working Groups I, II and III to the Fifth Assessment Report of the Intergovernmental Panel on Climate Change,” IPCC, Geneva, 2014.

20. Buzby, Wells, and Hyman, “The Estimated Amount, Value, and Calories of Postharvested Food and Retail and Consumer Levels in the United States.”

21. American Society of Civil Engineers, “Report Card for America’s Infrastructure,” 2021, https://infrastructurereportcard.org/cat-item/solid-waste-infrastructure/#:~:text=Estimates%20show%20that%20more%20than,and%20along%20the%20East%20Coast.

22. US Environmental Protection Agency, “Overview of Greenhouse Gases,” accessed December 16, 2023, https://www.epa.gov/ghgemissions/overview-greenhouse-gases#methane.

23. Melissa, “Why Does Moist, Baled and Stacked Hay Spontaneously Catch Fire?,” Today I Found Out, September 29, 2014, https://www.todayifoundout.com/index.php/2014/09/moist-baled-stacked-hay-catch-fire/.

24. Office of Resource Conservation and Recovery, “Municipal Solid Waste Generation, Recycling, and Disposal in the United States: Tables and Figures for 2012,” US Environmental Protection Agency, February 2014, https://www.epa.gov/sites/default/files/2015-09/documents/2012_msw_dat_tbls.pdf.

25. David B. Fischer, “Energy Aspects of Manure Management,” Dairy Cattle Illinois Livestock Trail, 1998, http://livestocktrail.illinois.edu/dairynet/paperDisplay.cfm?ContentID=274.

26. Rich Pirog et al., “Food, Fuel, and Freeways: An Iowa Perspective on How Far Food Travels, Fuel Usage, and Greenhouse Gas Emissions,” Leopold Center for Sustainable Agriculture, Ames, Iowa, June 2001, https://dr.lib.iastate.edu/server/api/core/bitstreams/bd4f9881-468f-4cfe-b17b-1251ebf36ba7/content.

27. Greenfield, “How to End the Food Waste Fiasco.”

28. Jessica Aldred, “Agriculture and Overuse Greater Threats to Wildlife Than Climate Change,” *The Guardian*, August 10, 2016, https://www.theguardian.com/environment/2016/aug/10/agriculture-and-overuse-greater-threats-to-wildlife-than-climate-change-study.

29. Kate Lyons et al., “Produced but Never Eaten: A Visual Guide to Food Waste,” *The Guardian*, August 12, 2015, https://www.theguardian.com/environment/ng-interactive/2015/aug/12/produced-but-never-eaten-a-visual-guide-to-food-waste.

30. Daniel Hellerstein et al., “Agricultural Resources and Environmental Indicators, 2019,” US Department of Agriculture,

Economic Research Service, Economic Bulletin 208, May 2019, http://www.ers.usda.gov/publications/arei/eib16.

31. Martin Heller and Gregory Keoleian, "Life Cycle–Based Sustainability Indicators for Assessment of the U.S. Food System," Center for Sustainable Systems, University of Michigan, December 6, 2000, https://css.umich.edu/publications/research-publications/life-cycle-based-sustainability-indicators-assessment-us-food.

32. Juul, "Stop Wasting Food."

33. C. Nellemann et al., "The Environmental Food Crisis: The Environment's Role in Averting Future Food Crises. A UNEP Rapid Response Assessment," United Nations Environment Programme, February 2009, https://cld.bz/bookdata/QCodPZo/basic-html/page-1.html# .

34. World Food Programme, "A Global Food Crisis," 2023, https://www.wfp.org/global-hunger-crisis#:~:text=2022%3A%20a%20year%20of%20unprecedented%20hunger&text=As%20many%20as%20828%20million,on%20the%20edge%20of%20famine.

35. Peter Lehner, "A Recipe for Cutting Food Waste | Peter Lehner | TedxManhattan," YouTube, March 4, 2013, https://www.youtube.com/watch?v=UwOHpWTRsbE&t=223s.

36. Alisha Coleman-Jensen et al., "Household Food Security in the United States in 2021," US Department of Agriculture, Economic Research Service, Economic Research Report 309, September 2022, https://www.ers.usda.gov/publications/pub-details/?pubid=104655.

37. Ibid.

38. Juul, "Stop Wasting Food."

39. UN Office for the Coordination of Humanitarian Affairs, "Global Humanitarian Overview 2023," December 1, 2022, https://reliefweb.int/report/world/global-humanitarian-overview-2023-enaresfr.

40. Gunders, "Wasted."

41. Food and Agriculture Organization of the United Nations, "Food Wastage Footprint Full-Cost Accounting," 2014, https://www.fao.org/3/i3991e/i3991e.pdf.

42. James Hitching-Hales, "Guess What? Food Waste Costs the UK More Than Foreign Aid," Global Citizen, January 13, 2017, https://www.globalcitizen.org/en/content/uk-food-waste-foreign-aid-daily-mail/.

43. Lehner, "A Recipe for Cutting Food Waste."

44. Ibid.

45. Jonathan Bloom, *American Wasteland: How America Throws Away Nearly Half of Its Food (and What We Can Do About It)* (Boston: Da Capo Lifelong Books, 2010), 175.

46. The Kroger Company, "2023 ESG Report," 2023, https://www.thekrogerco.com/wp-content/uploads/2023/09/Kroger-Co-2023-ESG-Report_Final.pdf.

47. City Harvest, "Our Story," accessed December 19, 2023, https://www.cityharvest.org/our-story/.

48. I Value Food, home page, accessed December 19, 2023, www.ivaluefood.com.

49. Bloom, *American Wasteland,* 179.

50. James Haley, "The Legal Guide to the Bill Emerson Good Samaritan Food Donation Act," Arkansas Law Notes, 2013, http://media.law.uark.edu/arklawnotes/2013/08/08/the-legal-guide-to-the-bill-emerson-good-samaritan-food-donation-act/.

Chapter 2

1. US Environmental Protection Agency, "Sustainable Management of Food, December 15, 2023, https://www.epa.gov/sustainable-management-food/composting#:~:text=In%202019%2C%2066.2%20million%20tons,that%20wasted%20food%20was%20composted.&text=In%20the%20U.S.%2C%20food%20is,percent%20of%20municipal%20solid%20waste.
2. Greenfield, "How to End the Food Waste Fiasco."
3. FoodHero, "What Food Waste, Climate Change, and Methane Gas Have in Common," October 14, 2019, https://foodhero.com/blogs/food-waste-and-climate-change.
4. Tim Johns, "California's New Composting Law in Effect: What You Need to Know," ABC7 News, January 2, 2022, https://abc7news.com/ca-composting-law-compost-how-to-california-new/11416032/.
5. Jill Richardson, "Sewage Sludge as Fertilizer: Safe?," *Food Safety News*, October 4, 2010, https://www.foodsafetynews.com/2010/10/sewage-sludge-as-fertilizer-safe/#:~:text=Currently%2C%20sewage%20sludge%20is%20disposed,percent%20of%20the%20nation's%20farmland.
6. US Department of Agriculture, "Food Waste FAQs," accessed December 19, 2023, https://www.usda.gov/foodwaste/faqs#:~:text=In%20the%20United%20States%2C%20food,worth%20of%20food%20in%202010.
7. Anna Burke, "Can Dogs Eat Onions?," American Kennel Club, August 31, 2023, https://www.akc.org/expert-advice/nutrition/can-dogs-eat-onions/#:~:text=It%20only%20takes%20100%20grams,to%20experience%20dangerous%20toxicity%20levels.

8. National Hog Farmer, "Upcycled Animal Feed: Sustainable Solution to Food Waste Problem," December 29, 2021, https://www.nationalhogfarmer.com/feed/upcycled-animal-feed-sustainable-solution-food-waste-problem.

9. Gunders, *Waste-Free Kitchen Handbook.*

10. Greenfield, "How to End the Food Waste Fiasco."

11. Rose Eveleth, "'Sell By' and 'Best By' Dates on Food Are Basically Made Up—but Hard to Get Rid Of," *Smithsonian Magazine*, March 28, 2014, https://www.smithsonianmag.com/smart-news/sell-and-best-dates-food-are-basically-made-hard-get-rid-180950304/.

12. Jonathan Bloom, "Dear Wasted Food Dude—Date Label Hell(p)," Wasted Food, May 16, 2016, http://www.wastedfood.com/2016/05/26/dear-wasted-food-dude-date-label-hellp/.

13. K. D. Hall et al., "The Progressive Increase of Food Waste in America and Its Environmental Impact," *PLoS ONE* 4, no. 11 (November 25, 2009): e7940, https://doi.org/10.1371/journal.pone.0007940.

14. Gunders, *Waste-Free Kitchen Handbook*, 82–84.

15. Food Standards Agency (UK), "Chilling: How to Chill, Freeze, and Defrost Food Safely," December 24, 2020, https://www.food.gov.uk/safety-hygiene/chilling.

16. Ibid.

Chapter 3

1. Ryan Cooper, "Food Waste in America: Facts and Statistics," Rubicon, July 25, 2023, https://www.rubicon.com/blog/food-waste-facts/.

2. Gunders, *Waste-Free Kitchen Handbook*, 86.

3. Amy Leibrock, "Solving the Problem of Moving Day Food Waste," Sustainable America, September 29, 2015, https://sustainableamerica.org/blog/solving-the-problem-of-moving-day-food-waste/.

Chapter 4

1. Bloom, *American Wasteland*, 83.
2. Gerlock, "To End Food Waste."
3. Nicole Rogers, "Glad Takes on Food Waste," Sustainable America, October 30, 2013, http://www.sustainableamerica.org/blog/glad-takes-on-food-waste/.
4. Love Food, Hate Waste, "25% of the Food We Throw Away at Home Is Due to Having Cooked, Served, or Prepared Too Much," X (formerly Twitter), April 12, 2022, https://twitter.com/LFHW_UK/status/1513760329523736576.
5. Stuart Elliott, "Ore-Ida Campaign Focuses on Authenticity of Tater Tots," *New York Times*, August 25, 2014, https://www.nytimes.com/2014/08/25/business/media/ore-ida-campaign-focuses-on-authenticity-of-tater-tots.html.

Chapter 7

1. Food Empowerment Project, "Bitter Brew: The Stirring Reality of Coffee," accessed December 19, 2023, http://www.foodispower.org/coffee/.
2. Food Empowerment Project, "Child Labor and Slavery in the Chocolate Industry," January 2022, http://www.foodispower.org/slavery-chocolate/.
3. Bureau of International Labor Affairs, "List of Goods Produced by Child Labor or Forced Labor," US Department of Labor, accessed December 19, 2023, https://www.dol.gov/agencies/ilab/reports/child-labor/list-of-goods.

4. National Institute of Diabetes and Digestive and Kidney Diseases, "Diabetes Statistics," National Institutes of Health, February 2023, https://www.niddk.nih.gov/health-information/health-statistics/diabetes-statistics.
5. Alexandria White, "Nearly 1 in 4 Americans without a Credit Card Don't Qualify-Here's Why You May Be Denied." CNBC, February 1, 2021. https://www.cnbc.com/select/nearly-1-in-4-americans-without-a-credit-card-dont-qualify-heres-why/#:~:text=About%2024%25%20of%20Americans%20without%20a%20credit%20card,in%20conjunction%20with%20Morning%20Consult%20in%20May%202019.
6. Board of Governors of the Federal Reserve System, "Report on the Economic Well-Being of U.S. Households in 2018–May 2019," June 14, 2022, https://www.federalreserve.gov/publications/2019-economic-well-being-of-us-households-in-2018-dealing-with-unexpected-expenses.htm.

Chapter 8

1. Douglas Broom, "South Korea Once Recycled 2% of Its Food Waste. Now It Recycles 95%," World Economic Forum, April 12, 2019, https://www.weforum.org/agenda/2019/04/south-korea-recycling-food-waste/.
2. Carl Samson, "How South Korea Reduced Food Waste by 300 Tons a Day," Next Shark, June 26, 2017, https://nextshark.com/south-korea-reduced-food-waste-300-tons-day/.
3. Bloom, *American Wasteland*, 87.
4. Republic Services, "Organics Recycling in California (SB 1383)," accessed December 19, 2023, https://www.republicservices.com/organics-sb-1383.
5. Cole Rosengren, "Is California's 2025 Organics Diversion

Target Still Viable?," Wastedive, November 14, 2022, https://www.wastedive.com/news/california-sb-1383-part-seven-compost-digestion-target-procurement/636468/.

6. Gov.UK, "Progress Report on Recycling and Recovery Targets for England 2020," January 5, 2022, https://www.gov.uk/government/publications/progress-report-on-recycling-and-recovery-targets-for-england-2020/progress-report-on-recycling-and-recovery-targets-for-england-2020#:~:text=Although%20progress%20has%20been%20made,impact%20the%20COVID%2D19%20pandemic.

7. Mara Weinraub, "Why Food Waste Is the 'Dumbest Problem Ever'—and the Fascinating Ways We Might Actually Solve It," The Kitchn, April 19, 2022, https://www.thekitchn.com/food-waste-reduction-2022-23312163.

8. ReFED. "New Data from ReFED Reveals Amount of Food Waste Has Leveled Off after Increasing 11.9% since 2012," February 2, 2021, https://refed.org/articles/new-data-from-refed-reveals-amount-of-food-wastehas-leveled-off-after-increasing-11-9-since-2010/.

9. Don't Tell Comedy, "Fly Like an Eagle: Julio Diaz," YouTube, April 6, 2023, https://www.youtube.com/watch?v=vmbzdLqhRCM.

Acknowledgments

When you tell your friends and family an idea and their faces light up, you know you have a good one. Thank you to everyone who supported me, asked questions, shared recipes, and told me about changes they were making in your own kitchens. Your passion for this project means so much.

Every writer "stands on the shoulders of giants," so I want to thank all the researchers and activists who provided the information I needed to write this book. I'd particularly like to thank Dana Gunders, who pioneered the food-waste movement by bringing the issue to light.

Thank you to all my beta readers, teachers, and writing friends for guiding me on the path to publication, especially my writing mentor, Kris Waldherr. I've learned more about writing and publishing from you than anyone else. Thank you to my writing group the Hub City Writers, and thank you to all the folks at the Historical Novel Society. I may not have published a novel yet, but your support has still been fantastic.

Thank you to my parents, who always believed in me. They supported my dream of being a writer since I was eight years old, and I don't know where I'd be without their faith.

Thank you to all the food-waste warriors on Reddit. The growth of the r/noscrapleftbehind subreddit demonstrated to me and my editor how great the market is for this book. Your involvement in this movement is going to have a ripple effect. I can't wait to see what you and my book readers will accomplish.

Thank you, Darcie Abbene, my editor, for taking a chance on me, and to everyone at Health Communications, Inc. You have been so supportive, and I appreciate it.

I'm grateful for my two girls! They support me and never complain about our waste-free lifestyle. It's so satisfying to hear them use the phrase, "We don't waste food in this house!" They are also good examples to the people around them, including their friends at school. It gives me hope that we can change the next generation.

The biggest thank-you of all goes to my husband. I am so lucky to have a partner who supports my dreams and who goes along with my crazy ideas! I love you. You have been the greatest blessing of my life.

About the Author

Teralyn Pilgrim is a passionate activist, a mother, and a lifetime food-waste warrior. She is the author of the hilarious parenting book *Don't Dance on the Toilet: and Other Things I Never Thought I'd Say to My Kids* and *100 Easy Ways to Change the World: The Heart Project Challenge Book*. She has an MFA in creative writing from Western New England University and a BA in English from Brigham Young University. Teralyn lives in the Pacific Northwest, in a forest that is definitely filled with fairies, with her husband and three children.